THE CLIMB UP AND AWAY

FROM THE SLUMS OF SUMMER LANE: PART TWO - WE CLIMBED A MOUNTAIN

by

Thomas Lewin

Grosvenor House
Publishing Limited

This book is published by
Grosvenor House Publishing Ltd
Link House
140 The Broadway, Tolworth, Surrey, KT6 7HT.
www.grosvenorhousepublishing.co.uk

A CIP record for this book
is available from the British Library

ISBN 978-1-83975-479-1

Given that this is a real-life account of events in my life, I have not tidied up the language, which, in places, is somewhat colourful. If you are easily offended, then you have been warned!

ACKNOWLEDGEMENTS

BETTY JEAN LEWIN, my wife, my life. I will love you every day till the day I die and beyond. I thank you, and I treasure your memories. I'm just sorry I took everything you did for granted. If only I could have told you more often how much I loved you. If only I could have seen more clearly what a diamond you were.

TO OUR CHILDREN:

To Rachael, the Yin, and the Yang. Hmmm. As parents, we all want the best for our children. My mom and dad gave us a few snippets. When we lifted you up to reach for the stars, it was my arms that carried you, but behind me was your mother helping and pushing. If I slipped a few times, she was still, quietly always there. Without her, in whatever I did, I could not have done alone. Even in death, her final impetus was to push me on. So, when someone gives you outside guidance, always consider the motives. There are lots of Yins out there. Maybe with a good education, possibly one drug-addled son who thinks they know better, they are the bank managers with the umbrella when the sun is out, the friend or tutor who knows what's best for you when everything is going fine. But when the shit hits the fan, as it does very often in life, as many people have found out, the Yins tend to disappear. Sadly, also with what happens in life, the Yang's, may tend to drawback the bridges. For what you achieved, what Kristy has achieved, me and your mom were immensely proud. All your mom ever wanted was for a bit of that pride to shine back on her.

To Andrew, Nicky, Kristy. Ditto. I remember the ice on the inside of those windows, almost kicking the bucket with double pneumonia, my dad's army coat on the bed. But it was our home, our mom and dad's home, and we respected that. If we didn't, we were kicked out or got out. Simple.

To Louise, Bobbie, Sammy, Mitch, Riley, and the Other One. Thank you truly for the pleasure you have given us over the years. None demanding, none grasping. I will forget, or not remember, your birthdays, but you will know I love you. Those little breaks - abroad or at home in England - were and will continue to be enjoyed. I cannot tell you how much joy and pleasure you gave me with just a couple of days in Barmouth.

TO TREVOR KAVANAGH. A journalist from The Sun newspaper who I have admired over the years for his frank and incisive views kindly reviewed my first book, Against The Odds from Summer Lane, and gave me some constructive advice. Part of which was to give some further insight into my ex-schoolteacher, a lady named Ruth Smith, our relationship and how it benefited me, possibly more than I even realised at the time and for many years after. So my first thank you is to Trevor Kavanagh. For reminding me.

TO RUTH SMITH. Ruth Smith came to our school, Charles Arthur Street, commonly referred to as Charlie, as a part-time English/music teacher. Her job? Well. To teach us music and a bit of English. What the fuck she was going to teach us in the few months we had left, I don't know. Most of us couldn't even spell music. I don't think any of us had any interest in the music or the English she was supposed to be teaching us. Personally, I think she was just dumped on us to give her a job and tick the boxes till we left.

Miss Smith was a battle-axe. Grey hair, square head and very serious. She spoke in a high-pitch posh voice. Loud. No nonsense. She must have been at least 65. Her arse alone was as wide as a barn door. She would stride in. Teach us a bit of English, then bash away at her piano. It was utterly fucking boring. To alleviate the boredom and the pain, we would just chatter away and do our own thing. One day I must have been a touch too loud... "Lewin. Get out there." Humiliated, I was made to sit cross-legged behind her and in front of the blackboard. To teach her a lesson, I picked up a piece of chalk and wrote 'fuck off' in big wide letters. She never noticed a thing. Unfortunately, the whole school saw it. And everyone knew I was the culprit, summoned before the headmaster, Dan Troop. He suggested another school might be the answer. Unfortunately, again, no other school wanted me either. I was dumped into the back of another class. Run by the formidable Miss White. Ignored and just left to stagnate. It suited me.

One day, Miss Smith called me after school and asked me if I would be interested in doing some gardening at her home. With the train fare paid and a few pennies in my pocket. I was up for it. This became a regular thing. Many times, Miss Smith picked me up in her little Morris Minor. But soon, the gossip started, and the tongues were wagging. I was shagging Miss Smith. There was no other alternative. No one, especially schoolteachers, takes an interest in their pupils, especially Nechells, Aston, or Summer Lane. Here, the teachers couldn't wait to escape to their nice little houses in Sutton. It was bad enough having to spend time with us at cricket or football for an extra hour.

First, it was my brothers. "What are you up to with her? You dirty little bastard." Then it was my big mouth, malicious sister-in-law Teresa. "He's at it with her. She ain't giving him money for nothing." Then my mom and dad started. They couldn't prove anything, but the insinuations were too strong to ignore. After all. They couldn't all be wrong, could they? But they were. Eventually, my mom saw it. Then my dad. But not the rest. No. I was fourteen, and I was shagging a sixty-five-year-old pensioner for money.

But Ruth Smith was nothing more than a decent Music teacher. A spinster who had never been married, who just wanted to help me. I just didn't see it for years. Once, after belting a copper (and he deserved it), Miss Smith got me onto a farming course before being allocated a farm in Wales. She would take me to posh restaurants, in Sutton or in the country. I was often humiliated as she would speak in that high-pitch loud voice so everyone could hear. But over the years, I got used to it. Not her voice so much as the posh restaurants.

Going to her house, I started to learn how to act and talk to posh people. Only to find, slowly, that many were not posh at all. Yes, some were. And I could feel them looking down on me as I was introduced. Miss Smith, bless her heart, had no clue that some of her friends thought there was something dodgy about the whole thing as well. You might have had to deal with these low lives from the slums, but you just don't bring them into your personal world. I think most of them thought I would rob her. Maybe even kill her.

But Miss Smith showed me a world that I could aspire to be part of. That anyone could aspire to be part of if shown the way. At 22, I bought our first house just down the road from Miss Smith, overlooking Sutton park. It took me another thirty years to realise the influence she had had on my life. Sadly, as is par for the course with me, it is too late to thank her properly.

Ruth Smith was a classically trained pianist. She devoted her life to music. She could have played for the philharmonic orchestra, but then she met me.

TO THE READER WHO TAKES THE TROUBLE TO READ THIS BOOK (HOPEFULLY MORE THAN ONE): Thank you. In the greater scheme of things, I don't think we achieved anything exceptional. Certainly, I know a couple of pals who achieved far more than we did in life. But when I look back - having written these books - it only dawned on me later what we had to continually put up with from bent, stupid, malicious, vindictive coppers, putting the poison in at any given opportunity, from the landscaping, clearances, building, to hotels. It was always the little word in the ear at each stage. I just said, "fuck you," and carried on. I never thought of any impact it may have had on us; maybe more educated people may assess it better than me. But someone, someday, might question how many others, with far less determination than me, are or have been getting the same shit. In comparison to Richard Branson, Alan Sugar, or that know-all ego on legs prat, Duncan Bannatyne, I have achieved very little. At least two of them are far more crooked than me, or my dad could ever be, and at least two of them are out and out nasty bullies. I would venture that at least Bannatyne wouldn't have a pot to piss in next to, say Bill Gates. So, it all becomes a bit irrelevant, really.

FOREWORD

Following the publication of my first book, AGAINST THE ODDS, I cannot help but feel humbled at the positive reaction I have received, and at how well the book is selling. I left school with no education to speak of. I'm still the snot-nosed kid from Nechells and Summer Lane and I go along in life quite content and happy with my lot. However, I have received the odd message asking me if I feel justified in naming people, bent scrap dealers, police informers etc. Also, many people can guess others who I am referring to even though I have changed their names, slightly.

Let me explain ...

There were a great many decent people who I grew up with in Nechells, some ex-criminals, maybe some who still are, others who have never stolen anything in their lives. They are still my friends, many from the age of ten or earlier, that means a lot to me, but there were and still are a lot of mongrels. In the main, I don't condone stealing or many types of robbery, but back in the day, I fully sympathise with many of the crooks and villains I looked up to. The people I knew who came into our house had honour and self-respect. They came out of a war, not of their making, after forced conscription. They came out to a land fit for heroes, which in reality was a shit hole house in a slum with no visible future. It was expected that you had to work for meagre wages. With hindsight, this was a short-sighted view. Now, looking back, I see that there were a great many opportunities, but back then, the future looked bleak.

History had shown a war had taken place on average every twenty years. But when you're on the bottom rung of the ladder, it's very difficult to see your way to the top. My uncle, Jimmy' Pussyfoot' Littleford, was a very clever man, he had a potentially very good pressing company by the Barton arms in Aston employing several women on the presses, but he wasn't making a fortune. Things were going slow for him, and one night, the little factory went up in flames. Pussyfoot put in a claim for twenty grand and got it.

At the time, in 1961, the average wage was eight quid a week. Sadly, instead of using it to grow, Pussyfoot, like many others, blew it. The same happened with Albert Walker. Albert was a lovely bloke and a good mate, he was given a lift up by Bernard Haywood, the exhaust specialist, and another mate. In next to no time, Albert had a chain of three exhaust fitting outlets. But what did he do? Tube's investments offered him ten grand for the company. They didn't want the business. They just wanted the name. Birmingham Exhaust Equipment (B.E.E). Harry thought all his Christmases had come at once. I think he blew that ten grand in as many months; it was very short-sighted. But at least they had a crack and didn't hurt anyone in the community.

I think it's fair to say many looked up to them with a measure of respect. I don't think that's the same with the police informers or other users like the steel stockholders. They simply used people for their own ends. Lining their own pockets whilst paying wages to the lads who then went along with any bit of dodgy business, in the belief that they were the best of friends. Whilst I have no sympathy for those who went along with it, it also exposed those in the business as users and abusers, ready and prepared to stuff anyone for a few grand. The very worst of the worst, to me, was the police informers, the grasses, like Charlie. Quite simply, they got into the teams which they had grown up with, participated fully in the robberies, enjoying all the rewards that came with it. Until they got nicked a couple of times, then their bottles fell out.

And there were lots of them. Instead of being like men, admitting their bottles had gone and getting out of the game, they decided that the gains were too lucrative to give up. Carrying on, they found it easier to throw bodies in, in all cases their pals and friends. If anyone thinks that's clever or honourable, well, knock me down with a feather. Nothing has been gained. The police had to resort to corrupt methods to get the results, hence the mass exodus from Lloyd house. Crime hasn't gone down; it's just shifted. So no, I have no qualms about naming them or people guessing who they are. Some of them are dead, some are alive, but their kids are all there. Charlie's kids think he is a hero and a respectable, now retired gangster. No he ain't; no doubt others think the same. If they feel or want to come and try having a pop at me, so be it, please feel free to try. I daresay they could ask one or two of their police pals to give them my whereabouts; I ain't hiding. Likewise, I can tell you, judging by the cop's reactions to whatever happens to me, as outlined in this and my first book —well, they ain't going to do eff all. Have a good life.

If Only ...

Not all police are bent; I know that. I believe the majority join the force out of decent intent, but most of the police I remember, as a kid, were bent. Because of our background, my brother and I were viewed as fair game. We were even once stopped in a country lane in Lincolnshire by rural cops. My brother Kenny and I (he was sixteen, and I was eighteen) were robbed of a couple of watches after being taken to a local cop shop for questioning. We had done nothing wrong, yet out of half a dozen cops, two watches had been nicked. How would one cop have been able to do that without the knowledge of any of the others? I have had cops boast to me about how they loved to volunteer when the miners' strikes were on, as the riots were taking place in Handsworth, ostensibly for the overtime as well as being able to bash a few heads. Was that just *one* cop boasting for himself when he said, "we?" They knew that they had gotten the odds with them; no one wants to risk a few years in the nick for belting a copper, much as they might deserve it. Now, in many cases, it's payback time both here in England and in America. The cops don't like it; they don't like getting the smacking's regularly. How many of those miners or those miner's sons are seething with hatred from the memories of what those cops did all those years ago? How must those black people feel from their treatment not all that many years ago when they were brought over here for cheap labour? Is anyone stupid enough to think they would just get over it and forget about it? We see the answer to that both here and in America. My brothers, like myself, have never wished to tell our kids what we've seen, *what we know,* simply because we didn't want to poison our kids. But I should imagine there are thousands more, in the mining towns and in the black heartlands of the major cities, making sure their kids *do* know, buried in their hearts.

Yes, I know the police are learning or trying to. However, I suspect it's going to be an uphill struggle because you have too many with their own agendas and hang-ups. Even worse and more tragic is when we read about some decent cop getting belted or even killed. It's probably the bad'uns who caused the problems in the first place. The fact is, the police are institutionally corrupt and racist, as is the judicial system, heavily weighted against the working class. The whole of the judicial system in this country needs shaking up from top to bottom. The average person will never see the inside of a courtroom except as a witness or maybe a jury member. As such, we trust the law, *the police,* to be acting in the interests of us all, *for* us all for the greater good. Well, that may be so from their point of view, but then you want to ask yourself why it's illegal to video a case unless *they* decide to do so. You might need to ask yourself why so many billions of pounds yes, *billions of pounds* are wasted, public money wasted, on useless, inadequate solicitors just going through the motions while making money for the firms they work for. Bloody disgraceful.

People need to ask themselves the reasoning and the purpose of so many senior judges and police officers of a certain level being members of the masons. Even having their own lodge, having to stand on one leg with trousers pulled up whilst swearing on oath to uphold the secrecy. I've had a couple of friends who belong to the masons, and knowing them as I have, I know they joined it for what they got out of it. Both were businessmen, and both let me know at various times how helpful everyone is if you're a fully paid-up member. If there's a contract going, the mason gets it. When we had a shop, a local farmer gave me the masonic palm greeting. When I didn't respond, that was it; I never got the better deal. It was not the first time. What do the cops get or the judges?

Here is how the penny drops …

First, you have six Irishmen on the night train to Belfast. The ticket collector hears them laughing in the Irish accents. It has been on the news about the bombings in Birmingham. A guy puts two and two together and comes up with six, phones the cops thinking they may have done the bombing and are on their way home. The cops go steaming in and arrest six of them because they're Irish, and they look and sound guilty. First of all, they don't have any evidence except that they are paddies. Sure look guilty, so the cops bring in Pip the Planter or one of Pip's many clones, and there are a lot in Birmingham central alone. When Pip turns up, the first thing he clocks is that the two of them have criminal records. That's it, they're fucked. By the time it gets to court, they've got unsigned statements from them and some evidence of their fingers from playing with the cards. The crowds are baying for blood because now everyone knows they're guilty. All the case needs now is a judge and a prosecutor who thinks they're guilty.

After that, with a half-disinterested defence barrister on legal aid, and a jury who knows 90percent that they are guilty just by the look of them, they may as well throw their hands up. Sentenced to life, there is no way they are going to get out because now they really are guilty, and the possibility of the establishment having to admit they cocked up is nigh on impossible. The establishment does not make mistakes. They served twenty years before five of them got out. One died in prison. The five who got out were awarded a million quid each, with at least one of their lives destroyed. Nine times out of ten, the cops have been getting away with this because the accused is, in fact, guilty. All it needed was a bit of help. The prosecution is in on it, the judges know about it, the defence is not too concerned. Trust me, I've seen their faces; if I ain't guilty of the one offence, I'm guilty of something.

I had had a day of work at Pilkington Glass when I was stuck at home, and Pip the Planter charged around. The borrowed car? 'Course I'm guilty. The same thing happened with Barry George, who was found guilty of killing the presenter, Jill Dando. The only difference was George was lucky. After only serving seven years, he got out but was told to "piss off" with no compensation because he couldn't prove he was innocent. I tell you, you couldn't make it up; no one else was ever arrested, so her family still feels George was guilty. With the Birmingham Six, the murdered peoples' families are running around spitting blood for someone to pay. The government doesn't want to know because Tony Blair gave all the bombers a get out of jail card to bring peace to the country. FINE, but that in itself is a joke because the government caused the problems in the first-place, hundreds of years ago. All the time, no one gives a shit about the Birmingham six, and you can bet your bottom dollar no cop would ever hold his head down in guilt. No, they were guilty, somehow.

For years I was perplexed at the treatment me and my family received from the cops and then the courts. I just couldn't figure it out when there was clearly some doubt about the circumstances, like the tenant attacking me in my own flats who had no right to be in those flats in the first place and the two plumbers who came to my house and parked almost half a mile away. They repeatedly lied in court and contradicted themselves, yet the single handpicked judge still found me guilty, after the local inspector apologised.

Sadly, I know exactly how my book will be perceived by the average Joe citizen. Perhaps the majority. But when I look back, I feel, deliberately or otherwise, that I had a lot of unnecessary harassment by stupid or corrupt police. All the incidents I recall are the truth. Outside or inside the courtroom. I would defy anyone to prove me wrong. How many others are there? Not just in Birmingham but throughout the country? A lot.

The real irony, the really funny part, is that the actions of the cops and the courts are such that instead of deterring people from crime, it merely makes them more corrupt. You only have to look around to realise this. But maybe that's the master plan; maybe our leaders are so clever that that's the real plan, and we simply never had the brains to see it. The more corrupt we become; the more work presents itself to the lawmakers. When work starts dying down, simple, bring in a load of immigrants from third world countries. Two problems solved at once. Repeatedly, Pip the Planter was brought in to arrest me and my dad and my two brothers, Reg, and Johnny. Each time, we were fitted or verballed up so blatantly it was beyond belief; yet who was there to fight our case or shout out against corruption? No one. Yet I would bet twenty grand that the judges knew all about these bent cops, which makes them just as corrupt. I can't see how anyone can think otherwise. Sort that rot out at the top, and you might clear some of the rot at the bottom because I know for a fact that if you ask any villain or petty crook (anyone who has been involved in a crime of any kind) they will agree with me that the police certainly are bent.

Why would so many say that? Sour grapes. Bullshit. Some, yes, but not all. The fact is the law - the whole of the law - should be impeccable. But it ain't. Sadly, it's almost always the decent copper you see getting run over, shot, or belted. Take Susan. Susan was a nice respectable girl. She was in the motor home with me when we had a couple of days in Matlock Bath. At least half a dozen cop cars surrounded my motor home; it had been picked up as stolen. Yet very quickly, anyone with half a brain or common sense would have seen the van was *not* stolen. There had been no change of plates, the van was lived in, and my wife's pictures were all over the place, yet some stupid female cop saw fit to frighten the life out of Susan by asking her, "Do you know who you're dealing with?" Her head was spinning with what kind of monster I was, yet we're still friends.

They tried to poison my friends and family against me. They tried to say such things to my wife. My wife, Bet, and I were married for forty-five years before she passed away. I can't have been bad. After Bet passed away, I met Carolyn. Carolyn was a beautiful bird: classy and a very clever businesswoman. She contacted me through Facebook. She had various businesses, including jewellery shops; she wore designer gear and knew how to carry herself. We had been seeing each other for two years before she died of cancer, yet she adored me. She told me she felt safe in my arms. How could she say that if I was some kind of monster?

How many customers have *they* put the poison into like that over the years? How many other people have they destroyed or tried to destroy? The problem is, these fucking idiots - on gossip, innuendo, and blatant muck spreading - see themselves as the judges and juries, based simply on the number of books they have read parrot-fashion. I am certainly not bitter; that does not run through my blood. I've never felt like a victim. In many cases, I was simply in the wrong place at the wrong time, but I consider myself lucky. Despite what the bastards have done to me, I still come up smiling. I know there are many more held back, dragged down, or wasting in prison. If I am sad, it is because my wife is not sharing my life. All my brothers except Reg were married for life. Like my mom and dad, they died married to each other. Johnny married a harridan, yet never raised his hand. Kirby never hit his wife or partner. Yet to hear the cops talk, the prosecution, we were all "violent nut jobs" - still *are* violent nut jobs - and raise a few questions. And the biggest crook of all, Tony Blair, the ex-prime minister, and warmonger/criminal, is strutting around on the world stage, earning millions in the process, and probably giving that masonic signal as he trots along. Yet he's responsible for the death of thousands still ongoing with the terrorists in our country today. Very clever. He's got the Lord behind him, and his wife.

Having the misfortune, yet again, to live next to another cop before my wife died, I had reason on more than one occasion to see how petty-minded he was. But after calling the cops one day, yet again, for self-protection against yet another plumber, I must have flagged up to the idiot next door who made it very clear in his attitude that he "knew who I was," and therein lies my problem. Some little rat or grass complains against me for whatever reason, the cops click on a button, and not only does my name flair up, but God-knows what else with it that some unknown cop has added to it. There are many ways I could enrich my life as well as others with time, experience, and ability. I could have had a go at being a porter in a hospital, tried helping in a food queue - which I volunteered for and was refused - helping some of the vulnerable, but fuck-it. No, thank you. I suspect many others feel the same. I'm alright, Jack.

I am not whining in my book or in my life, far from it. I feel quite lucky with my lot; I have a good life - *a good quality of life*. I can virtually fuck off and do what I want when I want. Many of my friends like my sense of humour. If I was stuck in a council house today on some estate, or down Nechells, god forbid, I think I might be tempted to be bitter, but my glass is always half full. My parents lived for the day - a good night in the boozer - as did many people of the time. There had been a war every twenty years throughout history. Now, coming out of WWII, they were expected to face poverty and hardship and be grateful for it. We were used as slave labour, with everyone else looking down their noses at us. Here today, in Sutton, people have aspirations – optimism, everyone! Every young kid in Sutton is expected to aim for the stars; there are no limits. In Nechells, I well remember that Hughes, the Welsh teacher, drew our future out for us. I suspect it's still the same for many today in those areas. My only sadness - my only regret - is for all the planning. By the time my wife, Bet, got to the stage where our kids had flown the nest, she could buy nice clothes and spend as she wanted, she had her stroke. But that, you can't plan for. Que sera sera.

FROM THE BACK STREETS AND SLUMS, AGAINST THE ODDS

We Climbed a Mountain

Leaving Stafford prison was a massive relief; my experience was such that at times I worried for my mental health. My feeling – and observation - is that prison serves no purpose at all except to keep people locked up and away from the general public whilst the majority should not even be in there. The hardened ten percent, the professionals, just took in on the chin as part of their lifestyle. If bank robbery or any other kind of robbery doesn't work, they just decide to shift course and steer in a different direction - that is, drugs. The odd few, like me, will make a determined effort to gain a foothold in business. Ray, who did the coop, turned his life around and got into business. It's accepted that some of the major criminals like the Krays could have made a success in business. I know that many former crooks made well when they turned to business.

The problem is, many of my generation and my father's generation were brainwashed, from when we first started school, to have limited expectations: building sites or the factories for the men, and shops or factories for the women before they turned twenty and before getting married. We were also brainwashed into accepting that only the elite - those who went to Eton or other top public schools - had a right to a career, to run a business, to be successful. We just had to doff our caps and get on with it. For the rest, the majority, they will just return again and again till they get worn down in the process. Many of them will become mentally damaged. I didn't think I was, but it certainly damaged me. But that manifested itself in different ways as I went about my life. I wasn't bitter - a bit angry, yes. Being fitted up was a bit par for the course. Lots of villains I knew - some guilty of the charge, some not –accepted it. It wasn't much worth fighting; the judges were in on it and it became difficult to wonder who was involved in the conspiracy and who was not. How can you have so many bent detectives...not only *on* the take, but blatantly fitting people up? They not only owned the town, but their reputation was also known throughout the force. Besides the villains themselves (they were the mafia), other cops would boast about them. "Oooohh, if Pip gets hold of you, you'll be in for it."

Don't tell me the solicitors didn't know or the judges didn't know...and if they didn't, then they must be that stupid they shouldn't be in the job of sentencing people in the first place. Sometime after - and coincidentally - Lloyd House, the main police investigating headquarters, was subject to a major purge. I don't think one bent detective or copper was charged with any crime such as fitting up; a few were sacked, some were given early retirement or took early retirement, some resigned on health grounds, others resigned. I think in all about 70 percent of Lloyd House was emptied of bent coppers, all quickly brushed under the carpet with one big headline in the local papers before dying away into obscurity. Great; that spoke volumes about how the corruption was looked upon by the law and judiciary in general. I often wondered if one of the main reasons they started getting caught out - quite apart from the most blatant way they were doing it - was because of their arrogance spreading to the IRA. Now they were entering into the political side of things. We might call them murderers and terrorists, but to their own they were soldiers fighting a just war, as such they had a lot of politicians, lawyers etc. on their side.

Seeing Bet was a delight; she kept calm and kept her feelings under check. We were both nervous; I had set the bar high (getting out of nick was bad enough anyway). Setting our goals so high was something else: the first being to set up somehow in business. I realised Bet was putting all her own life on the line to back me; if I failed or fucked up, she would have nothing either. We both knew it; we had seen it time after time again ourselves. Many in prison - especially those in a relationship - come out with aspirations, hopes and goals, and most people on the outside don't even realise how difficult that can be - or is. Most fail, and I was determined not to fail, but the first few months would be the cruncher.

We got off to a good start. I'd gotten a car with the help of Ruth Smith, and I'd started the taxi driving with an old family friend. Then I brought a lorry, then another lorry, and within a few months I felt confident that we could be in a position to buy our first house. We were offered our council house in Kitts Green, but I didn't want to know. In actual fact, it was Bet's house. She had the security of tenure. We were offered it for two-grand, but no, I knew best; she followed me blindly without question. My aspirations were a lot higher when Bet told me about Johnny Mack's eight-year-old kid being smacked by a local copper then her giving him a kick before being threatened with assaulting a police officer. Fortunately, when his inspector turned up and threatened to arrest her for assault, she had the bottle to tell him. Go on then, and I'll have him done for assaulting an eight-year-old minor. The inspector bottled it they both walked off bolloxed. If you've got a criminal record, you can be any cop's punch bag; but with no record, it's a different story. Bet had no criminal record; the kid was eight years of age.

One morning, we were having breakfast when there was a knock on the door. Two cops stood on the other side asking if they could search my house. I asked them why. They told me there had been an early morning armed robbery at the Marston Green post office. Turning to the kids, they pointed out I hadn't been out of the house. I should have told them to fuck off at that point, but I let them do a quick cursory search.

They knew it was nothing to do with me but went through the motions anyway, probably just to let me know. I was sick of these fucking coppers and their constant bullying attitude. Joe public sits back in the knowledge that the police are doing their job in the interests of the same Joe public. In the one respect they are, but it also gives them the opportunity to harass, bully, and intimidate anyone with a criminal record. I had served my time for the crime I was fitted up and charged with. I had gotten out of prison and now here we were seeing all this; it was a fucking joke. It was harassment. Everything I was doing was totally legal, yet I could imagine their brains spinning around like a fucking top on overdrive. Hang about. How many lorries has that Lewin got? And what about that big earthmoving machine on the top of his waggon? The landlord at the tavern pub pulled me over one night (he had given me permission to park one of my ten tonners on there) drott sitting on the top. The cops had been in asking about me: How long had my lorries been parked there? Did he know anything about me?? Actually, I was finding it quite funny really. After all, I'm a thick villain. These have got brains, maybe an O-level; no one can work or make money that fast. It wasn't just the cops, one or two were questioning us. Ray Kirby couldn't believe we were moving and buying a house in Sutton Coldfield. Susan even asked if we felt we were better than them. It was unbelievable. Have a look? See what we are having to put up with within weeks of getting out of prison, harassment, house turned over, almost getting nicked again for bent scaffolding? That I knew, fuck all about, that's without the potential charge of conspiracy to defraud a metal company just by being around on the scene; it was getting bloody ridiculous. Now I wanted out - out of the road, out of the area. It was the only way we were going to be able to succeed. My resolve was given even more impetus when Bet told me all about the little sting that took place a few months earlier.

A friend's daughter had called in to babysit for Bet. Pointing to her meter cupboard, she asked Bet if she'd gotten her meter fixed. Well Bet hadn't a clue what she was on about and looked suitably blank. The girl was fourteen years of age and was talking like a wizened old villain. Bet brushed her off telling her she wouldn't consider something so stupid. A few weeks later, her uncle - the gangster - was having a bit of a party. These things are quite spontaneous coming at the end of the night with everyone involved agreeing to buy a couple of crates of beer, maybe a bottle of scotch and heading off to one of their homes. This particular night, a group of about eight of them set of together with a couple of locals who were in the tavern. Once settled into the house, and after another slurp of booze, the question was asked: "How have you got your meter fixed?" Then, the one gangster goes over to his meter box, opens the door and shows this massive fucking needle stuck into the side of the meter box, almost as big as a fucking knitting needle. With that, and after some deep examination, his cousin jumps in: "Oh, mine's a lot better than that. You won't even see my needle; it's that clever." With that, a deep discussion took place on the merits of who had got the best method of fixing the meter, everyone taking it in turns to examine the meter. It was like Leonardo de Vinci showing of one of his inventions. Two days later, the whole lot of them were raided early in the morning, simultaneously at 7am, each electric company employee accompanied by two cops, making it impossible for anyone to ring the others up.

Most of them had just enough time to pull their needles out before the cops came charging in and the meters being taken out for examination. It wasn't hard to find the holes in the meters. Being unable to prosecute them, they were all put on notice that they would be monitored for the following six months, their readings taken, and the usage backdated for the previous five years. Failure to pay would mean them being taken to court and prosecuted for the full amount. Well, as you can imagine, they were shitting themselves for the following six months. Going around their houses was a revelation; all lights were diligently turned off at every opportunity, much of the time sitting in darkness. All of them had got calor gas heaters stuck in the centre of the room, so terrified were they of having there heating on. It was fucking hilarious. I would burst out laughing and they would be huddled up, overcoats on, too embarrassed to look me in the eye. The problem really was that you have a nice little perk: instead of being discreet and keeping your gob shut, you feel like doing your neighbour a favour. Well, they are struggling a bit, but having told your neighbour to keep their gobs shut, they feel like giving their neighbour - or brother or cousin - the benefit of their newfound little perk, and before you know it, the whole fucking road is fiddling their meters, with consumption going through the roof yet reading going down to zero. To save a tenner...no, we had to get out.

I reckoned we could afford a nine-grand mortgage. That took us around a nice semi in Walmley or Great Barr, but the fact that most had garages at the back garden put me off. Then we happened to see a nice house in Sutton overlooking the park at thirteen-grand. Knowing we couldn't afford it, we decided to have a look just to make a comparison. That was a big mistake. As soon as we walked inside the house, that was it. I looked at Bet's face and said, "Shall we go for it?" She didn't have to answer; we put an offer in and got the mortgage company to send a letter to Amy Roadstone via my pal Tommy Hobday. Tommy just past me the questionnaire and I filled it out myself and posted it, and we were offered the mortgage within the week. Before moving, the knives had already started coming out. Susan wanted to know if we thought we were too good for them. "Why don't you buy around here Tommy? Marston Green?" For Christ's sake, she didn't get it. It was just up the road within distance of the cops with easy access for them to bring a bit of gear by. "Store this, Tom." Oh, thanks very fucking much; I store some gear for them, then I get nicked. It's good old sound Tommy muggins; no thank you, I've had enough.

Bet's brother John pops up with his wife, Anne. Anne wants to know how we can afford to buy a house in Sutton Coldfield when her and John have been struggling for years to afford a house. "We're still living in the back room of my dad's hairdressing shop in Witton, after all, so you must be doing something bent." How do you answer that? At least John had the decency to point out that she had room to talk; her dad was just as bent at fiddling his taxes. Most of the money going into his chain of shops was all cash.

We actually completed on the house on a Friday but decided to move in on Saturday. On the Friday night, we drove up and pulled onto the drive for Bet to measure up for curtains and take notes of anything we would need. This is when we not only got our first cultural shock, but a real insight into why these people in Sutton could afford the houses in the first place. It's called the "hock-up." Coming out of the side gate were our neighbours, the Morrison's. She was carrying a prop, and he was carrying a great big chunk of rockery, for fuck's sake. I couldn't believe my fucking eyes. Knowing what was coming, Bet ducked down below the dashboard and I jumped out the car yelling, "What the bloody hell do you think you are doing?" They both went bright red, put the items down and walked out, shoulders bent over in embarrassment. I'm in fucking shock. I've left Kitts Green to get away from the villains, and here I am in posh Sutton Coldfield, my neighbours nicking out of my fucking garden. I was gutted, to say the least. We never spoke to the Morrison's again.

Walking into the house was another shock. The vendors had stripped the house bare: all the lightshades, all the loose shelving out of rear storerooms, even the bamboo poles in the garden together with plants, for fuck's sake. How cheap must these people be? I've got thieves next door and a vendor who was a right cheapskate. I wouldn't mind, but he wasn't a kid; he was well into his 50's. Bet came walking in behind me and I looked her in the eye. And we're the crooks? What kind of neighbours did we have around us? Tony, the scrap-dealer's partner, had warned us not to buy in the road. "They're two-penny-half-pennies, Tom." He lived on the Roman Road private estate. I told him I can't afford any more, I'm already overstretched.

Well, we got over it and moved in, and after the initial culture shock, the kids rapidly adapted and settled down to a totally different lifestyle to what they were used to. Andrew was Johnny Macs son's mate, and I could see which way that would be going if he remained, so we were now middle class.

I had sold a couple of lorries - was not doing the haulage anymore - and had also stopped doing the taxying. My brother Kenny had mentioned that a relative of his by marriage had offered him a free franchise in a car rustproofing company that he had established on the Tyburn road. It sounded amazing and was a sure money-maker. Up till then, car manufacturers didn't rust-proof their cars. What he offered was a rust-proofing service with a ten-year guarantee, and the sweetest part were the conditions attached to the guarantee. First you had to book the car in for its annual service check-up every year within a twenty-four-hour period. The first year lost 25 percent, and by the third year almost 80 percent had lost their guarantee. Most people sold their car after three years, and the next condition was they had to register their ownership of the car within twenty-four hours in person, taking their car in for check-up. Very few realised, or bothered to do this, which reduced the coverage to less than one percent. It was a licence to print money. We asked our older brother Billy to come in with us, but after lots of bluster, he bottled out. As I didn't have enough money, I couldn't take the risk, especially buying our house. In truth, none of us had a clue what we would be getting into. Shame, really. The company waiting room was chock-a-block every day with businessmen queuing up to pay for a franchise, that's where the real big money lay.

Desperate for money and to make a living, I decided to do rubbish removals, placing adverts in local papers and living by the seat of my pants. I'd gotten my brother-in-law on board, and we went out mooching and touting for work. A butcher gave us a job of clearing his daughter's garden prior to her divorce and selling her house. Out of the fiver I made, I gave George two quid, put one quid in the tank, taking home two quid for Bet. "I'm sorry, that's all I've made," I tell her, and with her usual chirpiness she said, "Don't worry, I'll manage." And she did, bless her. Moving rubbish was hard work, but George was as strong as an ox, and I was as fit as a fiddle - so fit that I even started going back and doing some boxing.

We were picking up little jobs and contracts slowly but surely, and we started getting builders ringing us up. We were nicknamed the JCBs because of the rate we could load my lorry, an eight-ton load which two of us could do in just over an hour. One day, the boss of one company asked me if I would be interested in doing a concrete drive to the front of one of their houses they were renovating. The company not only did building work but also managed houses for landlords. If we could work our way in with them, we could crack it. The only downfall was the slowness in settling their bills. My brother Kenny was doing a bit for me but was a total pain. I love all my brothers, but to get him on board meant I had to first pick him up from Kitts Green, over ten miles away, then go to the job doing the concrete drive. Kenny asked how much I was getting for the job and when I told him, he buried his little head and carried on working. The next day, he trotted onto the job to tell me he had been talking to tommy O'Malley who had advised him that I wasn't charging enough for the job, to say I was a bit pissed off was putting it mildly, especially as I knew what O'Malley was doing, ;tarmacking. Tommy had no right to educate me, not in the house he was living in either. Sadly, Kenny never worked for me again.

Seeing the potential, I asked my brother Billy to come and work for me. Now Billy had had a few businesses, mainly in the retail side, shops warehouses etc, but like all things, the barrel was getting emptier, and the perks were going out of the window. Unfortunately times were changing very quickly, Billy had been burning his bridges thinking things were never going to change. Sadly, again, Billy let his pride jump to the fore.

"Er, how much am I getting?" His little chest swelling with indignation.

"Well, I'll give you what I can afford, say 70 quid a week."

"Well how much are *you* getting?"

I said I have to draw 100 quid a week.

"Well, if you're on 100 quid a week, then I want 100 quid a week."

I looked at him in disbelief. "Are you fucking joking? I've got five kids and a mortgage to pay for, plus advertising and maintenance costs." But Billy had set his mind. "Oh well, I'm not taking less."

Well, that was the end of me and Bill's business relationship. I then asked Johnny if he wanted a job, but he lasted one day, letting me know throughout that he was only doing it as a favour to help me out and didn't need the money. What the fucking hell is the matter with these people? Can't they see the benefits of working as a team? Can't they see the end result - the light at the end of the tunnel? If only they could see that by working together, we would all benefit in the long-term; but no, when pride enters into it, brains go out the fucking window.

Dealing with the Greeks and the Asians I had always, even from an early age seen the benefits of working together as a team. i mean, it doesn't take a lot of brains does it. Work your nuts of saving twenty quid a week gives you a grand at the end of the year. Five brothers working together putting aside five hundred pounds a week in savings gives you twenty five grand at the end of a year.

I had seen the Asians doing this very same thing, then buying a house for cash in small heath or alum rock, move in then start all over again,- after five years all the family will have a house each paid for cash,-- it's not happening all the time, as time progresses, a lot of the Asians adopt the western lifestyle and habit of me, me, me. But in principle I know a few none Asian people who have done it and done well.

As a kid leaving school I remember thinking I would have worked for my dad or Billy for peanuts, unfortunately we lived in a period where it was me myself and my own. It wasn't just around Nechell's, in northern towns workers would take a pound or so out of there wage packets before handing it over to their wives, if they even did that.

In Nechell's it was, or seemed to me, every man for himself. Wherever I turned I realised you couldn't form partnerships or do much business with each other or others without them trying to roll you over for a couple of quid. It was a case of get in first before the other one ripped you of.. I had realised that whatever I did, I had to do it alone.

We kept on plodding along, and having done a few jobs, I decided to get myself into the landscaping business. Well, it can't be that hard; I'd done a bit of concreting, and any idiot can lay a lawn...jeezzz, it's only a matter of levelling the ground and roll out the turf. After getting a bit of work, I decided to go for the full Monty and place a half-page add in the yellow pages. If nothing else, I had balls. We got the yellow pages rep out, giving him the company name in big letters... LEWINS' Garden Landscaping. That was a big mistake, but I was nothing if not optimistic. The ad was placed in the September for the following year and the pages started being delivered in March. I was pooping myself. I'd gotten no work, had no money, and the yellow pages had thrown their bill in. How the hell could I pay it? All of a sudden, the phone started off the hook. I'd also decided to join the Federation of Master Builders. I'd produced a couple of completed jobs for references, and the biggest selling point was, "Well, of course, Mr. Lewin, being a member of the Master Builders Federation will be reflected in your prices." He was right; not only did the work come flying in, but it also meant I could literally treble my prices. I wasn't slow there, either. I couldn't believe it; just by having that certificate and a few stickers, I could expect so much.

I'd gotten a little company over Four Oaks who would call me up to do some business, usually factory clearance in there engineering company. "Mr Lewin are those of any interest to you?" they'd say, pointing to some straddle stones, bloody antique straddle stones - about eight of them – and on the lorry they went and into my garden, selling four along the way for a hundred quid each. Another day: "Mr Lewin, would your services stretch to felling those two trees? I did have someone give me a price, but they've refused to turn up. They quoted me three hundred pounds which I will be happy to pay you." Three hundred quid? I've got to get adjusted to the difference in values here in Sutton. It took us half a day to cut it down and get rid of the wood. Whilst doing that, the boss pointed to a very tidy Austin A55 with two months tax left on it. "Do you think you could get rid of that, Mr Lewin?" Of course.

I was getting used to training my face to show no response. A commercial copying machine I sold to another company wanted to speak to the engineering company to clarify it wasn't stolen. Of course, and as I spoke to the one partner - an ex-cop - I could feel the slight resentment at my entrepreneurial ability. As for the A55, I did a deal with Andy Neary, pal from Kitts Green. A few weeks later, I get a knock on the door.

"Two old bill, ahh, Mr Lewin? You sold a A55 van to a Mr Andrew Neary?"

"Yea, so what?"

Andy, bright as he was fucking not, had put a false tax disc on the motor, and when he got nicked showed he was even brighter by throwing me in as having sold him the van with the tax disc. "Look, I sold Neary that van over a month ago with nearly two months tax on it."

"Can you prove that Mr Lewin?"

I could feel the panic come over me. I know what's going to happen here. If I tell them the company name, they will go to them and see fit to inform them that I am [known to them] the usual term. I had no choice. Again, I was bolloxed. I gave them the name, true to form. The company never called me again. The police have a lot of nicknames besides Mr Plod, Old Bill, Bobby or Filth Pigs… all I think fit them very well.

The proof of the dates would have been enough to prove the van was taxed. Why on earth did the cops have to put the poison in with a company that was very lucrative to me? The engineering company had been using me to great satisfaction for nearly two years. Following one innocent incident, I was cut off - no more work. Those cops truly are filthy bastards. Half a brain would tell them I'm living in a nice house, I'm working hard - trying to build a business, yet the mongrels put the poison in for me. It's fucking never-ending. We got out of Kitts Green to get away from vindictive cops, gossiping friends, and even in-laws constantly putting the poison in. Teresa, my sister-in-law, was a prime one, while Johnny was a quite unassuming brother. His wife, for some reason, felt she was better than anyone else, and that her kids were better than my sister's kids. It's pathetic why are people like this.

In contrast, living in Sutton was totally different. The neighbours hardly spoke to each other. You would see them leave in the early morning and return at night. You could drive down our road after 7pm and barely one light would be on in the majority of houses. In Kitts Green, everyone lived in the one room: the front room. Here in Sutton, most lived in the back, using the front to eat, or as the best room. Weekends would be spent socialising, but where? The road was not much different to midweek. Sunday seemed the only activity day where everyone would pop out and clean their cars and mow their lawns. You would just see or hear the occasional "hello," "good morning," "nice day, isn't it?" - that was it. Me and Bet were finding it very difficult to come to terms with. It was never like this in Nechells or Kitts Green, so it was quite a culture shock. We were forever saying, "shhhh, shhhh, shut up," to the kids, even in the back garden. "Shut up, you little fuckers, the neighbours will hear you," in a loud whisper.

One day, after many months, Bet had had enough. "bugger this," she said. "I'm sick of whispering in my own garden." At that, she bawled out loud, "Ay, you lot, get in the bloody house!" My shoulders hunched up in fear, fucking hell. But the kids soon ran in.

One day, after a few months, she said, "I'm sick of this... this falseness. These lot ain't any better than us." We've got one neighbour on one side we caught thieving, all the others not talking to each other. Tony's partner was right; it's all kippers and curtains. I'd rather be back where we came from, Kitts Green, where the neighbours said hello and spoke their minds. I was half inclined to agree with her, but we'd made our bed and we had to stick it out.

In truth, we were totally and utterly wrong. We were steeped that much in our background, our own upbringing. We just couldn't see that these people, our neighbours, had busy lives to lead - full lives, working hard to enjoy the lifestyles they had. Plus, many were living on a tight budget to have and enjoy that lifestyle. They didn't have the time or the inclination to gossip about non-essential matters. And being more educated, they made sure to get to know each other before making friendships. Mainly, their friendships came from their work and their colleagues.

Christopher, our next-door neighbour, was the exception. Christopher was the only son of Muriel and Chip, our neighbours on the other side of us. Christopher was a lovely, friendly kid who would often pop around our house for a chat, enjoying our company. I think he enjoyed my company as I was just down to earth. "Good Lord, Thomas," in his little posh voice, "you're not going to eat all that, are you?" As he sat beside me, my dinner in front of me on a chair, I'd had the usual hard day, and Bet had put me a big dinner out. Christopher's eyes were out on stalks. I couldn't understand what he was on about till I popped round his house one

Sunday at lunch time. There the three of them sat around the table, all posh and correct, a nice view out onto the road. On a small plate sat a small piece of packaged cod, a few potatoes, and a spoonful of peas. This was my first example of portion control. As they sat eating, they would push a bit of potatoes to the side of the plate, then a portion of peas. This was pre-programmed within them and was carried out automatically, each one not saying a word.

Fuck me; I knew what it was all about, of course. This was common practice in Sutton, and we were starting to notice that everyone carried out this little ritual. It was for the hotpot I was used to seeing, Ruth Smith doing it on a regular basis. You would save a bit from each meal, pushing a few morsels to the side of the plate, and by, say, Thursday, the day before payday, you'd have a nice little dish of food. The hot pot, enough to provide a meal for the family, was heated up; it was another dinner. It was done automatically, and it forever amazed me. It was a regular event with Ruth; she was a single elderly woman and could be spending maybe two weeks building up her little pot. The problem with this came out when she invited me to bring Rodger-the-Dodger Hardiman to do a bit of work in her garden with the promise of being paid and a meal to follow. The Dodger was always up for this, as with nineteen in his family it was always a fight to get something to eat; Dodger was always starving. Having carried out the work, we were called down for dinner. Dodger was down at the gallop, dashing into the dining room and setting himself at the table, taking the hot dish and placing it on the table. Dodger couldn't wait. Whilst I was still bringing in the cutlery, etc., Dodger had started. All of a sudden, I heard Dodger crying out and groaning very loudly, "Where's the toilet?" Fortunately, the toilet was under the stairs opposite the dining room. Dodger just about made it before spewing his guts up. Ruth was mortified. Dodger wasn't putting on an act; his face turned from yellow to green. Dodger never went to Miss Smith's house ever again, and I never tried her hotpot.

Again, I couldn't get my head around this practice, most of all the double standards. These people had the nerve to look down on people like my mom and dad, yet they would never dream of doing something like this. Yes, we had the stew that lasted for days, but it was all fresh ingredients. We had the Sunday fry-up, but that was a treat for the whole household. Mom would make a big dinner, and any leftover meat or food out of the saucepans - usually a few potatoes and cabbage, maybe a few carrots or peas - was all fried up on the Sunday night for a nice supper, the fry-up. But this - the hot pot? It was a fucking joke.

Christopher turned to me one day as we stood on the drive. "Thomas, Thomas with the capital T, what do you think about us, as in us in Sutton Coldfield, subsidising these council house tenants?"

I thought, at first, that he was taking the piss and knew we had come from a council house background, but he wasn't, he was being very genuine. "Christ, so far," I replied, looking at him, "Christopher with the big C, how do you get that? Subsidising? Listen, we were in a council house and I feel sorry for anyone in a council house because they will be paying rent for the rest of their lives, and when they die, someone else will move into that council house and *they* will be paying rent for the rest of *their* lives, increasing every year."

Christopher's face dropped. He'd never thought that out. "Oh, I never thought of it that way, Thomas."

"Tell me Christopher, how much did your parents pay for their house?"

"£2000, but it's all paid off now, Thomas."

"Exactly, Christopher. Those council tenants will never have that pleasure. Subsidised, indeed. That's a propaganda piece of bullshit." Then I threw the googly at him. "And what about you, Christopher? What will *you* do when you need to buy a house?"

"Oh, good Lord, Thomas. I could never afford to buy a house. I shall just wait till Mommy-n-Daddy pass." Well for fuck sake, that's typical of the people's attitudes that lived here in Sutton, as I was beginning to find out on a daily basis. Christopher was a lovely lad, but I swear they lived in their own little bubble.

Bet came in one day and said, "You'll never believe who I met up the Ante Natal clinic today."

"No, who?"

"Well, the nurse came out and introduced me to another woman saying, 'You two ladies should get to know each other; you both live on the same road.'"

By a coincidence, her name was Brenda and she not only went to the same school on Tinkers Farm Road in Northfield - twenty miles on the opposite side of Birmingham - but she was also a friend of Bet's sisters. Bet had found a friend and I was pleased for her. Then she said the woman's husband was a copper. "A copper?"

"Yes, I told her, all coppers are bent. Brenda agreed."

Don't I know it. It wasn't the only coincidence. A few days later, I'm on the drive having a nice friendly chat with our neighbours, Chris and his mom and dad, when something funny was said. I had got a big laugh on my face when who should walk past? Tim, the copper I had smacked a few years before on Nechells Green when I was fifteen. I didn't know whether to fall back in shock or forward. I could feel the smile freeze on my face. He was walking with a woman - obviously his wife - and as they passed, he was looking at me full in the face.

Bet said, "Oh, that's my new friend, Brenda."

"Yes," I said. "And that's the fucking copper I smacked on Nechells Green as a kid."

We both stood stunned, knowing we were fucked. Oh great, the bastard is going to put the poison in now with all the neighbours. But to be fair, he did no such thing. A few nights later, he invited us up to his house a few doors up and asked us in for a beer. This was a newbie for me, and I couldn't. I didn't know quite what to make of it. What was his motive? We were never going to be pals, of course, and I hoped being neighbours that he wasn't expecting me to be his little buddy informant because he could fuck off. Tim had gotten his house with the help of his superior - bonny from Bloomsbury Street - Nick, who had sold him the house, otherwise, he wouldn't have been able to afford it. "Of course, you are now middle class," he pointed out.

"Middle class?" I said to Bet later. It's a fucking joke, this is. Last week we were council tenants, the next we are middle class. It's like we'd gotten a mask that we could switch on and off like a fucking light bulb. Middle class. It didn't help much that Brenda was leaning on the table and let go a little fart. That only added to the stiffness of the atmosphere.

But to be fair, Tim did put himself out to be friendly, even to the extent of showing out to me if he was hanging with one of his mates on duty in plain clothes. I could see by his mate's stiff face, though, telling he wasn't too pleased. Tim would overlook silly little things if I was in my untaxed car. He never asked me any personal questions about my mates or about different names. His kids became friends with my kids and would be in each other's houses; mainly it was my kids in Tim's house. I started to clock that Tim was keeping a beady eye on me. I also clocked that he was a very strong Catholic. Maybe there were some honest cops, but he was one of 130,000.

One day, I got another call come in to view a job. I was slowly getting used to dealing with a variety of people of different classes, different levels of wealth – surprisingly - and much to my amazement, the more money people had, the least snobby they were, from the Roman Road private estate to the Four Oaks estate. If they were professionals - doctors, company directors, etc. - they were refined, but down to earth; very few were snobbish. If they were self-made, they had nothing to prove. "Hi," "Hello," then, "I recognise that accent," and they would admit to coming from Summer Lane or Aston. Only a few were up their own arse; most recognised that they had nothing to prove. Certainly no one looked down on me; most had been where I was, they had simply climbed up higher on the ladder. Many had made a few dodgy moves to get where they were or make a few quid – "Put this job down to the company, would you Tom?"—"Yes, sure, no problem." So, his company pays for his patio or garden landscape, and it doesn't cost him a fucking carrot.

My newfound friend, Gordon, was always moaning about the stress he was under, running his own companies, but I clocked he was having a load of work done on his houses: new extensions - all built by his own workers, all paid for by the company. Our Billy used to do the same or similar with his shops and warehouses, only that was classed as *fraud*, which I was learning every fucking day. I estimated that the profit on two of his houses (one on Rosemary Hill Road and the other on the Four Oaks estate) that due to the extra work, it would have been upwards of 150 grand - tax free - and he reckons he was "hard done by." This call was a very polite gentleman who asked me to call at his home in view of looking at a job. Driving along Walmley Road, I get my book out to check the address. What the hell is going on here? I'm on the Walmley Road, but I've got no number, just Newhall. Well, that's bleeding great, Walmley Road is a big road. After going up and down a few times, I'm just about to bugger off back home when I happen to see two big pillars with the word Newhall on them. Driving through the gates, I notice a guy standing by a cottage inside the gates. I'm still slow. "Hello mate, I'm looking for a Mr Abbot?" "Yes," he replied. "Just carry on up the drive and it's the big house on the left."

As I pulled up outside the house, I was met by the gentleman I had spoken to on the phone. "Ahh, good afternoon, Mr Lewin. Thank you for turning up." As he turned, this silver haired lady came walking from inside the house. I missed it, but I knew I had fucked up before even starting. I had three-days-worth of growth on my face, big heavy boots caked in mud, a big donkey jacket tied with a piece of string; no way was I going to get this job.

"Oh, please come through, Mr Lewin. You were highly recommended to us."

"Oh, who by?"

"The fencing contractors who had put my fencing up."

As I followed her into the side kitchen, she started to lead me through the house. I was spluttering all over the place. "I can't come in here; I've got my dirty boots on, ma'am." She looked at me in admonishment and said, "Nonsense, Mr Lewin. I fully expect that you've been working." And with that, she walked me through the house. There were pictures on the wall of her and her husband in robes, meeting the queen, and great big solid silver punch bowls on the side cabinets. Oh-my-fucking-god, my bottle was completely falling out. This was Lady Owen and her husband's house. He was passed, *was* Sir Alfred Owen, and had been a director of the car parts manufacturer's Rubery Owen over in the Black Country. I knew I was fucked and out of my depth.

Taking me out to the patio at the back, I could see that the fencers had made a garden out of the fields for the house. This house had belonged to the head estate manager. Sir and Lady Owen had lived in the big, moated mill further up that was going to be turned into a five-star hotel. The patio was a total mess running about 50-60 feet along the whole length of the house. In the middle stood a cut-down oak tree, about four-feet high and two feet in diameter. Lady Owen looked at me in hesitation and then asked, "What do you think, Mr Lewin?"

It was shit or bust; I knew I hadn't gotten the job anyway, so I started giving it the extravagant gestures, with all the arm waving and confidence I just didn't have. "Well, for starters, you cannot touch the tree - that must remain and must be a feature of the patio."

Lady Owen looked at me with thrilled admiration. "Mr Lewin, I'm so glad you came. I'm so pleased. That's exactly what I thought."

Stagger me, I'd gotten the job. Sending in the quote was just a formality. As we walked back through the kitchen, Lady

Owen insisted that tea, coffee, and milk would be put out for me and my men, and we should help ourselves as she would be going away whilst the work was going on. My bottle was going yet again, and I could feel the panic rising in me. "No, no, ma'am, please, I'd rather not." All that solid silver? If that was nicked, I would be in deep shit. But Lady Owen insisted.

Once I got home, I made some enquiries. It seemed the Owens were notorious for not paying their bills. This led to quite a few small shops in Walmley Village coming close to bankruptcy. This was something I couldn't afford. I rang my bank up for advice. "No, no, Mr Lewin - don't worry. They were very slow at paying their bills but following a big outcry, there was a big shake-up at the estate, now the bills are paid promptly." Well thank the Lord for that. The next thing I needed to do was work out a suitable price. I sat down, worked the sizes out, then the materials: how many tons of sand, how many bags of cement, then how many slabs for the patio? After doing this, I looked at the total bill, sat back, and considered the possibility that they just might delay paying me, and decided to adjust the bill upwards a bit. Going over the prices again, I realised that I hadn't allowed for my new status as a member of the Master Builder's Federation, so decided to adjust the price up a little bit more. In all, I readjusted the price three or four times before sending it off. Blow me down with a feather, but my price was accepted with an immediate start. We were off and running. Lady Owen was more than pleased with the job and I was paid within a couple of weeks. I heaved a great sigh of relief that nothing was nicked while we were there. I don't know whether Lady Owen actually moved into the house, but shortly after the mill was turned into a top hotel, and the land - well, some of the land became a big housing estate. Bloody lovely money if you can get it.

My brother Reg came up one day and we sat in the sun enjoying a cup of coffee. Reg was a bit concerned about my swearing in the garden where I could possibly be heard by the neighbours. I said "Reg, Reg, trust me; these all swear as much as me, and rest assured there are more crooks up here than anywhere down Summer Lane." Reg was so naïve in many ways; the porridge had puddled his brain. He looked at me in total astonishment and disbelief.

I was invited to quote for another job further down the road, a nice big corner detached house. Turning up, I was met by a very nice buxom blonde with a nice smile. She wanted a patio built at the back of the garden for a barbeque. The price was accepted, and we started shortly after. The job was fairly straight forward, and just involved building a small dwarf wall in a semi-circular shape in the corner of the garden, enclosing a slabbed patio area. I was getting to feel comfortable in my new surroundings and getting comfortable in how to deal with people. Her husband asked me if I did any other building work. Of course, I said, "What do you want done? He brought the plans out and I could see it was a nice extension to the rear. "Take the plans with you, Tom, and work out a price. If your price is ok, you can have the job." With that, I folded the plans up and took them home. We finished the patio job in about a week and I presented her with the bill. She was very enthusiastic about her new patio and told me her and her husband had had a few friends around the previous night for a barbeque. Everyone liked the patio, even one of her friends, who was a detective. Oh yeah. After a bit more chit chat, she said, "Oh Tom, are you related to the Kirby's?" That's it; the frigging coppers put the poison in again. I could feel the bomb explode in my brain. The filthy mongrel. Of course, she wouldn't know that or see the significance, but I knew he'd put the poison in. For what reason? He would have my address; he would know where I lived. Why would he think he was being of any service or kindness to his [friends]? What was I going to do, come back at night and rob their bloody house?

The next day I went back to pick my cheque up for the work and when I got back, Bet asked what happened with the job. "Nothing, why?" "Well, shortly after you left this morning, the woman's husband knocked on the door asking for his plans back. He was sweating and panic-stricken saying he needed them." I could see the puzzlement on her face, and I explained exactly what had happened. She was resigned to it. So not only had the copper put the poison in to my now ex-customers, but the other guests at the barbeque would also be in on the little secret. Maybe six? Eight? More? So, they ain't going to give me a call, are they? And how many more will they tell? I was beginning to realise that Sutton was a small place. People work on recommendations: neighbours, friends, etc. This didn't bode well for me, and it wasn't the first time this had happened.

Any yearnings to move back to Kitts Green had now receded. The kids were happy at school, we were settling in fine, and I was getting forward financially. But always at the back of my mind was that nagging fear: when is it all going to collapse in on me? Each week I thought the cops might come screaming round if there had been a burglary at one of the houses I worked on, or if I lost customers due to the poison going in. We had a big mortgage and we only needed a bit of bad luck to lose the lot.

I tried to put any uncertainties to the back of my mind. Our garden was some 130 feet long, so I decided to build a good size pool to the back - part ornamental, part dipping for the kids in the hot summers. Next to it, I built a chicken pen, my mom and dad's enterprise in me at all times. Then next I got us a few ducks. 'round Ronnie Broadhurst's. One day, he introduced us to his lamb, Mary. Ronnie had a couple of cottages in Wales and had decided to bring it home for a few weeks. My eyes lit up at the thought of what our kids would make of it. Ronnie was happy for us to take it home for a few days. I got her home and - true to form – the kids went berserk. We had got a proper little farm going on: ducks, chickens, and now a sheep. From early morning till late at night, we would hear the bleating of the lamb. After a couple of days, the phone went. "Oh hello, is this Mrs. Lewin?" After giving a cautious "yes," the caller apologised and pointed out that she was from the RSPCA and she'd received an inquiry as to whether it was legal or lawful to keep a sheep in the back garden. "Oh," we told them, "there is nothing illegal at all in keeping a sheep in the back garden. In fact, you can keep an elephant if you wish." "But Mrs. Lewin, could I come around and have a look? I can assure you its only curiosity. We here just can't believe that someone in Sutton Coldfield would want to keep a sheep in the back garden of a house in Sutton Coldfield." Bet said yes of course, and within the hour, a young RSPCA inspector turned up at the door. Bet led her through to the back room where she could see the sheep at the top of the garden. The girl was bemused. Bet opened the patio doors and suggested she call out to Mary. With some scepticism, the girl did, and like a shot, the sheep came bolting down the garden. The girl couldn't get her breath after bursting out laughing. She said, "Now I've seen it all. They will never believe this back at the office." With that, and a bit of friendly chatting, she waved goodbye and got in her car. We were intrigued. Was it Tim the cop making sure we weren't doing anything illegal? After all, Brenda did comment that they had heard the sheep and knew only the Lewins would do something like that. Or could it have been one of our neighbours? Just as they say, "inquiring?"

Chick and his wife, Christopher's parents from next door, were a very nice couple but quite innocent of the world. With the experience of the next-door neighbours nicking from our garden, we had decided to put up six-foot fencing all around. One or two of the panels had knot holes in them, and once or twice Bet had caught Chick nosing through the holes. He always seemed to be intrigued with what we were doing. Bet would take to having the hose pipe ready, and when she heard Chick loitering around, she would grab the hose, wait for Chick's eyeball to show in the knot hole, then give it a good blast with the hose. It took Chick a couple of blasts to stop him nosing. A few days after the sheep incident, I was talking to Mrs Walton on the drive. I decided to wind her up a little bit. "Ahhhh, Mrs Walton," in that over-exaggerated put-upon posh voice. "I've been having a think and wondered if you and Chick would like to join in our Dig for Britain project." Mrs Walton's eyes started swirling around like a screaming dervish, wildly looking to see where Chick was. "W-w-what do you mean, Thomas?" It was always Thomas, never Tommy. "Well, Mrs Walton, you do remember Winston Churchill's cry to the country to dig for Britain?" Her eyeballs were whizzing around even faster now. I said, "Its ok; I've spoken to the Morrisons next door and they are fully in agreement. They feel you might like to participate. The only thing I'm going to ask you is for now please keep it confidential because I can tell you, if the neighbours find out they will all want to get in on the acts." By now Mrs Walton was in real panic, wondering what to expect. "Look, you know we've got some ducks, chicken and a sheep. Our gardens are far too big for us. I mean look at yours; the last fifty yards are just unused. What we propose is this: I will increase my chickens to about fifty. This will keep you, me, and the Morrisons next door in eggs all year round, even the odd chicken for the Sunday roast. We will increase the duck by the same amount, which will give us each a duck for the Sunday roast. The Morrisons have suggested that they keep a nice jersey cow, which will supply our milk all year round. The rest of the garden they will turn over to potatoes. We will cut a line right across the top of our gardens and you can keep the pigs." That was it, pigs. Mrs Walton really went into panic mode. She was sweating, her lips were trembling, and before she had a chance to reply I got it in quick and said, "Now don't worry; we do appreciate that you might not like keeping pigs. The Morrisons have agreed to keep the pigs if you don't want to and you can keep the cow and grow the potatoes. How about that? Is that fair enough?" I knew they never spoke to the Morrisons, but with her nerves falling to bits, and her lips trembling, she said she would have to discuss it with Chick and get back to me. Mrs Walton avoided me like the plague for a good few weeks after that.

I was still worried about the work situation with coppers putting the poison in against me. Whichever way I looked at it, I came from a so-called notorious extended family, and I was a convicted thief - innocent or not. No one in Sutton was going to employ someone they thought might break into their house after finishing a job. I know what people are like, which reminds me of an expression: "fair weather friends didn't just crop up for no reason." When the shit hits the fan, people fan out quick sharpish. Plus, the mortgage was still a heavy weight around my neck. We now had five kids and it felt like we were always living hand-to-mouth. Even the newly taken on tree felling went out the back door. Yes, it was very lucrative, but I didn't carry any insurance and the last job had been a bit too close to comfort. A guy had rung me up for a price to cut a beech tree down on the Birmingham Road. Looking at it, the beech was at the rear of his garden. His garden backed on to a side road which was handy for getting rid of the wood. It was also plenty of distance from his house and greenhouse. I gave him a price, which he accepted, and we turned up on the due day to start work.

Steve Hewston, Tommie's brother, was working for me. Steve was a nice kid and was drawing the dole. Now Steve typically thought I was loaded, and one Friday night Bet had gotten out a T-bone steak for my dinner. "Ohh, look at that. T-bone steak, ay?" I was giving Steve seventy quid a week, and when I asked him, he admitted that he would spend all that on the Friday and Saturday night. He just wouldn't have it that I was on not much more than him. But fair play, Steve had bottle, and on turning up on the job, we parked the lorry in the side road. We got the ladder up against the trunk which gave me time to have a good look at it. It was big, and I could feel myself twitching a little bit. The main trunk was about two-and-a-half-feet in diameter by about forty-feet high. Three quarters of the way up, two heavy branches spread out from it. I instructed Steve to climb up the trunk and cut the one branch of before tackling the other. As he started to climb, I looked around and noticed the old boy was out videoing us. Oh Jesus Christ; that's all I need. Making a cut underneath, Steve then proceeded to cut above the branch. He'd gotten a 30-inch chainsaw that I had taken out on hire. Too late: as the branch cracked and dropped off the tree, the tree sprung ten feet, and with the loss of weight, the chainsaw came spinning to the ground. Steve threw his arms around the trunk, clinging on for dear life. The trunk landed on the ground just inches from me and my bottle completely fell out. I looked around to see the owner still with his video camera, and in my loudest voice - and trying to keep as calm as possible - I shouted, "Yes, that's fine...FINE. Exactly right, come on down and have a rest." Checking to make sure the chainsaw was ok, I asked Steve if he was alright. "That was a bit bloody close, Steve." Thankfully, I pushed the blame onto him, and he accepted it. My hands shaking, I instructed Steve to get back up the tree. "Right, now see where that trunk splits off? I want you to cut a cheese on the opposite side, then come around this side and start the cut a couple of inches above the cheese. First tie this rope ten feet above the cut. I'll tie the rope around me, and when it goes, I'll help it along by pulling on the rope. That way we'll just cut it up and put it on the lorry." Instructions passed, and both in agreement, Steve starts back up the ladder. He ties the rope, works his way back down, and begins the cut. I make myself round to the other side of the tree, tying the rope a few times around my body and bracing myself. Steve shouts, "It's coming!" I look down the garden and I can see the owner is still at it, videoing every bit of it. I could feel the sweat bouncing off my bonce and I wish he would piss off.

I could hear the crack, braced myself - ready to ease the trunk over - but it wasn't coming. It was going the other bleeding way! I could feel the weight pulling on me, and quick-sharpish, I whipped the rope from around my waist. Looking up, I saw Steve had flung the chainsaw to the ground and gripped the trunk as tightly as he could, the top half of the tree slowly coming down on top of him. My bottle was completely going. He's frigging dead. I know the tree is going to hit him. Looking across, the guy is still filming, the tree is falling towards him, and if it doesn't hit him, it's going to hit the greenhouse. It took me all my strength to stop screaming and, miraculously, the tree missed the greenhouse by about six feet. The owner was that busy videoing he never even noticed. I walked as slowly as I could and shouted up at Steve as calmly as I could muster. "That could have been a bit further over that way, Steve, but never mind, it's good enough. WELL-DONE!" I couldn't look at the bloke at all, and when I got to him, I said, "Steve, you made the cut too high up, son." Steve nodded in apology. That was it; I couldn't take any more of this kind of stress. Only the week before, some council tree fellas had done a similar job. The branch fell, the tree whipped away, and the young lad cutting the branch lost his head completely as the chainsaw sprung back and against him. Birmingham council stopped tree felling from that moment on and stopped using chainsaws. I felt the same. Steve was casual; he was on the dole. The publicity was unthinkable. The thoughts were horrifying, yet he could have died. No, that was it. My tree felling days were over. We finished the job of, got rid of the timber, got my cheque, and that was it - out of it.

I was doing well in the boxing, keeping as fit as fiddle, winning every fight. I was now doing a bit for Sheldon Heath, with some good boxers among them. Paul and Ian Murry, who went on to become good friends, Johnny Burns, and Lloyd Hibbert, a welter weight who later went on to win the Lonsdale belt. All good kids. The club had major plans for me to fight in the ABAs, but I knew I was too old. Even one of Jackie Turpins family wanted me to turn pro after watching me win by knockout, cobblers to that with not too much reluctance. I informed my old trainer, Wally Cox, that I had got too much worry on with my business to carry on with the boxing. I was telling the truth. If anything, I should have turned pro years ago; now it was too late.

It's surprising what desperation can bring out in you. Each builder or self-employed guy I spoke to taught me a new lesson. The carpenter from great bar had gotten a double garage to the side of his house; this was his workshop. He specialised in building and fitting porches. He would visit the customer, measure up, then make the porch in his garage. Before delivering it to the job and fitting it, I had ordered a porch of him for my own house. In talking to him, he admitted to digging his own footings out, laying the bricks to take the porch, putting the concrete in and tiling on top, even fitting the felt roof. Oh, bugger that he said, "I just got fed up with either waiting for brickies to turn up, or not turn up at all." He was right, of course; I had been having the same problem, so on my first small job of a dwarf wall, I decided to have a crack at it myself. After a bit of practice, it didn't look half bad. After a few more practice runs, I could build a decent wall. Eventually I could build a small extension. My friend John had started life as a chippy - a carpenter. When I met him, he had called me up to clear the rubbish from an extension he had built with his partner, Roger. Together they did the whole lot, from digging the footings out to the whole build, only calling in a specialist for the one of jobs like the electrics...even doing their own plumbing.

John was a miserable little git, alright; shoulders always hunched over with the burden of living, always got a roll up in his mouth and a dew drop on his nose. I was forever expecting the dew drop to drop on his fag. I never saw him in any clean clothes, and often wondered what his home life was like. I was to find out. John had a very nice, big house in Great Barr with over an acre of land to the rear. The land was full of trees that had a protection order on them. This really pissed John off because he knew with planning permission, his fortune was staring him in the face. I never knew why, or if it was that which made him so miserable...or the fact that his missus kept having affairs behind his back. Walking around with a constant fag in his mouth and a dew drop on his nose made me question if anyone could blame his missus. But John, for all his miserableness, was a friendly enough guy, and built my extension for me on our first house. When I wanted my bathroom plumbing done, John was good enough to spend half the day fitting in my bath sink and toilet. I decided to have a bash myself, so I disconnected all his work and refitted it all myself, this time burying all the pipework under the floorboards and out of sight. Easy when you know how. From that moment, on I did all my own plumbing - same with plastering and tiling. Really, the biggest lesson I learned in life was it all boils down to the groundwork you put in first. It was a lesson instilled in me from boxing: unless you do the training and the exercise, you won't win the fight. It was the same with any type of work. To lay a lawn, the easiest part is laying the turf. The hard work is getting the ground prepared: don't get the concrete footings level and your brickwork will go all over the place, as will your tiles on an uneven floor. The more I did, the more I learned, and the more I learned the more I realised how ignorant I really was. When needed, it's surprising what you can do.

One night, I got a phone call from John. "Hello, Tom. I'm just ringing to see how you are. Good-bye; you're a good mate, Tom." The alarm bells went off in my brainbox, and when he put the phone down, I rang Sutton police right quick-sharpish. "Get over there, he's going to kill himself!" Where the hell was his missus? The cops got to him just in time. He was unconscious, so they broke the door down. A week later, a sheepish John came around the house with his wife to apologise and thank me for saving his life. I looked at his wife trying to figure out what he'd done to make her go off having affairs. He'd had no reason to come around thanking me; it was just luck, really. That made sense after what he did. John left with his wife after that, and, sadly, I never heard from him again. Too embarrassed, I suppose.

Building and landscaping was too hit-and-miss for me, and I realised my shortcomings: I was your typical jack-of-all-trades, good at none. Plus, there was still that cop threat. I decided to sell our house and buy something cheaper that needed refurbishment. Putting the house up, we were chuffed to find the house had almost quadrupled in the four years we had lived in it, no doubt about it. It fully justified our actions in buying private in a nice area. I put a couple of adds in the local paper covering Sutton and Great Barr. The idea was sound; the practicalities were not. I started getting every comic with a bit of a crappy house ringing me up asking top-bat. I'd needed to look around. When you chase, you always get the knockback - whether it be a bird, an item for sale, or a property. People think you're desperate, so the price goes up. Then Bet pointed to an advert in the Sutton News: a cottage for sale over Aldridge. We drove over to have a look. This was a 200-year-old cottage - falling apart - in over half an acre of land, right opposite a nice little park. Ok, a brick quarry to the side, alongside a transport yard, but it had great potential. It was all there for us: a potential four-bedroom house with enough land to set up a small garden centre, and we had enough money to pay cash for it. No one else was interested except a building company who wanted to finish off the development of six houses they had already completed to the edge of the land. The owner was a church minister who had inherited the property from his father. The cottage had been in the family over 200 years and was, in fact, a Wesleyan chapel at some stage. The last thing he wanted was for it to be demolished and built on. We suited him down to the ground and he agreed to sell the cottage to us. We were up, up, and away...almost.

IT'S EASY TO MAKE MONEY WHEN YOU'VE GOT MONEY

My dad never spoke to us a lot as we grew up; he more or less left us to our own devices. Some may condemn him for that - especially the do-gooders, judges or probation officers - but he didn't allow for our complex personalities. His idea was to let us grow in ourselves, find our own way as we went along in life, make our own mistakes and learn from them. For sure he had given up with the older ones, but in Sutton there were lots of parents who did exactly the same thing: leaving their kids to fend for themselves because both parents were out working. Latch-key kids, and more than one teacher. But going along, he would drop the odd nugget out, and I never forgot it: "When you've got your first grand together, you will have cracked it," he told me when we set up in business and brought our first house in Sutton. Yes, Pops, but what you never allowed for was inflation. By the time I'd gotten my first grand, it was worthless. It was ten grand I needed, and by the time I'd gotten ten grand it was thirty grand...it never stopped rising. It was like I was always ten grand behind.

The cottage was a wreck; maybe we had bitten off more than we could chew. There was a bathroom so the kids could have a bath and use the toilet, the kitchen was abysmal, and the lounge had quarry tiles on the floor. This was a right comedown from our lovely house in Sutton but Bet never said a word. Sometimes I could never figure out how her mind worked. Worse, we were utterly totally skint; we'd used every penny to pay cash for the cottage. Well, almost. We decided to get a little caravan for our kids to sleep in because the house was so bad for them. We must have looked a right bunch of Nesbit's to the neighbours, but our friend John would come around with his son Andrew, even letting him stop overnight with our kids. So exciting, as he thought it was. John was a solicitor who worked for a big company in Walsall and had never heard of my name. We kept it that way. "Tom, what a bloody little gold mine you've got here. Look at the potential." He couldn't get over it, but there were quite a few people in Sutton like that - bank managers, professionals. Some would buy a house every five years, making as much from a house as they did in a year of working. Each time they would be moving up the ladder. I wondered whether we were working our way down. Still, we'd got to crack on - shit or bust.

It's interesting how different people see things so differently. I would have thought the very people who would look down their nose at you living rough in a wreck like we were, living in were the so-called snobby middle-class people in Sutton, but far from it; they were the very people who saw what you were up to and what you were planning.

Tim and his wife Brenda popped round to say hello. Why? I was never quite sure. Whether it was to have a little nose at what I was up to or what we had bought, I didn't know. Tim basically had known me since I was a kid of fifteen, but I just don't think he could weigh me up. My brother Reg came round one day with my niece, Teresa. Teresa was a nice kid, but I reckon she and her siblings had been poisoned about me and Bet, so she didn't say a lot.

I had offered Reg the use of a chunk of land to the side of the cottage to set up a little fence manufacturing business. All it needed was fencing off, a template set up, and a bench saw - relatively cheap, really. But Reg was just not business minded. Charlie, the grass, had offered him a job in his fencing yard leading to a directorship. Well, I just looked at Reg in astonishment. "Are you fxxxg joking? Heinz is a grass; he threw me and Dad in!" But Reg wouldn't have it in a month of

Sundays. It did infuriate me that by getting Reg to work for him, Charlie was showing everyone that my accusations were a load of cobblers. There's naivety, then there's stupidity. I couldn't figure out what came first. I said Reg, "Billy Kirby lost his arm working for him. He had no insurance, so he buttered Billy up with the promise of his jag and a directorship. Billy stood for it. The directorship never materialised, and after twelve months, Billy was out on his ear. Charlie was not only a grass, but he was also a mongrel." Sadly, Reg was blinded with the same offer; the directorship never materialised, and true to form, once Reg had served his purpose, everyone had clocked Reg Lewin working for Charlie, he was sacked. Now here he was slagging me off for putting our kids through this disgraceful experience.

"This is disgusting, what you are putting these kids through. How can you take those kids from a lovely house in Sutton Coldfield and put them through this?" Reg just couldn't see it. "Look, Reg, this ain't going to hurt the kids for a few months. It will educate them, if anything. Besides, what we are doing is all for them anyway." He still couldn't see it. Mind, I don't think many of the neighbours did either. A builder lived opposite, and he took the opportunity one day to introduce himself. Well, that's what I thought, but it didn't take him long to puff his little chest up and say, "'Course, I did look at this myself, but I wouldn't touch it with a bargepole." Well, I bet that made him feel superior, the dickhead. Maybe he couldn't see what we thought we could see, but he changed his mind right rapid a few months later.

We had rung the local planning office up to pay us a visit and give us some advice, and within a few days, two gentlemen from the planning office turned up. Looking at Bet, he said, "Where do you come from, love?" When she told him, he looked around and said, "Well, there you are. You don't want to live around here, do you?" Well, I must admit it wasn't the most salubrious area; much of it was private, some nice big houses, but they were iggly piggly - mostly self-built and full of gypoes. Nicky had been attacked by a bunch of kids from her new school who didn't like her posh accent, knocking her black and blue. The cops didn't want to do bugger all about it, par for the bloody course. Me and Bet were far from snobs, but this was worse than Kitts Green. Besides, they were amya and bammyas - black country. "Look," he carried on. "We will give you planning permission to extend the bungalow and an adjoining builder's yard, but what we'd rather see is this site finished off with housing. You'd get eight or ten on here." With that, they walked away and left us to mull things over. It didn't take too long, and within the week, we'd gotten a draughtsman who worked out that we could get ten detached houses on the land. Planning permission was put forward and it was just a question of us sitting back, getting the plans through, then getting the agent in to sell them. In the meantime, we would just have to sit it out. That was the hard part. We couldn't do anything; we couldn't spend any money on the place. All we could do it sit it out.

With the park opposite, we had brought a pony for the kids to have some fun with, keep them distracted. One night, Bet got so depressed, she got pissed, went outside and sat cuddling the pony and singing songs to it. She would wind me up about the minister's ghost being in the bedroom. "Look there," she pointed one night. We had put a carpet down over the quarry tiles to give some warmth to the place, and Bet had pointed to the floor in the corner of the room. It was moving. Each night it was moving along, and I couldn't make out if it was a mouse or a rat. "No, it's too big for a rat. Go over and lift the carpet up," I told her. "I'm not lifting it up," she told me. There was no choice; I'd have to pull the carpet back and take a look. Bet ran out the room staring in from the window, and with great caution I started pulling up the carpet, only to be met with a weed so big it was growing across the bleeding floor! It was like a frigging triffid. Bet gave a nervous laugh, but it only added to our depression and desperation to get out of there. This was 1980, and we were in the middle of a bad recession.

Interest rates were up to fifteen percent, but we were getting quite a lot of interest in the development. The prices coming up were very nice, indeed, so in anticipation, we started looking back over Sutton for a nice house. We had started selling some items we no longer needed, including a new window. A couple phoned up and came over, buying it straight away. They were very nice, very friendly, and very interested in the cottage and what we were doing. Their names were Ken and Janet, and we swapped phone numbers, promising to keep in touch. One of the neighbours told us that the builder opposite was pig sick. I never thought there was that much room. We took great pleasure in his discomfort whenever we passed each other. Eventually, the plans were passed, and we'd gotten builders/developers lined up to buy the plot, minus another that we had decided to keep for later on as an investment. It felt like all our Christmases had come at once. Hard work and suffering, yes, but very worthwhile. A friend, Harold Green, hearing the news, asked us to buy his builder's yard with detached bungalow. It was a great proposition. Harold wanted to retire to his villa in the canaries. Really, he was offering us a very nice deal, but I didn't think I was up to taking anything like that on. Plus, it would have meant borrowing money, and at the current interest rates, I just didn't fancy taking the risk. No, after the past twelve months, we deserved a break. It was an offer I very much regretted, but we make our choices in life. We bought a nice four-bedroom detached house in Sutton, had money in the bank, plus another building plot back over Aldridge. We had, at last, gotten that pot my old man was on about.

The house in Sutton was very nice. There was a big, long garden, so we decided to build a stable for the horse we had brought Andrew, a beautiful three-quarter Arab gelding. There was a spinney opposite us, and we were only a short walk again from Sutton Park. On one side we had a couple who, for some reason, grew rapidly pissed off with us. Why? I don't know. We'd never met them before. Was it the horse, or the knowledge we'd paid cash for the house? I didn't know; I didn't much care. Opposite lived a very nice bank manager and his family. Next to Frank and Mary Dillon, a builder and his wife who became firm friends with Bet. Next door on the other side lived a teacher, his wife, and two kids. True to form, Dave would confirm to me every reason why I despised teachers. In the garden one day, he deigned to introduce himself. "Ahhh," in that lofty, snobby little voice. "My name is David, and I teach at Sandwell Valley. Poor working class, of course, but quite nice." "Ahhh, yes," I replied. "I went to a similar school." Why do teachers have to be such assholes? What gives him the right to think he is so superior to someone from a so-called working-class background? He couldn't bloody afford to live in the house himself. Bet was in the butchers one day in Boldmere, and the teacher's wife was in front of her. When she clocked Bet, she went bright red. "Oh Betty, would you like to go first?" "No, it's ok," Bet said. "I'm in no rush." The teacher's wife placed her order: "Two slices of ham, please, and two slices of corned beef." Oh, well for Christ's sake, that was dinner then. Corned beef for the kids. As she paid up, the butcher turned to Bet. "What will you have, love?" "Oh, two T-bone steaks, please." It gave Bet a smile as she watched the teacher's wife walking out, cheeks of her arse squeaking. "Oh, you would never believe what some of them ask for in here," the butcher told her. We do. We were starting to clock on. Bet was cleaning the car one day. On her hands and knees, she was doing the hub caps when she heard Dave come out and start doing the lawn. Then his two kids came out and joined him in the garden. Polishing away, she could see he was getting pissed off. "Go in, children." They weren't listening. "Go in, children." They still weren't listening. After a couple more times, he let go. "You two, get in the fucking house now!" They shot in the house. Bet was mortified. "I couldn't get up," she said. "He would have known I'd heard him." "Exactly," I said. "You should have gotten up, ha-ha." It wasn't the swearing that got me, or the shouting, nor the corned beef slices. It was the bloody hypocrisy of people like that. Why did they have to look down on others who came from a so-called poor background, when in truth, they couldn't afford to live there themselves?

We got a knock on the door one day. I go to answer it only to be confronted by a copper in uniform. Squeezing my buttocks in, I scrambled my brain trying to think what I had done. The cop, seeing my discomfort, bent over backwards to reassure me. "It's ok, sir. I do apologise. It's only this speeding fine that had dropped in yesterday. I knew automatically that you had obviously overlooked it, so I decided to come round personally to save you any trouble." Well, this indeed was a turn-up for the books. A *copper* apologising to *me*. Little did he know. I invited him in while I got him the money for the fine. As I was white and middle-class, he saw fit to let me know how he and his mates were all looking forward to volunteering for the miner's strikes. "Oh, we love it, sir. Gives us a chance to knock a few heads together and getting paid overtime for it." "Oh, oh...oh yes, I bet," I said, thinking I was in full agreement. He then went on to tell me how they all had a fine old time when the riots were going on in Handworth. Now in full flow, he started boasting how the bosses were having to start refusing them, such was the clamour for the overtime. Oh, oh, oh, so many white police officers were clamouring to batter all those black heads. I was just sorry I never had a tape recorder. I couldn't believe it; how arrogant was he to think I would automatically condone his behaviour because of the assumption that I was white and middle class. I was astounded.

I was still doing the landscaping and building and was picking up some work from the Greeks. Greeks, like Asians, had a different way of looking at things when it came to money. Asians I wouldn't work for. I'd had a couple of experiences with them, and found that whatever you told them, they would start bartering. To get the job, you had to cut the price. Having cut the price, you then had to cut the job.

In the end, you ended up codging the job up anyway. Greeks were different. Greeks worked hard, made a lot of money, and paid for the job if they thought it was reasonable. I was getting recommendations. To each other, they all owned fish-n-chips shops and they were all related – cousins. If one was happy with you, they would recommend you to their cousin, or friend, their friend would recommend you to their cousin, and they all had plenty of cash. I had done a nice job for George, who had a fish shop in Sutton and a very nice, detached house in Four Oaks. He told me he had recommended me to his cousin, Chris, and maybe I would give him a bit of a discount. I was grateful and did. A couple of weeks later, Chris duly rung me up. He had gotten a very nice, detached house in Four Oaks off Rosemary Hill Road. It was a new development, and his was the last one of four, as such the builders gave him a big discount. I was envious. Chris was a nice guy, as were many of the Greeks I dealt with - modest, unassuming, hardworking. I think every Greek has a natural ability to cook food, and they all do good fish-n-chips.

Chris wanted the whole of his rear garden landscaping - at least half an acre, including the obligatory barbeque on the newly built patio - all cash, of course. I gave him my quote, which he accepted without question. We started work the following week. First, we built the patio, then the barbeque. Whilst we were working away, we couldn't help but notice that while we were outside beavering away, Chris and his family were beavering away inside. There was beautiful French furniture being brought in, a branded curtain shop coming in fitting the best curtains and drapes. In the end, my curiosity got the better of me. It was only after I realised how cheeky I was. Chris had come out to have a chat with us. "Chris, I hope you don't mind my asking, but do you gamble?" I asked. "Only I couldn't help but notice that you're spending money here like there's no tomorrow." Chris gave me a smile and with no indication of any resentment, told me, "No, Tom, we Greeks do gamble, but it's not for the big money - we play for pennies - it's the game that we enjoy. The truth is our accountant told me we got to buy a house as we were making too much money. The wife didn't like the kitchen that the builders were putting in, so we paid an extra £5,000, for a better kitchen, that's all."

I said, "I only ask because my cousin has a fish-n-chip shop just down the road from you, and he's still living in the flat above his chip shop." At that, Chris looked at me and said, "Ronnie? Is he your cousin? I know Ronnie. Look, he has his potatoes of the same potato man as me Dave."

We have the same fish supplier, the only difference is, Ronnie uses oil to cook with and we use lard." I couldn't figure it out; my cousin was directly opposite the university, yet he must have been earning a fortune. Whilst my little brain was letting this sink in, Chris said, "Where the difference lies, Tom, is your Ronnie employs two staff: that's£200 per week, £10,000 per year. In five years, that's a detached house in Sutton." Such a simple logic, yet how many of us truly think about it. Chris went on to tell me, "The thing is, Tom, we Greeks work together; our kids do a bit in the shop before going to school, then they work in the shop when they come back. My mother, who's 80, does a bit of cleaning in the shop. Not a lot; she's old, but every bit helps." Mazda - that's why my cousin, lovely as he was - was still living in a cramped flat, while Chris here was moving into a luxurious four-bedroom detached house in Four Oaks.

I also knew my cousin was spending a fortune on insurance bonds and other investments. What do those companies do with your money? Invest it in land, etc. Why not just bung all your dough into the best house you can afford? My brother-in-law had tried to do the same with me years earlier. "Tom, buy some insurance bonds. That's what I do." Clive was a manager for an insurance company. Obviously, he was looking to earn commission of me. "Clive, I can barely afford my mortgage," I told him. As it happened, without realising it, I had been right. Chris told me he had also got to find five thousand pounds to put into a pot for yet another cousin who was arriving soon from Cyprus. That was his whack; this was how the Greeks worked. How bloody admirable. So, they all bung in. The guy has a wad of cash, he then goes to my cousin with a carrier bag full of cash, which had happened. "I only have £8,000 pounds, to buy a new car," he told me, as he wanted to sell his Mercedes on the drive. I had learned some valuable lessons. I also did a deal with Chris and ended up having his Mercedes. It was a decision I came to regret. Chris certainly got the best end of the deal on that one. I found a lot of the Asians worked the same way. The father will knock out his kids. He will then take, say, £100 wage of each child per week; five children equal £500, and after twelve months that comes to £25,000 - enough to buy a house in Handsworth or Alum Rock. After five years, the whole family has their own home. Very simple, very clever. The auction houses are chock-a-block with Asians buying houses. Why can't we English think like that?

Doing some work on the roof one day, my back went. I mean *really* went. It was a problem that affects many bricklayers and builders. I could hardly get down from the roof to drag myself into the house and into my bed where I lay for three days in agony. When I finally managed to get to the doctors, he recommended me to a specialist who diagnosed me with a crushed vertebrae and arthritis to the spine. However, I looked at it, my gardening and building business was out of the way for sure.

Me and Bet decided to have a break in Devon with a couple of the kids. We had seen one of these little advertising posters in the local post office window. It was a small hotel run by a Sutton guy named Terry, and his wife. Devon was a lovely place; the sun was out, and we were enjoying a nice break. Terry and his missus were a nice couple, but we clocked after a couple of days that. Whoever was doing the cooking just couldn't cook. Everything we were eating was frozen. One night, while eating our evening dinner, I commented, "You know, these pair can't cook to save their lives." Bet was quick to agree. That night's meal was fish in breadcrumbs, always a dead giveaway. Frozen fish and frozen chips. It was the same with breakfast - the only thing that wasn't frozen were the eggs.

We also noticed how quiet it was. Because of our financial circumstances, we never gave much thought to the financial circumstances governing these Hoteliers, or people like Terry and his wife. We had owned and sold our cottage for cash, brought our new house for cash, and had money in the bank. The reality of borrowing money at fifteen percent never hit us or occurred to us, but most Hoteliers were borrowing money. Most were hocked up to the eyeballs with debt, including Terry and his wife, no doubt judging by the fact he had to borrow bottles of spirits on demand. "Course," I said to Bet, without thinking about it, "I recon we could run a hotel better than them." With that, Bet bit. "Well, I could cook better than this crap, that's for sure." That was it; the seed was planted. We both started getting carried away with the thought that we could own and run a hotel. Down in the town, as we started looking around, enjoying the sun, we started looking in estate agent windows. We couldn't believe how cheap some of the hotels were. We got a local accountant on board who advised us not to go too big in hotel bedrooms due to the difficulties and having to pay the extra tax. Looking around, we found we could buy a twenty-bedroom hotel for not much more than our house was worth.

We looked at a very nice seventeen-bedroom hotel directly on the sea front. The rear patio overlooked the Bristol channel. The owners were two couples who had been friends from Derbyshire who decided to go into partnership together. Both me and Bet fell in love with it and the idea of owning it. We went back to the hotel, and later on in the bar we dropped it out to Terry and his wife what our plans were. They were both very receptive and helpful. Sometimes ignorance is bliss, alright, and if nothing else, I had an inbuilt sense of ignorance up to the eyeballs. I didn't look too much around the corner: what it fully entailed, how to get the customers in, if it would pay. As far as Bet was concerned, I think she thought I was the great Tommy Lewin and could do anything. As usual, she seemed well up for it and showed no fear. That gave me the confidence to go blindly ahead. In all sense of the word, it was the blind leading the blind.

With no more to do, we put an offer in on the hotel which was accepted straight away. That night, with a minor celebratory drink in the bar with the owners, Terry dropped it out that another brummy couple owned the hotel just a few doors up from our hotel. When he mentioned their name, I realised it was Bernard Hunt and his family. Bernard was a former scrap dealer and a friend of my older brothers. This was very encouraging, and we felt it was great to have a friend close by in a strange town. It was to be a bit over-optimistic on my part. Without further ado, we started planning and getting to know the town. Bet had been talking to a lady who was sitting on a bench overlooking the harbour, and on saying hello to the lady they started chatting. When Bet excitedly told her we were buying a hotel, she replied, "You'll be sorry," with a sense of bitterness. We shrugged it off and dismissed it from our minds. Obviously, she wasn't too happy with her experience of the town - whatever that was.

By the end of the week's holiday, we felt comfortable with our decision and set off home to discuss it with the kids. We sat them down and talked about the hotel: the position, the sea, and that we thought we were offering them a great opportunity that we could all grow into. Andrew had joined the army, but Nicky was now almost sixteen, so she would be the waitress, Bet the cook, I would run the bar, and we would all muck in on the cleaning and chambering. Sutton was a very nice place to live, but I had always recognised the benefits of being self-employed. Working for someone else is great if you've got the education; you are valued as an asset to the company, whether in sales, marketing, or management, with a view to promotion. As a labourer with no education, that's it. You were looked down upon, paid crap wages and sacked at a moment's notice. Not for me, thank you very much. It was my experiences of life and Bet's experiences that helped us in our choices.

The kids were all happy with the decision. Andrew was so happy he wanted to get out of the army. We all learn in life from different slices of life. A businessman, friend of my brother Billy, had a small engineering business and once standing at the bar in a pub advised me always to borrow money of the bank even when you don't need it. I couldn't see the purpose of getting into debt with the banks just for the sake of it, but I could see the logic. I read a book once by the great actor Errol Flynn. Out of work for a long period, he was offered a job running a cotton plantation in south America for a friend/acquaintance. Flynn was the first to admit that he hadn't had a clue about business or running a business, but the plantation had a full workforce and a foreman who oversaw the plantation. That was enough for him. He knew that the foreman would know his job and would effectively run the place. All Flynn had to do was ride around two or three times a day on horseback to show his presence. If he had any queries, the foreman could sort it or answer him. That, together with my dad's advice that you can do anything in life if you set your mind to it, gave me the confidence to go for it. In truth, my ignorance played a great part in it as well. I only saw the positives, never the negatives. I only saw the negatives when they jumped up and smacked me in the mouth.

Taking another leaf from the Asian and Greek community, I insisted that Bet be allowed to spend a week in the hotel learning the job of cooking and working in the kitchen, getting to learn the running of the hotel. I grew up with smart arses around Nechells, and the wider area that never offered any input on anything spoken or talked about. I'm thinking of buying a lorry and getting into haulage...the look goes around the room, eye to eye, a little raised eyebrow, the cxxxxt. It took me years to figure it out. Why do people do that? React that way? It's the ultimate put-down; the knockback, certainly. If I'd turned to my brother Billy and said, "I'm buying a hotel, son," he would have looked at me in total disbelief, paused a bit, then might say, "What?" Don't be a cxxxnt. Going to be a labourer on the building site? Fine, that was about your barrer, it was the teachers' mantra. Want to be a boxer? Fine. Want to be a champion boxer? Don't be a cxxxt. The Asians had a totally different attitude to business; it must be in built within their culture or from the poverty they went through. The people I grew up with went through poverty as well, yet they couldn't wait to knock you down. What a mug. Once one learned his business, he would teach his sibling or friend. The Greek community would bring a cousin or family member over from cypress, everyone throwing a few grand into the pot teaching him how to buy, cook, and sell fish and chips. He, in turn, would get stuck in, work hard, then return the loans and be available to return the favour...and so the cycle went on. The Asians have the same mentality, but they take it to a different level. The Asian will look at a business, work out its potential, then agree to buy the business, offering to keep the existing staff on. I've seen them do it many times with shops, garages, petrol stations, and property. Once they are in the business – say, the petrol station - they will sit back in the background pouring over the books while all the time watching the staff and learning from them. Once they learn enough, they may well sack that staff then put their own family in. By another year most of the original staff have disappeared and been replaced, one token staff kept to front the counter.

I've had people say to me, "Oh, those Asians are hard workers you know," in awe and with bated breath. It's a mantra that's sunk into our culture, yet it's always amazed me. How many do you see with a shovel on the building sites? On the roads digging holes? Not many, I'll be bound. You will see them in a shop sitting there from eight in the morning till twelve at night, because that's what they are used to. In Asia or north Africa, you will see them sitting all day in there Djellab, selling from a stall, waiting all day to earn pennies. It comes naturally to them as they sit drinking mint tea. Likewise, they come from a culture where its normal to sleep crammed into a small room. When they come to England prepared to take the lower wage of the native English, it's of no consequence to them to share a room in the same manner. It makes common sense; it's only a small step from that to buying their first house, and so it grows. Very clever.

We had now started to make preparations for our move to Devon. Ken and Janet, having now become firm friends, had offered to help us move. they had had the good fortune to buy a nine-bedroom house in Sutton. We would have dived in for it ourselves, if given the opportunity, but they had gotten it and good luck to them. It needed a great deal of work doing to it, but the potential for a small guest house, letting rooms, as well as giving their family a home was a great incentive. But then we got a bit of news that created another problem. One of Nicky's friends approached me in the street and asked me about the belting Nicky had had. What do you mean? She had gotten a black eye as she had been talking to a lad she knew just a few roads away from us. That night, I pulled Nicky aside and asked what had happened. It seemed she had been talking to her boyfriend outside his home, when a young lad walked past and gave them a bit of verbal. The lad had apparently been trying to chat up my daughter a few times over the previous few weeks only to get a knockback. This did not sit well with him when he saw her talking to another young lad. After a bit of verbal, he's done no more than march over, give her boyfriend a right-hander, her a black eye, and when the boyfriend's mother ran out, gave her a smack too. It was only when Michael's brother Steve came out, all guns charging, that the bully ran off. Michael's mother called the police, who sent an officer around to his house. The cop turned up, got his report sheet out and started taking details.

Michael not only had bruises, but a fractured jaw as well. When it came to his job, Michael replied that he was in the navy. At that, the cop tore up the complaints sheet saying, "Oh, well this is a complete waste of time. By the time this gets to court you could be the other side of the world. Look, my advice is taking a couple of lads up and give him a good hiding." With that, he got up and walked out of the door.

That is so fxxxxg typical of the cops. Anything like hard work and they throw the towel in. It's got to be headline-catching or laid on a plate for them. To me, I'm used to it. Nicky was set upon by a group of kids over Aldridge just a few months earlier simply because she had a different accent. When the cops came into it, they wanted to treat it as a simple group altercation. The cops like to keep brainwashing the public into thinking they are human beings just like the rest of us. No, they are not, unless it suits them. They love nothing more than nicking people, unless it gets a bit difficult or the nicking is too difficult, and the end doesn't justify the needs. I felt I had no alternative but to take the matter into my own hands - find and chastise the yellow bxxxd. This, under normal circumstances, should do the trick. This is how it worked when I was a kid growing up in Nechells. It was accepted practice. There is always someone bigger than yourself. Bullies were very few and far between.

To me, I was dealing with a young kid - a bully - who hung about on the street corner up the bush picking on anyone who was an easy target walking in the area. It was their entertainment. My intention was to admonish the little toe rag, maybe give him a clip around the earhole. Andrew knew who the kid was, so I asked him to point him out, giving him strict instructions not to move out of the car. There were three of them sitting on the shop doorstep as I walked across - big lads, about eighteen or so. I started off asking the little toe rag if he was the lad concerned. Big mistake. These lads are on the ball. This is what they did: before I knew it, they were up of the step throwing punches and jumping on my back. I felt

Andrew run up behind me. He had seen one of them with a baseball bat, ran up, grabbed the bat and hit the one who then - with the other two - ran off around the corner. "I told you to sit in the car!" "But he was hitting you." Fair enough. How could I chastise him? That wasn't the end of it. These little toe rags were back within seconds with baseball bats the lot, plus an extra couple of their gang. Soon others gathered around, running up and down like little dervishes. I stood my ground holding Andrew behind me. Eventually, and typical of bullies, they ran off without further ado.

Getting home, I felt the only way to handle this was to find out where the little toe rag lived and confront his parents. This was getting ridiculous. The next night I drove around to his house in Kingstanding, only to see a mob of about fifteen standing outside his house with his parents. I realised this was going nowhere so decided to drop it and get home. Going around the block I was confronted by about twenty of the little toe rags spread across the road, pickaxe handle and god knows what else. Putting my foot down, I drove through them on the wrong side of the road. Getting home I debated about calling the cops. Bet quite rightly pointed out it would be a waste of time and reminded me of the last time I called the cops. She also reminded me we'd be in Devon soon. She was right, but I was bloody angry. These cops, idiots as they were, are encouraging this kind of behaviour by turning a blind eye to it in the first place. It was happening in schools, in the playground, and in the streets, and both the cops and the schools turn a blind eye. Boxing is being banned all over the country, yet boxing is the ideal discipline against bullying. In the first world war, it was said that we were lions led by donkeys. Things are not changing. We are still being led by donkeys - no common sense. Eight o'clock, the doorbell went. Going to answer it I found myself facing a young copper looking confused and a bit nervous. I saw there were three squad cars and a van. "Obviously the house has thrown them a bit, Mr Lewin." I invited the copper in. "Well, we received a complaint that you tried to run someone over earlier on this evening." Here we frigging go again. "Would you like to come down to Erdington police station to clear this up?"

"Yea sure."

So, we go down to Erdington. This time the cops are sitting back a bit; they can't quite add it up, that's obvious. Without much prodding, I explained to the cops exactly what happened. Far from me attempting to run them over - a very serious offence - they were trying to attack me.

"Well," the one cop told me. "We've got him in the cells here, and he's a right bolshie little shit, shouting his mouth of to high heaven."

"Let me in the cell with him for ten minutes and I'll soon shut the little toe rag up." It was all very relaxed, and I wasn't under arrest or felt under arrest at any time. I could feel the cops were quite sympathetic. After half an hour or so, a group of cops came walking in, all smiles on their faces, carrying two pickaxe handles.

"Well, this proves you were telling the truth." With this, and shortly after, I was released. I thought that was the end of it: no charges, and complaints were dropped. That's how it should have been, till my ex-neighbour, Tim, stepped in. Now how Tim found out, I don't know, but there must obviously be some kind of alert system. He is CID after all. At any rate, two days later, two cops come to the door asking for Andrew.

"What do you want my son for?"

"Well, we received a complaint that your son assaulted a young man regarding the incident the other night." Andrew was on a short four-day break from the army, and I didn't bloody want his career being jeopardised, but I had no choice. I agreed to go to Erdington police station later on that day only to be confronted by Tim. Now the two cops told me that there had been uproar with Tim going up to Sutton police station and giving them a right rollicking for not doing their bloody job in the first place. Quite right too.

Now whilst I know Tim ain't my best friend or anything, him being a cop and all, I thought I had a bit of moral support and understanding, knowing that he knew me and my family on a personal level and knew I wasn't the fruitcake I was being made to appear. The first thing Tim did was volunteer to take Andrew's fingerprints. He had volunteered to do this rather than have some strange cop do it. "Why didn't you just put a balaclava on your head and go and belt them?" Tim asked me. These cops never fail to amaze me with their super intelligence, always after the frigging event. "Because I thought I was only dealing with a young delinquent for one thing, and I didn't realize he was a three-time ABA boxing champ." I'm sure these cops lose sense of reality once they get their uniforms on. Off duty or on, they are quick to flash their warrant cards at any sign of trouble. But for the rest of us, we've got three choices: ring the cops - mostly hit and miss - walk away or confront the situation.

It appeared that when I went to confront this little bully, Andrew, by hitting the one over the nut, had caused him to have a few stitches. I looked at Tim in shock and disbelief. "Tim, they were fucking attacking me. Andrew came to my aid."

"It was self-defence, yes Tom, but there are twenty witnesses."

"Twenty fucking witnesses? Those were the twenty who were attacking us. It's fucking ridiculous."

But Tim was having none of it. Well, at the time I just assumed, again, thinking that because Tim knew me, and his wife was an old school friend of my wife, that he was just trying to be helpful. It was others behind the scenes who were doing the dictating. We were duly charged with assault. Why not the attempted murder charge? It's funny how the cops can alter the charges to suit themselves. If there are twenty witnesses accusing me of attempting to run them down, why are they not believed, yet they are of the assault? Obviously, what I found difficult to understand - or see - was this was messy; it needed to be tidied up. Fuck Tommy Lewin and his son, Andrew.

This is how much our society is changing in this country. This kind of nonsense would have been unheard of years ago. First off, the cops had a bit of common sense; they were being paid to be coppers and that's it. Today they are paid to rack up nicking's, just as the factory workers are being paid on piece time, like robots. Someone up top has decided to apply the same rules to the police. You want promotion? Nick some bodies.

Likewise, with little toe rags like these lot, years ago no one would have the neck to go out, cause trouble, then go squealing to the police. It was the lowest of the low. Even if you felt like squealing, your peers pulled you back in, acting as a moral brake. It was taught from school: if you came in crying that your teacher had wacked you, you were given another whack and told not to complain. Today, grassing is becoming the norm and the cops are loving it. Well, they were.

Tim had recommended I speak to a solicitor, and from experience, felt one was as bad as another. Besides, I thought he was genuinely concerned. To anyone who thinks otherwise, I can tell you categorically that Birmingham law courts are literally a law unto themselves. The law is not black and white, but a dirty grey. Those scales are not even-handed. If you are Lily white with no criminal record from a non-criminal family or background, you have the chance of a fair trial. No, lets rephrase that: you will *get* a fair trial. Hence, people may pick the paper up and see that someone found "not guilty" will wonder if common sense has flown out the window. It makes you wonder why. You will see famous sportsmen accused of rape, or maybe assault, found not guilty, or advised by the judge to find that particular person not guilty. 'Course, it helps that he's going to pay thousands in legal fees. Even better that he pays hundreds of thousands in tax too. Funny, really. One of the most debilitating diseases hitting this country is drugs, yet from the 60s, pop stars have openly smoked dope. MPs and even prime ministers boast about smoking it. Former druggies are given knighthoods, then we wonder why drugs are rife in the country. It's a joke, duh.

Rob a house in one town, you'll get six-month's probation. Make the same mistake in another town and you're likely to get two years in the clink. One case that always amazed me was the couple who had fell out with some animosity. Both professionals. After quite a bit of bitterness passing back and forth, the boyfriend invites his girlfriend around to one last peace-making goodbye. Sitting at the kitchen table, the girlfriend notices a glass of orange juice on the table. How the orange got there wasn't clear; the report was a bit vague on that point. How it happened to have acid in it as well was another bit of a vague issue. I mean, what are the odds of a couple having bitter rows for months on end, and then getting together with a glass of orange on the table laced with acid - further, in front of her boyfriend - decides to pick the orange up and take a drink, mainly because the heating was quite high in the room making her hot and uncomfortable. What are the odds of her picking up a random glass on the table and taking a drink without her ex-boyfriend saying a word, even if he was in the room? Billions to one? Worse, having drunk from the glass, she then started to writhe in agony as the acid started to work on her guts, her boyfriend, for some reason, finding a reason not to ring the emergency services. When he did eventually dial 999, it was too late to save her. All the doctors could do was dose her up with high levels of morphine till she inevitably died, her intestines burnt to bits. Her ex-boyfriend was found not guilty of murder. Maybe he gave the masonic distress signal. It is very easy to accuse Birmingham law courts of being incompetent. That is an easy way out. To me, it's corrupt.

So, me and Andrew turned up at court expecting an initial hearing and a trial to be set. What a major mistake that was on my part. Far from doing me any favours. I was being set up, both me and Andrew, much to my sadness. They had re-awoken the complaint from Nicky and Michael, but without Michael and his fractured jaw for some reason, and the hearing was set for a couple of weeks later. Ideally, I would have liked to have gotten hold of the little toe rag and said, "Can't you see what's going on? Drop the charge and we will do likewise." No charges meant no criminal record, no cost to the taxpayers. But I knew I couldn't take that risk. I could just see the little scumbag squealing even louder, then me being right in it.

One of Andrew's senior officers had turned up to court with him. The knowledge was clear. If Andrew was found guilty, and anything other than a minor sentence was given, he would be kicked out of the army. As I was talking to my solicitor, another solicitor/barrister came across and motioned Andrew aside. I never paid much attention. Fifteen minutes later he came back and blurted it out, "I am afraid you have no choice. I have spoken to your son, and he will have choice but to plead guilty." Then I saw the look in my solicitor's eyes, a look of contempt towards the prosecution and police. I knew it; I caught it. We were being fucking set up. Andrew had never been in a court in his life; he had never committed a crime in his life. But he was my son, and, as such, he was guilty. It's hereditary, see, keep 'em on file as much as possible. Andrew was furious. "I'm not pleading guilty to this nonsense. I'm not guilty." But the poor fucker didn't know he *was* guilty because he was my son. Worse, I would be found guilty, because I was Tommy Lewin. The solicitor tried being kind and keeping a soft voice. His advice was clear. "Look, Mr Lewin, if we fight, it will mean a crown court trial. If we plead guilty, you will be given a minor fine. You can walk out of court, your son can resume his career, and his record can be wiped clean after two years." Andrew was still showing his anger at the thought of pleading guilty to a charge he was clearly innocent of. For myself, I could see the alternative, his senior officer's face in front of me, frozen and non-committal.

I felt I had no choice but to persuade Andrew to plead guilty…for both of us to plead guilty. With great reluctance, he nodded his head and we walked into the dock, pleading guilty when asked. Further proof of a fit up came when the clerk got up to read my criminal record. I felt myself stiffen up, shitting myself at the thought of Andrew - even worse, his colleague - hearing my record, but the judge waved him down. Fuck me, now I know it's a setup. Even the judge knows about it. Then our brief got up. "My client is a respectable businessman, your worship, and his son Andrew a young soldier with a promising career." I couldn't fucking believe it. Tidied up nicely, we were both given a nominal £20 fine - a pittance - all boxes ticked.

Two weeks later, Nicky had to appear in court as a witness against the squealing toe rag. After a bit of weak argument pleading not guilty, it was very clear he had no choice but to plead guilty as well. A nice result all around for the police and prosecution: cases closed; problems solved. The corruption stunk to high heaven, yet I was a lone voice in the world. Angry as Andrew was, and unfair as he thought it all was, even he didn't realise how fully corrupt the system was. Now, he was left open to having a criminal record, with a file that opened up bringing up all my history and my family history.

This case, once again, could have been resolved with no ill effects. If anything, the toe rag and his friends should have been charged with the original offences. But to me, and anyone with half a brain, it is further proof of how corrupt and incompetent the police and legal system is in this country. Why force us into such a situation? Why grab my son aside behind my back, a young kid, naïve to the ways of the world and certainly the court system? Was there deliberate thinking that because he's my son he needs to be put on file at any cost? It's fucking disgraceful. On paper, it would be argued that, well, you pleaded guilty. But I can assure you people don't realise what the blackmail is. We would have been found guilty. There was a possibility we could have lost the hotel business we were committed too. We went to court for and expecting a preliminary hearing. Instead, we were railroaded into a guilty plea. No doubt Tim and the cops would have you believe they were doing us a favour. They were not. They were doing themselves a favour, that's all. I will guarantee if it was their son it would be totally different. I tell you, cops shit themselves when their kids get nicked, as they do. Oh, ok, they went to the toe rag and asked him if he'd like to consider dropping the charges. Well of course he wouldn't, so then they charged him after with assault. Ha-ha, now it's too late to change his mind.

Getting home, Bet just accepted the verdict and the situation. Like me, she knew how bent the situation was, but she resigned herself to it. We had to refocus on what lay ahead for us. Andrew set off back to the army. We started planning. We had committed to the hotel now and thought it offered a great opportunity for all of us, as a family, to grow.

I needed some experience running a bar, so asked Jimmy Kirby if I could have a few days with him in his pub down Nechells. Straight away, I realised I had made a mistake asking. Jimmy was naturally suspicious of anyone getting close to his business or what he was up to. It was a natural instinct, I suppose. It pays to be a bit secretive. Quickly, I assured Jimmy of my motives and what I was intending. With that, Jimmy relaxed, and I turned up for work the next night. It was a Friday night and quite busy. Jimmy's bird was behind the counter. Pulling a pint and serving it was fairly straight forward; it was the cleaning of the pipes I wanted to know about, and without too much trouble, she took me down into the cellar and showed me the process. It was quite simple and straightforward, and after a couple of nights I was a bit glad to get out. For some reason I was having a nervous effect on everyone. My old mates were popping in and I could see their little brains spinning around like the exorcist, their mouths whispering in curiosity… "What's he doing here behind the bar? He must be buying the pub." For Jimmy's part, I recon he thought I was picking his brains to find out how much he was taking. It's so bleeding funny, really, and so transparent. These are supposed to be my pals, yet they can't ask me outright and just be honest.

My lovely Bet outside our first hotel

Our daughter Nicky sitting on the patio sea wall of our hotel.
We would boast about having the biggest swimming pool in the world

HOTELIERS

As promised, a week after we had signed the exchange contracts, Bet went down to Devon with Nicky to spend a week in the hotel they had booked into - our friend Bernard's hotel - popping into our prospective hotel each morning for breakfast and evening dinner. We would speak to each other every night to have catch up, and by the third day, I hesitantly asked how she was getting on. "Dead easy," she said. "These lot haven't got a clue; they don't even know how to make a decent soup." The soup of choice for most catering establishments is Maggie's soup, and there was a different variety for each day. The secret was down to consistency: too little and it was like water. To save money, the hoteliers had cut right down on the thickness, something that was very short-sighted and something that many people do. We are talking pennies, or fractions of a penny per bowl, but it puts the guest off. As soon as Bet caught on, she increased the thickness. It was noticeable straight away, and the guests told her, "Bloody hell, we can tell the difference now that you are making the soup."

The hoteliers were that confident of Bet's ability that they left her to it, cooking breakfast and evening dinners whilst they started organising their departure. It was the end of June and the hotel was packed. I was starting to shit myself at the thought of it. I could only admire Bet but wondered if she was bullshitting me. She just never seemed to be phased by anything. Nice house, big mortgage? No problem. Derelict cottage with overgrown land? No problem. Now this hotel: 17 bedrooms, 45 guests? Dead simple. All I had to do was get down to her nice and safe with all our furniture, and the kids, put the court case behind us - the set-up behind us.

Ignorance is bliss, and if there is one thing I've got plenty of, it's ignorance. The day came when we hired a van and loaded up to set off to Devon and our now hotel. Ken and Janet turned up and we loaded the van up. Ken had hired the van in his name for returning the next day. We deliberately set off early evening with the intention of getting to the hotel after midnight while the guests were asleep. Absolutely unbelievable, really; utterly stupid, but it worked. We got to the hotel, backed up and started unloading into the basement through to the kitchen and into our private accommodation, Bet guiding and instructing us as we went. Bet had allocated the kids one of the biggest guest's bedrooms on the first floor above the bar. Our new sofas to go into the guests' lounge, replacing those taken away by the exiting owners. What the guests thought of it, I don't know. As we were unloading, a cop car pulled up with two cops inside asking if everything was ok. "Yes," I replied with a smile, never giving it a thought why two cops should be turning up at 2 a.m. in a very quiet harbour town. Of course, I never gave it a thought, that they had come to clock me. Duh. After we had finished, we had time for a coffee before saying goodbye to Ken and Jan who set of home for Sutton. After a short chat, we got to bed only to get up three hours later for breakfast, Bet and Nicky, now sorted in their routine like proper little hoteliers: Bet cooking and sorting the breakfast, Nicky doing the waitressing. Like ducks to water. One of the main reasons we brought the hotel was because of how the kids were as children growing up. Nicky was absolutely bang-on, clever, loyal adaptable; she was babysitting at ten, cleaning and looking after the house at twelve onwards, and she had the right attitude and knew how to play the guests exactly right.

My job was the washer upper. Quite simple, really, but integral to the running of the hotel. As Nicky brought the plates dishes and cutlery in, my job was to clean it off and feed the big commercial washing machine, all of which was a piece of piss. Our next job, after the guests had left the hotel for the day, was to go upstairs and do the chambering (make the beds, etc.). In a small family hotel, most guests are clean, tidy, and careful to keep their rooms in good order. My job was to clean the toilets and then get into the bar to clean, tidy up, and check all the stock. After a few days, I felt this was enough for me. Besides, I wasn't too keen on cleaning the toilets. I've got a weak stomach; everyone knew this. I couldn't even pick a dog turd up without gagging all over the place. After a few days, and getting into the bar first, the girls automatically took over the toilet duties.

The first night behind the bar was the first time that both me and the guests had gotten the first sight of each other. These were ordinary working people, mainly from the north of England Liverpool, Doncaster etc. who had worked all year saving up for that one week or fortnight in our hotel. I soon came to feel humbled that they were choosing *us* to spend their hard-earned money and time with. Under normal circumstances, I would have considered it utterly stupid to buy, move in, and take over a hotel at such a busy time as this, but it worked for us. It really was a case of diving in at the deep end, and after the first week, a new bunch of guests rolled over who didn't know us or even that we had just taken over. Even if they did, they were unaware of the circumstances, thankfully.

Bet told me a bit about her first week with the previous owners. After five years in the job, the one couple had left with nothing at all to show for their hard work and efforts. The other couple had only £4000 to show for their efforts. For the past twelve months, they had been working in a fish-n-chip shop to build up some savings in order to buy the shop for themselves. We had started to see the wisdom of buying a smaller hotel rather than a bigger one, but the two couples also gave themselves away in their conversations with Bet. "You will be taking a wage out, won't you Bet?" Well Bet has this way of looking vague and puzzled; it was a mistake I made with her over many years. "What do you mean?"

"Well, you must take your wage. After all, you are working, you must be paid."

"Oh no, we don't work like that. We never take a wage out of the business." The looks went across; it's always the looks that give people away. Obviously, Bet was thick for not insisting on taking a wage up front. Then me and Bet give each other the look. £75 a week for two women is almost eight grand a year - £39,000 after the five years they had owned the hotel, and did the men take the same wage? All being equal, nearly £80,000 after five years? The mind frigging boggles. They are looking at Bet like she is stupid, and we are looking at them knowing *they* are stupid. The stupidity of these people absolutely staggers us both. We see it time and time again, in all sets of circumstances.

Examples are put in people's faces all the time. Paul Getty was a known miser and billionaire. We see wealthy people and assume because they have money coming out of their backsides, they are always big spenders. In fact, it's far from it. The history of most people starting from nothing is one of self-deprivation and hardship, going without, yet time and time again we see examples of such utter stupidity, selfishness and greed. Want a holiday? You have to save, want to build a business? You have to save, don't take a lot of brains does it.

Main season or not, we settled into the hotel quite easily and got on with the guests with ease. These were ordinary working-class people like us from working-class backgrounds. Me and Bet had no airs and graces and no feelings or wish to put an act on. We were just being ourselves, and the guests could see that. One night, a very nice Liverpool couple sat in the bar with their daughter. Being July, it was very warm -stifling - even though we had the windows open. The girl had already had a draft coke and was now asking for another, the dad's face frowning with the effort of finding yet more money.

I immediately felt for him. I'd been down that road many times; no doubt would again. I couldn't just give the girl a free drink; that would not only be silly, but it would also humiliate the father, so I decided to come up with a little competition. There were a few people in the bar, mainly because we kept the prices to local pub prices for how much we sold. I quickly looked on the bar as a loss leader - the main income coming from the hotel guests and the bookings into the hotel. Fill the hotel, and the bar will fill up automatically. Giving a bit away will be looked upon warmly.

"Ok kids, here's how it's going to be: if you do a conga, the first two best conga dancers get a free cocktail, ok?" Well, those kids didn't need asking twice. On goes the music, and the kids form into a line then off they go, out of the hotel down the harbour and back to the hotel. In the meantime, I've got the cocktail glasses out and started sugaring the rims with coloured dye, making a mix of orange or blackcurrant cordial. Coming back into the bar, the kids were all excited and happy at the thought of winning a cocktail. After a great deal of brow scratching and heavy thinking, I had to give up. "Well, look guys. I'm afraid I can't pick a winner." Faces drop. "No, no, it's only fair, I think you were all equally as good as each other." Dropped faces now smiling. "So, I'm going to say you've all won a cocktail." Now its laughter, giggles and screams all around as I handed out the cocktails. The relief and happiness on the parents' face spoke for itself. It was winner all around and cost me a few pennies.

One of the guests who returned the following year walked into the bar at the first opportunity and said, "I owe you an apology. We didn't expect you to be here." When I looked at her, puzzled, she explained. "Well, when we got back home, I spoke to a friend of ours who is an accountant and I told him you wouldn't be lasting another year by giving free drinks to the kids. The accountant asked if we were going back this year. I said yes, we love it, and the account said well there's your answer then."

"Look," I said. "Do you know how much a bottle of cordial costs? Each portion of cordial required to make a cocktail costs about a penny. The sugar and dye - nothing. The cocktail umbrella, another penny. So ten cocktails costs me about twenty, maybe thirty, pence, yet it's saving their parents at least a pound." I didn't set out with a deliberate plan to give free drinks, it just happened; but I could see it was a great relief to the parents, and indirectly helped in making them return the following year. By giving a bit, you get more back.

Before selling up, Andrew and I had joined the local Sutton BSAC to learn sub aqua diving. Our main aim was to reach the standard of class three, which enabled us to go out diving with an equally qualified diver. By now, Andrew was all excited and wanted to leave the army and join us in Devon. I found out and joined the local BSAC club, paying for both Andrew and me. I had also taken a twelve-month inshore navigation course, as it was my plan to spend some spare time diving and eventually cruising around the coast. Unfortunately, I saw the pettiness that I had experienced in the Sutton club. One of the local committee members had informed me of the pecking order and what I couldn't do. I rang up the very next day and cancelled my membership. This resulted in the local treasury officer to turn up in the bar the next afternoon apologising and begging us to rethink. Sitting in the bar, he expressed his regret that we were pulling out and that the club would find my bar ideal, as they didn't have a member who had a hotel bar - or a bar of any kind – and asked my reasons for not wanting to join. I explained to him: It cost some £130 for a year's membership of the local BSAQ, and at first it was great: training in the local pool first, then local quarries around the midlands. We soon passed our class three and were duly qualified to dive alone with another equally qualified diver - i.e., both me and Andrew - but then we started to notice how clicky and committee-minded it was. At any time, there might be twelve or fifteen divers on a meet, some with partners. The committee consisted of twelve members. On major diving events where the club boat was taken out, there was only ever room for the committee. Ok, maybe the odd member might get in, but it was rare, and when it came to the good dives - the interesting dives - all the committee turned up, the rest of us were confined to the quarries or rivers. I wasn't the only one to be dissatisfied. Another couple of guys conceded they had noticed the same thing. Oh, we're not interested anyway; all we want is the class three then we are off to do our own diving. The treasurer was disappointed, admitting that does go on in his club, but hope sprung up as he put forward, "But you can join the committee." I looked at him in disbelief. For Christ sake he's just compounded it. "No, I don't think so," I responded. And with that, he buggered of.

Walking into the hotel one day, Andrew mentioned that the night before he had been walking down the harbour when two cops in a panda pulled alongside him asking, "Are you Tom Lewin's son?" Looking puzzled, he replied, "Yes." With that, me and Bet looked at each other. She had already told me that when she turned up in court to apply for the drink licence, the magistrate asked the copper in the dock if he had any objections. After a deliberate and long, drawn-out pause, then a bit of coughing, he hesitantly replied that he had no objections. He was obviously sending a message to her that he knew. Bet, naturally, was utterly nervous. For fuck's sake, we had brought a small hotel in a sedate seaside resort. On the first or second night, I walked out of the hotel after closing the bar to get some fresh air. I walked down to the harbour a few yards away, and within minutes a cop car pulled up beside me asking me if I was alright. Without a thought I replied, "Yes, I'm fine, thank you. I've just had to come out for a breath of fresh air. A beautiful night, isn't it?" Am I stupid or what? I did think it was odd that two cops should be out at one in the morning in such a quiet place. In fact, it made me wonder if something was going on that I was missing. I had deliberately avoided any big resorts like Blackpool or Torquay because of the problems that would arise. Now here we were, barely three weeks into our venture and this was now four times these stupid prats had made their presence known. Did they think maybe I had robbed a fucking bank to buy the hotel? It's disgusting; I was entitled to be angry, but fortunately, it takes me a bit to get excited. I realised the futility of it. Did their senior officers tell them to go out and make themselves known to me to let me know? But why, Bet? Why, Andrew, for what purpose? What point?

There is a contradiction in this country that people - the general public - don't really take on board. People commit crimes - young, old, elderly, male, and female. If they are taken to court, they are dealt with accordingly. Maybe a fine, probation, a prison sentence - either way, when that sentence is served, that is supposed to be it. He/she has supposedly paid for their crime. As such, they are expected to get on with their lives...right? Yet when we pick up a newspaper and read about some police force boasting about dropping leaflets into criminals' letter boxes with warnings and/or signs saying we are watching you; we all give a sigh of relief or satisfaction that police are doing their job. So who is to say or assume that that person is committing any crime? If you're doing your job properly, watch them, keep your eye on them, then nick them. Instead, what they are doing is bloody harassing them. I have been harassed for years by stupid or bent cops who have never had the brains to say, ay, hang on a bit, isn't he a bit young to have pulled of a job like that? Or are we 100 percent sure this guy did commit an assault, or violence of any kind? No, the cops' mentality doesn't work like that. The first time, yes, you might get arrested and taken in for questioning. Any doubts and you will be released with no stain on your record. Once you've been convicted of an offence, you are on the watch file. I can get in the boxing ring and knock ten piles of shit out of someone but defend myself from a gang of kids in the street who have instigated the violence who then go squealing to the cops and I'm automatically the guilty party.

I despised the police when I was a young kid. I have witnessed their corruption first-hand. My natural reaction, along with my peers, was to say, "fuck you." We're doomed if we do, doomed if we don't. Now, here I am trying to run a respectable business, as far removed from any criminal activity as I can be, and I'm still being fucking harassed. I wouldn't mind if they had the balls to come down and confront me face to face: "Mr Lewin, I'm the local inspector and we notice you've brought a business in the town. Do you intend to go out on a robbing spree while you're here? Maybe knock the crap out of a few holidaymakers or guests in your hotel?" Or maybe even give me the opportunity of explaining what I have had to put up with; get to know me as a person. But no, it doesn't work like that; if you're guilty, you're guilty, no ifs or buts. They are very quick to find you guilty in this country, even hiding evidence from the defence in order to gain a conviction. And once convicted, to get an appeal heard and a not guilty verdict is almost impossible and take's years. I've known of people who were sent to prison for life and spending longer in prison by pleading not guilty than they would have done by pleading guilty in the first place; a great incentive to make you admit your guilt even when you're not. That is not a case of sour grapes on my part. It's a simple fact of life. Our judicial system is still entrenched in the middle ages when you were ducked in the local river. If you survived, you were guilty; if you died, you were innocent. Great.

We were making a major impact on the guests in the hotel. They liked Bet's home cooking and they liked my banter behind the bar. The fact is, they could see we were genuine and not out to rip them off. If someone wanted a lobster for supper, I would go down the harbour and buy two or three live lobsters for six quid. Bet would cook and dress them, then serve them in the bar with a bit of salad and a slice of bread. Again, it was goodwill on our part. Cost a few pennies, but we just charged them the six quid for the lobster. With the theatre just down the road, we were getting quite a few of the acts either coming to stop with us or even pop in for a night's drinking. Unknown to us, a family would book in from somewhere around the country only for us to find out they were here to support or watch their kids singing or dancing in the show. For a few nights, Frank Carson, the Irish comedian, would come round after his show and spend the night in the bar, much to the delight of the guests. Frank was exactly as he was on the telly - no airs or graces, just cracking jokes as they came to him. I reminded him that the last time I saw him was at Brendan Joyce's Garryowen in Birmingham. In that broad Irish accent he said, "Oh hi. BeJejus, the best steaks I've ever had." Another time, we got a block booking for a bunch of guys spending a weekend on a fishing and drinking spree. One of the groups brought his mom and dad who turned out to be Sylvia and Adrian Clapton. We never twigged at all who they were related to till their second visit when Sylvia dropped it out. They would come at least twice a year, sitting up till four in the morning playing cards after a day out fishing. After the first visit, we used to leave them in the bar to play and help themselves. They never gyped us. And Sylvia and Adrian became great friends.

The only one downside was some of the local drinkers who insisted, or tried to insist, on coming into the hotel after the pubs had closed. I knew from Skegness what the score was because I had spent time seeing the same thing myself where I went up for the work and the birds. A lot went and stayed there on the dole. This was the case here. I had assumed being a little fishing port it would not attract them, but in actual fact, the reverse was true. These were low life's who couldn't survive in their own cities of Liverpool or wherever, came down here for a bit of summer work, then quickly realised they didn't have to work at all. Then they would ring their sisters or other family members and tell them as well. Soon you'd have a load of them down; one city crowd worse than the other. Nicky, being a bit naïve, would be pleading with me in front of them, "Oh please dad. This is Stuart; he's really nice." A lot of the guests didn't like it. I could see immediately that the main reason many of them booked into the hotel was because of the privacy it afforded them, and the comfort it gave them to know they were sitting with fellow guests in the comfort of their own surroundings, especially the screws and their wives. These were prison officers from the north of England who would book in for a fortnight at a time, and between them with their wives' colleagues and kids almost filled the hotel. I could not afford to take that risk but having allowed them in in the first place it was doubly hard to get them out. Look lads, you can drink in here every night when the season ends, but you're making the guests nervous. The idiot's responses were that I was happy to make money out of them in the winter but not in the summer. "Look," I said. "I'll give you the drinks fucking free in the winter. I don't make money from you lot sipping a pint after hours."

The other hoteliers along the terrace tried different ways to keep them out. Hugh, who owned the bigger hotel next door, just re-sited his bar into the basement. The other hotel did the same, but some of the boozers found a way in through the back door via the sea wall. Jack and his family just resigned themselves to it. I was just getting pissed off by the week. One day I stood outside the hotel with Nicky during an afternoon break. I painted her a picture of how things could be. "Look, in three or four years we could own Hugh's hotel, or the Moonta. In eight -or ten- years' time, we could own the 80-bedroom Sunderland or Grosvenor. At that point, your mom will not be doing the cooking; we will employ a chef. You will not be doing the chambering but overseeing the chambermaids. Then, as the others grow up, they can take over different roles." I hoped it would sink in and be taken on board by her. In the meantime, I had to be a bit blunter with the drinkers who didn't take it too happily, but eventually stopped coming in. I just couldn't understand why the other hoteliers didn't seem to stick together on such a thing as this.

There again, I couldn't understand how anyone could be so stupid as to not take the hint when asked to stay out.

Our friend Bernard and his wife would pop in and say hello, having a drink at the bar with their daughter and son-in-law, Rick. Bernard was old school and a scrap dealer. The only problem was he thought like a scrap dealer, thinking everyone was a mug ripe for the plucking. He would talk to me in that cockney-type, wide-boy way, out of the side of his mouth. "Well, I did go round the local pubs, Tom, telling 'em they were all too cheap and that they should raise the pint by ten pence at least." They would all look at him with interest then carry on, totally ignoring his advice. He knew this and put them down as mugs. He just couldn't see that their pubs were full yet his was empty.

Bernard just didn't have a clue, nor did his son-in-law, yet they had a fantastic set-up. They had the large bar and leading out from the bar was a patio leading up to a veranda that stretched out over and alongside the sea wall with seating for at least forty or fifty. It was like being on a ship, looking down at the sea. Adjoining the pub was a ten-bedroom hotel. Blimey, they had got it cracked. Yet the pub was virtually empty. They were paying forty quid a night for a DJ, but instead of nicking all the drinkers from the other pubs by offering a DJ, they insulted the drinkers by ripping them off. I stood with him for a couple of hours one night and watched how they worked. First, they would charge different prices based on whoever was serving. If they went up to Bernard, he would charge one price, gyping them for an extra ten pence. If they went to Rick, it could be anything more. I never figured out if either one knew the other was doing it, or if they were just lining their own pockets. Either way, the customers clocked it quite rapid. Holiday makers in the main who came to our hotels were working class, and mainly from up north. Devon and anywhere south was equivalent to being abroad. It was the nearest thing to being abroad for them. If they had the money and could afford it, they would be spending their holidays abroad. As such, many were on a very tight budget. Me and Bet were very aware of that. On their first night, they would have a steady meander around the town, hitting different pubs, feeling the atmosphere, and - most importantly - checking the prices. Neither Bernard nor Rick seemed to grasp this. One afternoon, I popped in to say hello, and Bernard pointed to a couple sitting at one of his tables. In that wide-boy, scrap dealer way, he said, "Me and Rick have got 'em sussed, Tom. See them sitting there? They come in to listen to the music, but just sit there nursing a pint. WELL, we keep our eye on 'em and when they get down to the last inch, we watch 'em. Me or Rick will go over and ask if they're having another drink. They soon jump, Tom and they'll either say yes or get up and walk out."

I couldn't believe my bleeding ears. I looked at Bernard thinking maybe he was taking the piss - having a laugh. He was dead serious. He had a gold mine there, but they were both killing it: a ten-bedroom hotel, a pub that should be heaving, and a fantastic position. In the summer they should be making a killing, serving the food alone. Instead, he was boasting how they were borrowing ten grand of the brewery.

"Well, Tom, it's silly to refuse it. The interest rates are rock bottom. We'll spend a couple of grand on the pub, then have a nice holiday abroad." When I got back and told Bet, she just nodded in acceptance. I think she had already sussed out Bernard and his family. But this wasn't just confined to Bernard. The previous owners of our hotel had a similar attitude with the food they served up. Soon we started to see the same attitude amongst quite a few of the local businesses. The holiday makers were known as grockles, which I thought was utterly insulting. "Why do you call them grockles?" "Because they are, holiday makers." "But you were a grockle a few years ago." We thought that old image of the guest house owner or hotelier locking the doors as soon as the guests left after breakfast was a myth. It wasn't. Hugh had a 25-bedroom hotel next door to us, and the doors were shut right quick sharpish. He would be off to spend the day with his family, returning in time for evening dinner. They made me wonder, if only *my* family had caught on to all these shenanigans. We were seeing moves that we could never see in Nechells.

The phone went one day as I'm sitting in the bar without a customer. "'ello, Allan here." My brain started whizzing around. Allan? Allan? Who the hell is Allan? He must know me to speak so personally, but I didn't know any Allan. "Oh right, Allen who?" A gasp of irritation that I never recognised Allan straight away. "Allan Cliff from the Chandlers." Oh fuck. He was upset before I even knew him. "Ahh, yes, Allan." Straight away he dived in. "Did you say you wanted a boat?" "Well, yes," I said. "Well, I've got one down here in the harbour." "Ok, I'll pop down and have a look." Fifteen minutes later, I found the Chandlers and walked in to see Allan standing behind the counter. I knew it was Allan because he was the only bloke there. "Allan?" "Tom Lewin, yes, Tom." He obviously didn't know me or my name either. I didn't think I'd made a big deal out of putting it out that I was looking for a boat, but at any rate it had obviously flown around the town in no time at all. Allan led me over to the yacht which was sitting in the middle of the harbour. It was a nice 32-foot sailing ketch, and Allan explained that it belonged to a friend of his who needed to sell it. Looking across, he mentioned the price and that was enough for me. I wasn't an expert, but I felt my new friend, Allan, was trying to rip me off. We had a little chat, I made my excuses, and walked back to the hotel. Allan reminded me of my brother, Billy: walked stiff, upright, like he'd done a bit of time in the army, chest puffed up in self-importance. Allan was the kind of bloke that owned a shop yet acted like he owned a chain. I'd met a few like that over the years.

A couple of weeks later, I was down in the harbour when I looked across at the boat that seemed to be settled down a bit in the water. Tilting over on its mast was a sheriff's distress notice informing everyone that it was being put up for auction. It also stated that neither the highest nor lowest price would necessarily be the accepted bid. That seemed strange to me, as well as a bit vague. When the tide went out, I went over to have a look and noticed straight away that there was about eighteen inches of water in the cabin. A bit of damage had been caused to the rails that looked a bit deliberate to me, probably someone trying to devalue it. Getting back to the hotel, I rang the agent up enquiring about the yacht. It appears that Allan's friend had had his hotel snatched from him. The local sheriff had grabbed it in lieu of monies owed, hence the wording. If he came up with the money, he could have his boat back. Yes, my new mate Allan was certainly trying to rip me off. The agent asked me if I was interested in buying it. I said I might be if the price wasn't silly and I could get an answer, quick sharpish. "Well, what are you prepared to offer?" When I told him, I felt him sink back in his chair. "Well, I'll put that to the court Mr Lewin, but I don't think for a moment that your offer will be accepted. Would you like to reconsider?"

"I'm afraid not," I said, then I threw the googlie in. "And I must know by the end of the day, as I fear it will be sunk by this time tomorrow." I felt the gasp this time, then deathly silence for a second.

"Ok, I'll go down right now and have a look. Does your offer still stand if I get back to you?"

"Yes," I replied.

True to his word, he was back before closing time. "Mr Lewin, I've been on to the sheriff's office and they have accepted your offer, on condition that you get up to the office with a cheque before six p.m."

"Ok," I said. His bottle must have fell out. He wanted that cheque before the day was out. I was up to his office sharpish gave him the cheque, then got down to the yacht first thing after breakfast the next morning, on edge all night crapping myself that the boat never sank and now I was the proud owner of the yacht, Blue Spirit. I was dead chuffed. My first job was to get the water pumped out, the next to find a mechanic to rebuild the engine after it had seized up with water ingress. The boat wasn't as bad as I thought; the water had been seeping in for weeks, maybe months, a natural thing to happen together with the rain getting into the open to the skies cabin. I couldn't figure it out why no one had jumped on it sooner, but then I realised what was going on, most of the locals who were interested were playing the slagging game hoping to put everyone else out, jumping in at the last moment, hoping to pick up a bargain. Yet surely, they all must have noticed that it was lilting over with water. At any rate, I'd gotten it and planned to use it alongside the hotel. I hoped when my new pal, Allan, found out, it would piss him off. It did.

A NICE YACHT AND A BUSY CHRISTMAS

As we were coming to the end of the season, I felt that we had a couple of choices. It had paid off for us, coming in right at the height of the season; we had had a full hotel and we were still getting people in in bits and drabs. We could either pull our belts in tight for a long winter or open for Christmas, and if we were lucky and filled up the profit would pay for a winter holiday abroad. As usual, Bet was up for it. With that, I started whizzing around all the hotels picking up their Christmas brochures. We were very limited because we only had seventeen bedrooms, no ballroom or dance floor, just a lounge, dining room, and bar. We had to compromise. First, I got onto the local coach company who suggested that we share the coach with another hotel of the same size. Then I put my mind to the brochure. First, we offered a return coach trip from Birmingham to include a day trip out, then a half day to watch the hunt over Exmoor. That knocked out a day and a half. Then we set out a traditional skittles night at the local pub, a church choir visit, and singing a few carols. All that cost us a small donation to the church. Very quickly We had a full itinerary for the four-day Christmas period. Most hotels were charging over £110 pounds. We did our costing and worked it out: we could charge less than £100 and still make a good profit. It was a first for the hotel. We put one add in the Birmingham mercury and filled up straight away. At the same time, we re-worded our advertisement in the local tourist brochure. A picture of our yacht against the Devon coastline with the headline, **Come and enjoy a fortnight or weeks break in sunny Devon with a half-day cruise or fishing trip on our own ocean-going yacht.** Ok, it was a little bit of bullshit; it wasn't actually fit for ocean-going, but it looked the part. I just hoped I hadn't over egged it. The next thing we did, after the deposits came in of course, was book a six-week holiday in Morocco for January. Then we sat back.

Out of season in Devon came to life in a way that was pleasantly surprising. All the local hotelier workers and other staff came out to participate in the local darts and skittles groups. Then there were the invitations from caterers to other hoteliers putting events on. We were continually being surprised by how we can be treated by our perceived position or class. Now we have young lads, who I was enjoying my youth with just a few years ago, chasing my daughter because she was the daughter of hoteliers. Just a few short years ago, we were looked on as council house whallas, without a pot to piss in. Yet I know many a businessman earning very nice money who lived in council houses, many a friend earned far more net than a lot of people in fancy houses in Sutton Coldfield. As soon as we bought our own house - and in Sutton Coldfield we noticed the difference immediately - we were now "middle class." Now, here in Devon, we were now "hoteliers." The guests wanted to be our friends, the caterers were sending us invitations to do's and exhibitions, and we were treated with a newfound respect. Whilst it was all very nice, me and Bet thought it was quite hilarious. We never got carried away with it because at any time, we expected it to come crashing down around us.

One of the first invitations we received was a horse racing charity event at one of the local bigger hotels. Turning up, we quickly realised our first cock-up. I put on my best pin-striped suit, Bet her mink coat and jewellery; it was a charity event!! As we walked into the main bar, we were mortified to realise everyone had done the complete opposite and dressed right down in casual trousers and jumpers. Bet never said a word, as usual, so I didn't know how she felt. For my part, I felt a total prat. We never made that mistake again. It took some getting used to, though. Some events were formal wear, some casual, but we joined in with gusto.

The catering events were an eye opener. Me and Bet were used to eating fresh cooked food; we just couldn't eat processed, tinned, packaged or frozen meals. Oh ok, the odd one, but for every meal, no. Yet here, you could buy every meal under the sun that came in a plastic bag or package. Duck or maybe a nicely prepared fish in a choice of sauces; they catered for everyone, and all you had to do was put it in the microwave for three minutes, serve with a choice of vegetables nicely presented on the plate, and ay presto. You could charge the maximum price for very little effort. Some of the very top restaurants in the town were serving the very same food. On their menus, our eyes were constantly being opened. Very few restaurants or hotels sold fresh home-cooked food. We would often get some snobby restaurateur snootily refer to Bet's food as "adequate pub grub," which would lead me to start saying, "Well all of yours is out of a packet, old son."

Andrew had got himself a job in one of the restaurants in the town. It's big selling point was the lobster tank in the front window. It was massive, holding about ten or twelve lobsters. The owner was an ex-fisherman who was lucky enough to marry a bird with a few quid. This, in turn, helped him pack up the fishing, set up the restaurant, and treat himself to a nice 32-foot yacht. His brother, who was still a fisherman, would supply him with the lobsters and fresh fish. When you walked in as a customer, you were sat down at a table where your order would be taken. If you happened to order a lobster Thermidor, you were invited to choose your own lobster from the tank in the window. This was the big selling point. The lobster would be taken out with a flourish. The customer sits back down with some excitement, and the lobster would go out the back, and into another tank. The customer's lobster, much smaller, was taken out of another tank, cooked, split in half, and served in a creamy mix of cooked lobster meat, egg yolk and brandy stuffed into the lobster shell. With a bit of salad and Thermidor butter, it made a very nice meal, but not before half the lobster meat had been taken out for the next customer. Whatever colour that lobster was in the tank, by the time it hit the plate it was pink. No one could tell the difference, and the end result was a substantial meal on the plate. What a great con; not only were they doubling up on the lobster, they were charging top bat as well. I couldn't help but turn to Bet saying, "Fucking hell, my old man would be nicked for that, here it was accepted practice."

I had always felt that in life, most people needed a little scam to improve their standard of living, especially if you were on the kind of low wages that I had been used to seeing. Miners were allowed their own coal allowance, as with people I knew who worked in biscuit or chocolate factories. Here in catering, it had reached a whole new level. I thought we knew a bit but these lot were teaching us and opening our eyes right up. Without a doubt, Pip the Planter and his corrupt colleagues would have a field day here. If they'd had the brains.

These were businesspeople and entrepreneurs who were making moves to survive and improve. That never failed to make my eyes boggle. Nicky had got herself a part-time job with a local business owner who ran a drinks off-licence with his brother. He was also the local magistrate yet would buy anything that was stolen. Being a magistrate, finding him guilty of anything like that would have been nigh on impossible.

Initially, she had got herself a job in a local fish shop and restaurant that had an adjoining hotel. The owner had asked her to bring in a bucket of flour from the storeroom. It was dark, but as she went to open the bag, she thought she saw something moving in the flour. Jumping back in fright, she thought it might be a rat. She ran out to the owner, who came back with her to see what the fuss was about, shaking the bag and bringing out a bucket into the light. "Maggots!" Nicky shot back in horror. The owner just looked at her in mocking contempt. "It's only maggots, girl. They will disintegrate in the fat fryer. Besides, it's good protein." Nicky lasted another ten minutes before she walked out in disgust. Some of the scams were so simple, yet sometimes so ingenious. The local electric supplier was on the ball for anyone who whose electric bill was a little on the low side, charging in unexpectedly at the least unexpected times.

We kept our hotel open all year trying to grab what we could. We felt we were doing well - picking up one or two tradesmen that were working in the area from outside of the town - but we couldn't help but notice that as soon as the second week in September hit, the majority of the hotels closed down. It took us a couple of years to find out that many of them were signing on the dole. Fucking hell, we were slow. Technically, they were unemployed, as such they were entitled to unemployment benefits. Seven months winter season was a long period. Then there were the fishermen: we would often notice the boats in the harbour during the early or late season. Even during the season, only going out with the lucrative fishing trips full of tourists, I just assumed they didn't need to be working so hard because it was so lucrative. How wrong was I? Allan, the chandler, burst out laughing. "You must be joking! No, it is related to the Beaufort scale; this is the empirical measure that relates wind speed to conditions at sea. If it's over a certain level, they can claim dispensation. All they have to do is look at the weather report, pop into the local dole office, sign a chit, and they get paid." Blow me down with a feather; and it's all legal. Spread this around the country, Blackpool, Torquay, Skegness? And how much is being lost, yet the average person would never see this side of life? I had seen this from young kids in Skegness, signing on when there was plenty of work, but just focused it to that small minority. Now here it was before my eyes, seeing most of the fucking town at it.

At one of the hotels, we got chatting to a lady who had a very nice hotel a little bit out and away from the town centre. As we got chatting, she asked if we were opening up for Christmas. When I said that we were, she then asked how we were doing on our bookings. When I told her we were fully booked, she visibly jumped back in shock, her head spinning like the exorcist. "Fully booked? *Fully booked?* How did you manage that?" Well, I ain't going to tell her our little secrets, am I? But I asked what she was offering and for how much, she looked visibly hurt.

"Well, we're charging £120 per person, and we're just doing the usual, really."

"What's the usual?"

"Well, you know, a Christmas breakfast, Christmas dinner, and snacks laid out on the table for them to help themselves at night."

Me and Bet looked at each other. "Are you putting anything on? "Again, the indignant look. She had such a high opinion of her hotel that she felt the big selling point was the log fire and walks around the local beauty spots.

When she asked what we were charging and I told her £99, her little face pinched with indignation. "Oh, I wouldn't open my hotel for that." When I told her it included the coach from Birmingham and back, her face almost turned purple. "Oh, I definitely would not do anything like that." With that, the conversation ended, and I think any friendship that might have progressed from that point died a death, quick sharpish.

The more I learned, the more we both progressed in life; the more we were staggered by other people's stupidity. Both me and Bet had had no decent education. I'm not ashamed to admit that through the fault of bad teachers, I never learned a carrot at school. Getting my head banged off the desk at eight made me stop in my tracks to learn my times table. It was the same with the alphabet; I just could not get my head around learning parrot fashion A, B, C, D; but I can write a contract out for my wife to copy on a typewriter, and I can work out a contract - how much I want to earn or make, how much the materials with cost, and how much profit we will make. Yet we often encountered well-educated people - people with all the ology's you could wish for - to be as thick as two planks. It was astounding; that woman would rather remain empty than earn a good amount of money simply by offering just a little bit more, making more of an effort. After all our costings, we expected to make at least £2000 pounds, which would pay for our six-week holiday in the sun in Morocco.

A meal out, flies covering the meat behind Bet.

A NICE HOLIDAY AND MAKING NEW FRIENDS

The closed season leading up to Christmas for us was very enjoyable and passed quickly. As we tootled along, we made some friends along the way. Soon, December was here. We had decorated the hotel, putting some lights up on the sea wall, which worked to great effect. We booked all the food wines and drinks and started preparing ourselves for the arrival of the guests: who they were, how old they were - we hadn't got a clue. All we knew was that they were all couples except for one single person. We assumed they were all elderly. Our only hope was that we got on with them and could give them a good Christmas. We need not have worried; most people do not spend good money to come away and be miserable, but they are determined to have a good time.

Come the 23rd of December, the coach pulled up with all our guests on board. As expected, most were elderly, most were married and had come to get away from their families and the inevitable tensions that build up. All were looking to enjoy themselves and have a good time. Bet and me are genuine people. Yes, of course the money was important to us, but having got the money in the bank, our main concern now was to have a good time and make sure the guests had a good time with plenty of food and drink. Being a small hotel worked in our favour because we could be more intimate and friendly with the guests, where the bigger hotels couldn't. By the end of the first day We were all friends together. Four of the guests actually knew one of Bet's sisters, which put things on a more personal level. It was hectic and non-stop, the only break being when the guests went out for the day on a coach trip, and the half-day trip to see the local hunt which, was immensely enjoyable for them; something none of them had ever experienced before. The four days quickly flew by and before we knew it, the 27th had arrived. The coach pulled up, a few tears were shed, and we gave all the guests a small hamper of gateaux cakes and fruit to eat on the trip back home. All in all, the break was a fantastic success in every way possible. Walking back into the kitchen, we walked straight past the mountain of washing up, straight into bed where we remained till the early evening. From there, onto the sofas into the lounge. We never walked into the kitchen for two days.

It didn't take long for the end of January to come around and our trip to Morocco. Louise, Kristy, and Rachael came with us, Nicky stayed at home, looking after the hotel. Thankfully, we didn't find out till we got back that she'd almost fell off the sea wall trying to take the Christmas lights down during a force-ten gale and had had to ring the fire brigade.

Our winter holiday in Morocco was great and very relaxing. Never having been to Morocco before, we also found it a bit of an eye opener. The average wage was about £7 a week for the maids working a six-day week, twelve hours a day. The hotel was full, with mostly small business owners like ourselves who took the opportunity of the quiet period to take a break, whether it be a shop owner or builder. Then there was Mike and his wife Mary, from Canada. They were in the apartment opposite us and we became great friends. Mike spoke in a deep gruff voice and I started imitating him which tickled him pink. Little did I realise his gruffness was due to his cancer which eventually killed him.

"Tommy, what do you do back in England?"

"I own small Hotel Mike."

"Ahh, I do too. I bought a 300-bedroom hotel in Toronto for my son, Tommy."

I looked at Mike in some surprise. “Erm, Mike, there is a bit of a difference. Mine is only a 17-bedroom hotel.”

“That is of no matter, Tommy. A small hotel today becomes a big hotel tomorrow.” Which, as it happens, was exactly what we had in mind.

Mike originally came from Yugoslavia but left during the 1955 uprising. In Canada he was given a few acres of land as part of his settlement. He struggled for years trying to scratch a living from the land before breeding turkeys. This is where he made his fortune. Now he had got cancer and was on a six-month tour of Europe. We never found that out till quite a bit later. He and Mary were very reluctant to mix with others, but we soon persuaded them to join us and our newly made little gang for our evening shenanigans in the bar where entertainment was put on virtually every night. One of the entertainers was an English couple who sang and played the guitar. These, in turn, introduced us to Fatima, voted the best belly dancer in Morocco. Fatima on the dance floor looked fantastic, and much to Bet’s merriment fell in love with me. Fatima’s party trick was to grab you between the legs give your dick a big squeeze then say, “Ahhh, you like me, yes?” in that Berber accent. Close up, she had a mouth like horse with massive teeth, and thighs to match. After initially being attracted to her seeing her dancing, she quickly started to frighten the crap out of me. But she was good fun to be with and I made sure we would make the most of it.

One night, a little carrot head was in our group with his wife from Derby. Fatima had walked in ready to do her show. When she saw us, she waved hello and shouted to us from across the room that she would join us later. Carrot head was really impressed with our friendship and asked if we knew her. I told him she was a very good friend and asked if he wanted me to introduce him to her. A bit of colour crept up his face as he said yes.

Shortly after, Fatima appeared on stage and did her routine. The bar was packed, and, as usual, she looked fantastic and

Fatima the belly dancer. She said she loved me but had a disturbing habit of grabbing any man by the goolies.

oozed sex. Looking at carrot head, I could see he was awestruck. Finishing her act, she came past us asking us to give her five minutes to get changed before joining us. When she came to us, I immediately introduced her to Paul with the ginger hair. "This is Paul, Fatima, and he loves you." With that, Fatima whipped her hand up and between his legs giving his cobblers a real good fondle. Typically, the carrot head went bright red. His wife, who was sat on the far end of the table, flew back in shock. "PAUL! Put a stop to that." Fatima let go of his dick, but not before we could all see he was well aroused. His wife turned to Bet, and said, "I know what he's like. He's only got to be touched like that and he can't help himself." Another night, we were having yet another birthday party where the manager had allowed us to bring some food out to snack on the table. George was sat by me with his wife, and his father - also named George - sat at the opposite end of the table. Fatima came over and joined the table. She grabbed my nuts, much to the disgust of our daughter Louise, who never forgave me for weeks. "Fatima, why don't you join George there. He likes you very much." With that, she went over to join him. Now George was in a separate hotel to us and hadn't seen Fatima. Before pulling up a chair next to George, she did her party trick. George was a skinny little thing who had less fat on him than a chip. We could see him freeze with terror. At the same time, she spotted his hotel keys on the table, clocking that he was in one of the top hotels. Without further ado, she went to grab the keys saying, "Ahh, you are in the Sabina. I will take your key and join you later." George - who by now had gone as white as a sheet - went into panic mode. "No, no, no," making a grab for his keys. I could never make out whether Fatima was deadly serious in trying to grab any man, or merely winding us up with her party trick.

The maid, Zaida, asked us if we would like to join her and her husband one evening for dinner at her home. Intrigued and interested to see how the people really lived, we jumped at the offer. At six o' clock, after finishing her shift, we walked outside where her husband pulled up on his little scooter before setting off to buy and cook the evening dinner. Agadir was a fairly modern city, rebuilt after a major earthquake that destroyed the old city in 1961. It was easy to make the mistake of thinking - or comparing - it to Spain, but half a mile outside of the city it was like stepping back 2000 years. The taxi was soon manoeuvring across bumpy dirt roads and craggy hills, competing with donkey's pulling carts driving in between single-story concrete buildings with the shop fronts open and selling their wares: the butchers with chickens hanging up, smothered with flies. For fuck's sake, we wondered what we were getting into.

Eventually, we pulled into a large square with a water trough on each side and a tap. A group of women were lined up all in burkas filling up containers from the tap. In the one corner was the local mosque. Looking around, I was totally at a loss to understand where we were. How far had we got to go now to reach her home? Bet gave me the look and I could just about hear her say, *where the frigging hell are we?* I didn't know, either. Zaida started leading us away down into one of the many alleyways leading of the square, in between the single-story stables, and it slowly dawned on us that these were not stables, these were their homes. After a few yards, Zaida came to a stop and led us through a door into a big room that looked a bit like a scullery. This was the kitchen with another room to our right and another bigger room in front of us. A concrete block was set around two sides of the wall with cushions on top, a table in the centre. Sitting us down at the table, we thanked her for being so thoughtful, but there was no need to have gone to the trouble of putting candles out for us making it so romantic. Zaida spoke very little English so had brought a neighbour around who could and would act as translator. The only problem was, he could barely speak either and it was quickly obvious that he had jumped on the bandwagon to get a free meal. Between the two of them, we gleaned that they hadn't put the candles out to be all romantic but was merely waiting till the government lighting came on at 7 p.m. For two pounds a month, the government gave them lighting from 7 p.m. till midnight. Talk about control.

The first course of the meal was brought out, which consisted of popcorn. After picking at a few pieces of popcorn, the dish was taken away. After a few more moments, a chicken tagine was brought out consisting of a tagine dish piled into a pyramid with couscous. On top of the couscous was placed pieces of chicken and juice dribbled across. When we all sat down to eat. We all set too, picking at it with our fingers the proper way of eating was to pick a small piece of the meat up in your fingers, roll it to the bottom together with a bit of couscous and juice. As honoured guests, our hosts would gently push a bit of meat around the bottom of the dish in our direction. Zaida's husband never said a word, but he would push the first bit around to his wife who would then push it around to their interpreter who couldn't speak English. He would then gently flick it around in front of me suddenly the hygiene standards hit me between the eyes. I knew that they didn't wipe their backsides like us or use toilet paper; they go to the dunny with a bottle of water, use their hand, then wash themselves. The only problem is...what hand do they use? I'm pretty sure they wipe their arse with their left hand and eat with their right, but what about if they're dirty buggers or just keep forgetting? The thought didn't bare thinking about so rather than risk it, I flicked it around to Bet. She wasn't having it either, so she slowly flicked it around again. It seemed to me the same piece of meat was going around the dish in circles.

Eventually, the meal was finished, and some fruit was brought out for dessert, the translator got up and left us, and Zaida went out to get the taxi. Bet mentioned that she wanted the toilet, but I whispered out the side of my mouth shut up. Bet was nothing but persistent. After the third time, Zaida caught her whispering to me and indicated to follow her to the toilet which was the cubby hole of the kitchen. When she got back, she said, "That was disgusting; I wish I'd never gone." I said, "Well I did tell you the toilet was just a hole in the floor, below which led to a connecting sewage pipe from one home to another." Bet had to hold her knickers in one hand, her head on the door to keep it closed. I said, "It's just as well you didn't do a number two." Getting back to the hotel was a relief, but it was a great experience and a great way to find out how another culture lived. Fatima the stripper also invited us to her home, but she lived in the modern part of Agadir in a modern apartment block. This time it was a fish tagine, and it was her father doing the flicking around on the dish. We carried on the custom of sending the little lumps of fish around the dish wondering if any one of them was going to catch on.

Soon, our holiday winter break was coming to an end. It was a great experience and one we did for more than a couple of years. Morocco was an interesting experience, the culture utterly different and amazing. Sadly, we found the majority of the Europeans or English who visited the place never ventured more than a few yards from the hotels, maybe just down to the sea front then back again. Once used to it, we had some great fun winding some of the British holiday makers up. Saying goodbye, to Mike and Mary we promised to keep in touch when we got back home.

Getting home, everything was quiet and in its place. When we started to find out about the storm and near-tragedy, we had to reconsider how we left the hotel in future. Our next brainwave was to send our hotel brochure out to all our guests inviting them back at the previous year's prices instead of the current year with its ten percent increase, together with the latest brochure coming out with our yacht included. We could only wait with anticipation to see how we fared. Bit by bit, the bookings started to trickle in. Never having had the experience before, we just didn't know what to expect. Things were looking good, and we soon knew that the main season was going to be almost fully booked, if not fully. Even better, we were getting returns from last year; we must be doing something right. Walking down the harbour one day I made sure to ask the local fishermen for their cards. I was more than happy to take my guests out for a bit of fishing, or a half-day cruise along the coastline, but that did not include serious fishermen. They could go to the professionals who needed them for their income. My only goal was to ensure my guests had a good time and would return again.

Within a week, I got a phone call from someone telling me he was from the council.

"Mr Lewin?"

"Yes."

"This is Mr so-and-so here from the Devon council."

"Yes?"

"Mr Lewin, we have been informed that you are running a business taking customers out on your private yacht."

"Well, you've been informed wrong I told him." I could feel him formulating his next words over the phone.

"But you are taking your guests out in your yacht, are you not?"

"Yes, of course; is that a crime?" That threw him a bit, but not for long.

"W-w-well, you are indirectly profiting from your guests by encouraging them to stop at your hotel, as such you are charging them indirectly." I had never heard such bollox in my life.

"Look, out of the whole of my hotel guests, just a small number take up my offer of a short trip along the coast. And as I am encouraging people into the resort who may well not come, perhaps you should be grateful for my enterprise? In the meantime, if you're still not happy about it, I suggest you get your highly paid solicitors to contact me." That threw him. I put the phone down. Obviously, one of the fishermen had squealed on me.

Opposite our hotel was a couple of small shops. The one shop was run by a funny little couple, the husband having MS or some other physical disability. He was quite proud to tell us that due to the small income from the shop, they were getting some made up income support from the council. We would recommend them to our guests who might pop in to look at their goods. For this, they thanked me by nosing into our bar every night from his bedroom window. This came out one day when he happened to mention that he saw me doing something behind the bar. Clearly, he was a twitcher. The guy in the shop next door was also a funny bugger, as was his wife, a mousey little woman who ran the shop in the summer. He had a franchise selling and distributing car tools. I thought the shop might be a little earner for Andrew or Nicky. So, when he made it clear he wanted to rent his shop, I expressed an interest. Our hotel originally belonged to a former ship's captain, and the small cottages had belonged to various fishermen of some kind over the years. Now people brought them to live in. Someone, harking back to the good old days, had had the great idea of turning the front lounge into a little gift shop, but having expressed an interest, the guy showed me his books which - even with a bit of tampering with - didn't look too healthy. By the time we had paid his rent, there would be nothing left in the pot. There was no way, whatever way we tried, would we be able to make any kind of a living from it. We had to politely pull out from any interest we had. Now this really pissed him off. 'Course I never realised at the time that he must have felt he had taken me into his confidence, shown me his personal finances, and now I had walked away, "For Christ's sake, you're running a business, be business-like."

The season started picking up nicely, first Easter then the May bank holiday. If the sun was out, it made a big difference. The Easter and May bank holidays would we found be spur of the moment breaks. The main holiday season booked more in advance. Thankfully, very few wanted to go out on the boat, especially when I showed them how choppy the sea was. We were in the mouth of the Bristol channel, noted as one of the highest tides in the world. Any slight wind and the sea could get very choppy. Saying goodbye to the first of our main season's guests, the one had gone down to the harbour car park to collect his car. The one thing lacking in our hotel was there was no parking. We were grateful to realise that though there were yellow lines outside the hotel limiting parking, this was only respected most of the day except for loading and deliveries. The opposite side, where the shops were, was double yellow lines with absolutely no parking at all. Those in the cottages would have to park in the other alleyway, on the opposite sides of their properties, or if not somewhere along our side in front of the hotels. On the nights only I gather this had worked well for many years. Not now, the prat in the shop opposite, having copped the needle with me for not having his shop, had decided to teach me a lesson by parking his huge van directly in front of our hotel steps or bar window at night. Now I know for a fact that he had always parked his van quite a bit further down, so why stop now? If he stopped in front of the bar, that was bad enough, but at least it didn't unduly upset or affect the guests. But parking directly in front of our steps was ridiculous. It didn't go unnoticed by the guests, either. After a bit of this, I went over to try and reason with the guy, pointing out the problem. He knew exactly what the problem was but was quietly adamant that he couldn't help it. If he couldn't get further down, he had to park where he could. There was no need for this, but there was very little I could do about it, infuriating as it was. So, each night I would have to put up with him blocking my bar window or the biggest portion of my entrance steps.

Worse, someone was starting to squeal at the slightest opportunity. If someone was foolish enough to park outside at any time during the day. Now on this Saturday, this particular guest had brought his car up. Parked outside the hotel then gone up to his room to pack. After a few minutes, two coppers - one male, the other female - turned up outside. The male cop was doing the mouthing off. Initially, I thought he was just a bit pissed off - maybe with the heat, maybe the frustration at being called out yet again over the parking. Whatever it was, his gob was getting louder and louder. I was perplexed. What was this prat making such a big deal about? The car tailgate was open and up in the air, it was obvious a guest was loading. Outwardly, I was keeping very calm. Running a hotel is very much like being in a pressure cooker. We were seeing families laying into each other. Such were the tensions that could build up. But I knew I was in a vulnerable position. Frustrated, I said, "Excuse me, this is a guest who is loading his car." That went over his head; his face was now contorted, red with anger. There was something else to this; this was not normal behaviour. The female cop was not saying a word. I could feel my temper rising. This fucking idiot was right out of order. Was it me? Did he think he knew me on a personal basis and already realised that he hated me? "Get this car moved now or it will be towed away." With that, the guest walked out of the hotel and down the steps. He had been listening to the bust up, and as he walked down the steps he apologised to the cops and explained that he was only going to be a few minutes, and that he was loading up.

The cop did an immediate backpedal, accepted his explanation, then walked off with his female colleague. Now much of the time, I don't ask my guests what they do. Some volunteer - like the prison officers - most don't mention it. For my part, it's none of my business. I walked down into my kitchen, fuming, telling Bet about this prick copper. Surely it couldn't be personal. Yes, I came across this regularly in Birmingham, but this was Devon - these cops had no knowledge of me, surely?. After a few moments, and having calmed down to normal, I went upstairs to reception to say goodbye to the guests, and ready to depart was the guest with his wife. Trembling, he handed me a letter and said, "Tom, I am a serving police officer, and I must say I have never seen such disgraceful behaviour by a serving police officer. I have taken the liberty of writing this letter which I would be grateful if you could pass to the senior officer at your local town police station."

I thanked him and apologised for any bad feeling having spoilt his holiday. With that, he left, both not looking back. Looking at the letter, I could sense the shaking of his hand as he wrote. *Dear sirs: I am a serving police officer from the Birmingham police force*...and on he went expressing his anger and disgust at the manner in which he and the proprietor of the hotel had been treated. When I showed the letter to Bet, her only comment was, "Well, that shows it all really, don't it?"

I took a small amount of pleasure in taking it up to the local nick with the letter addressed to the chief constable. The letter was utterly scathing; no one was going to be happy about that. A few days later I was visited by a senior officer who came and apologised to me and Bet, explaining that the officer concerned had been relocated to another force. I could see he was apologising through gritted teeth. That's the modus operandi for the cops. They used to do this with Pip the Planter in Birmingham, together with the other bent cops: once things get a bit heavy, they are shifted out of town. Now this cop is just a uniform - give him a little bit of a rollicking, look, noddy, we're not blaming you-we'd like to do the same, just disappear for a bit, when you come back no one will recognise you. Ha-ha, nice. Well, perhaps you might have a word as well with the dickhead across the road who also seems fit to park his large van blocking my steps? I never knew if it was the twat opposite that had rung the cops up complaining. I suspected it was, but for what reason? Resentment? Jealousy? I was just over thirty; maybe it had got around we had paid cash for the hotel. The guy was over fifty, for Christ's sake, the cop? What was his motive? This is a holiday town; why come steaming in like that creating bad feelings when we - the town - needs all the custom we can get?

But throughout it all is another underlying concern. I have had cops in Birmingham telling customers that I am somehow to be wary of; I am related to other bigger criminals, maybe even that I *am* a fucking criminal. I was abandoned by an engineering firm after the cops paid them a visit. A customer whose patio I had built - a patio that she had invited a few guests to show off - one of her guests, a detective who obviously warned her who I was, who I was related to, and her husband very quickly snatched his extension plans back. Now here in Devon, these cobblers. This after being put on notice by idiot coppers, pulling my son and me, maybe they think I've robbed a bank or something, maybe they think I've got my money by ill-gotten gains. I mean, my neighbour Tim saw where I'd made my money. Obviously, he ain't going to go down the local nick and put a post-up, is he? I've observed this guy over the last few years; he's made his money legitimately. Oh no, so I go to another town? Well, well, well - what have we here then? Where's he get his poppy? I mean, he can't have brains like us; he's been nicked too many times. Either way, it's bloody disgraceful, and it was a bit worrying. Are these fuckers going to harass or hassle any other of my guests, this was only for starters. I never heard back from the guest again; he sure never made another booking. Maybe the local chiefs had got in touch with him, warned him who I was. That at all wouldn't surprise me. I was starting to get fucking paranoid. Of course, I hate and despise coppers for what they are and what they do. But I can put a bit of an act on if it's a case of earning a living. Besides, by coming into my hotel, I'm not going to make them my best buddies. They are just guests, and I am the friendly hotelier. That's it. I ain't going to be inclined into asking some cop from miles away if there's any chance for a bit of bribery. For what? It's that stupid; it doesn't bare thinking about. Anyone who thinks any offender has paid for his crime once his sentence is completed is very much wrong. Cops love nicking people; it's got naff all with stopping crime or protecting the general public, it's all about promotion, earning points.

As the season started to get underway, we started to get into the spirit with it, welcoming the guests, and enjoying their company. It was a rich diversity of people from across the country; most came in good spirits. We had a bunch of lads who came from Bristol and owned a chain of video shops. They drank a cocktail of Baileys, Drambuie and Tia Maria, costing eight quid a shot, thank you very much. My pal Bernard would ask me to recommend any of my guests to his bar as he was desperate for custom. One night, the Bristol lads came into the bar. "Did you say he was your mate, Tom?"

Bernard, "Yea, well, with mates like that, you'd be better off without." We went up last night for a drink and he tried to persuade us to stop at theirs next time, showing us around his hotel, but we wouldn't. He even tried to rip us off but thought you should know. Nice one, Bernard, a mate. I never recommended him again. What a dick head. He hadn't got the brains to build up his guests, so tried nicking others. What a mug. When I next saw Bernard, he commented on how much those lads of mine drank. "Blimey, Tom, they knock them cocktails back." "Yes, Bernard, but they won't be coming up to yours again."

The benefits of a smaller hotel kept coming home to us. We only needed a decent sized family or group to half fill us. The prison officers, with their wives and kids, would fill us up because of their job. Most chose the security of the bar to do their drinking, so when we were full, we were very busy. The Clapton's were a regular crowd who very quickly became our friends, even stopping with them on our way to or back from Gatwick airport. Everyone got on well with each other whilst keeping to their own space. The prison screws did volunteer the first time that they were in charge of young offenders, but I never asked, and I didn't particularly want to know. It was of no interest to me at all. The one year - and by coincidence, another screw - booked in from the north of England; he was a funny bugger indeed, hardly speaking to anyone, walking around like he was walking the landings to the prison that he was serving in. His missus was equally as funny, barely uttering a word to anyone, just nodding her head when he barked some order out to her. The other screws had a nickname for him because of the amount of overtime he did - Lockdown Willy. He spent more time in prison than he did at home. Watching them going about I could only wonder.

The season went quite quickly, and we decided to try and repeat the Christmas success of the previous year. This time we sent the new brochure to all the guests who had visited us the previous year, and amazingly - much to our surprise - all the guests, bar one, booked to return the following year. It was worthwhile to place one single advert to fill that one double room. In the meantime, to bring an extra few quid in, I took an invitation up to do a bit of taxi driving by a guy who was based in another town. I was enjoying my aqua diving and taking the yacht out and doing a bit of sailing. My hope for Bet and the kids to enjoy the time with me went by the wayside when she saw a couple of force ten gales. We were on the Bristol channel - it had one of the highest tides in the world, rising some thirty foot. At its highest, coupled with a severe gale, it was quite frightening to watch. After the first one, Bet said, "There is no way you are getting me to go out in that." She never stepped foot on the boat once. I can't say I blamed her, but it took a lot of the pleasure out of the sailing for me.

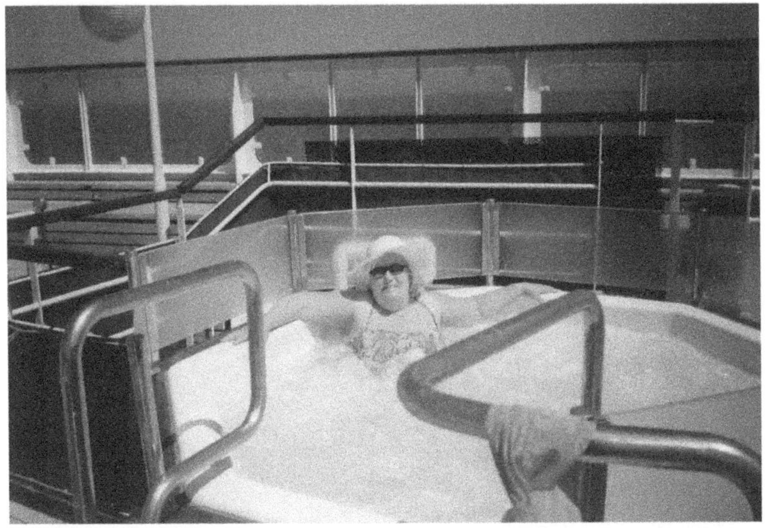

Bet chilling in the on-board jacuzzi

At Nicky's wedding. Sylvia and Adrian Clapton, still friends to this day.
The whole family often came twice a year.

Our first holiday in the works van.
All the sand and gravel cleaned out... mostly

Wedding number three: our daughter Rachel in Oxford

Nicky getting married – wedding number one

BUILDING A PROPERTY PORTFOLIO

Once we started getting our confidence in the hotel game and finding our feet, we started looking around the town, A block of six flats came up for sale at a very reasonable price. It was not showing a great profit, but the weekly income was more or less guaranteed, all paid for by the dole office to mainly young kids who enjoyed a bone idle lifestyle. The flats were run down and in poor condition, but we looked at it is as a long-term investment. Maybe it's the background I came from - the lessons I had learned from my mom and dad - but some of the lessons I had learned taught me not to live for today. In my dad's time a war was expected and had been a historical fact on average every twenty years, I could understand their thinking, but I didn't want to get to sixty and be skint, living on a state pension and without a pot to piss in. Neither did I much like the idea of having a mortgage for twenty-five years. I had seen too many people in different situations and job skills sit back thinking everything was hunky dory, only to find themselves sacked or laid off for a variety of reasons. One minute you're strutting around in life in a nice suit, a nice car on HP, and a mortgage that you can easily afford, the next you're in deep shit - a mortgage that hasn't decreased and a car that has. Someone once said the average person is only six wage packets away from a park bench. They were right; the thought of getting so far up the ladder then falling off again scares the living daylights out of me.

Sadly, midway through the following year, Nicky had decided she didn't want to work for us in the hotel any longer. She didn't mind a bit of part time, but she wanted her own independence. With no choice, we had to agree to it. Now we had to find a couple of hundred quid a week for part-time staff. She did the second Christmas with us, which was a relief, but this was only followed by more bad news. Bet had been going to the doctors regularly for a problem that they couldn't diagnose. Eventually, I suggested that she go back up to Birmingham and make a private appointment with our previous doctor and see what he said. He diagnosed that she needed a hysterectomy. He got her booked into the hospital for the middle of September. She would then spend the winter recuperating in readiness for the following year. This seemed like a great plan. In between times, she would be staying with Janet and Keith, which was very kind of them. Getting back to the hotel, we settled Bet into bed for a quite restful winter. Some bleeding luck, she then caught double pneumonia, which really knocked the cobblers out of her. Getting through the following season was going to be a challenge.

We struggled through the next season, welcoming old friends who were returning. The same prison officers returned with Lockdown Willy and his tired weary-looking wife. It was the same with the Bristol guys who would pop over once or twice a year. Also booked in was a police officer and his wife for the first time from Birmingham. Even without his uniform, I could sense he could be a nasty piece of work. His wife, however, was very pleasant and friendly. She was also out for a good time playing up with the Bristol lads. Things could get quite merry in the bar. After a day out, they would return to the bar, the cop standing by the bar with the Bristol lads winding his wife well up. It helped that she had a massive pair of tits. As the drinks flowed, she was getting merrier and merrier, and the Bristol lads were insisting I kept her and her husband's drinks topped up. He was standing by the bar zombified and not saying a word, to much goading. His missus was flashing her tits all over the place, the Bristol lads taking plenty of photos. I couldn't believe he could allow his wife to behave in such a manner. I couldn't help if they got up to anything else after I had closed the bar. What is it with these police officers and their wives? We had two couples come to us from the Derbyshire area: the one guy was a detective, and his wife was very nice-looking. Worse, she quickly made it obvious that she fancied the pants off me. Very obvious, I was surprised they had come back for a second time. At first, I thought it was just a bit of banter, then I thought she was doing it just to wind him up. She would bounce over to me outside of the bar flashing a lovely pair of tits in my face with people in the bar watching her. She was bleeding dangerous and I tried to keep well away from her. Her husband was having to go to his room early most nights to study for his work, leaving her to gallivant with her mate, but I heard them argue one night telling her to go back down to Tommy then if she wanted to. I locked the bar door quick sharpish.

One of the difficulties in running a business like a hotel is the question of familiarity: if you become too friendly, it becomes easy for guests to over familiarise themselves with you. I had come close to this a few times, and it was mainly with the women it happened with; one or two stepped over the line going even further. The guy who owned the yacht we brought had owned a small hotel like ours, and after a run of success, he brought a very nice big hotel overlooking the sea. It went to his head a bit; he started knocking it off with his female guests and his wife caught him bang at it where he had made the mistake of assuming he owned a big hotel and a nice yacht. In actual fact, he didn't. His wife walked out grabbing what she could; the bank grabbed the rest. It was a nightmarish thought.

Sandra and Dillies had met up the previous year with their husbands. They got on so well, they decided to return on the same dates the following year. Sandra, who was heavily pregnant, went to bed early with her husband. Dillies and her husband decided to stay in the bar, her husband going to bed early. After a bit, Dillies, well-pissed by the look of it, got up and then set off to bed. Leaving Lockdown Willy and Keith - another guest - when they went to bed. I locked the bar as usual and went to bed myself. I was woken the next morning by Bet coming into the room and asking me what happened the previous night. I looked at her blank...what are you on about? Going into the kitchen, it appears Sandra had poked her head around the kitchen door, telling Bet to have a word with me as she had heard me in the bathroom with Dillies. I was fucking mortified. The accusation was obvious: I had been knocking it off with Dillies.

Waiting for the breakfasts to finish, I went into the lounge dragging Elsie, our help, with us as a witness. Sandra was sitting on one sofa with her husband, Dillies on the other with hers. I asked Sandra what the hell she was on about. She was adamant she had heard me go into the toilet opposite her bedroom and heard Dillies giggling. I looked in turn from Sandra to Dillies, in shock, I then looked over to Dillies who was sitting there, blank and hungover. "Dillies, do you realise what she is saying? Don't you have anything to say?" Well, Dillies looked at me in that stupid northern way and whined, "I can't remember; I was fucking staggered." Staggered, in front of her husband, she's virtually admitted she was in the bathroom with me. I looked at Elsie just not knowing what to say. Why would someone make that accusation? From being in bed in a large bedroom to a bathroom across a large landing, I could only walk away with Elsie back down to the kitchen and swear my innocence to Bet. I don't think she could make up her mind what was going on for some time. Worse, Lockdown Willy had left the hotel, and Keith couldn't remember a thing. This was too much. Two weeks later, the phone went, and Bet answered it. It was the cop's wife asking how our name was spelt. He was from Stechford police station. Bet was looking puzzled, and I told her it was obvious, he knew we were from Birmingham and he clocked the name and checked it out when they got back. Bet could never get her head around anything like this. Why would coppers deliberately try to fuck your business up? I said, "Let's just hope he don't ring Lockdown Willy and his mates; that's half our hotel gone."

By now it had flown around Birmingham that Tom and Betty Lewin owned a hotel in Devon. I couldn't help but consider how unheard of this must have been to anyone who knew me - or thought they knew me. *A fucking hotel? Who does he think he is?* Yet if only they could ever realise, those gangsters and other clever clogs from the clubs and backstreets of Nechells and the bigger Birmingham, if only they could see. See how instead of dragging each other down, slagging every other one off they could all do well. My generation had certainly changed from my dad's generation. I very well remember how they would help each other; I used to see it with my own eyes. My dad was a ducker and diver, Arthur Daley and Del boy rolled into one. He was a capitalist with a strong sense of socialism mixed in. If you were skint, he'd bung you a fiver; if he had a good idea that didn't suit him, he would pass it on - willingly share it - as did many of his mates and my brother's mates. This was their downfall, really. I suspect this kind of mentality came from there army days, the knowledge of how everyone benefitted from sharing and helping each other. I had seen it within the Asian and Greek community: One or two become richer, but everyone gains. Sadly, I realised also that this is where my elder brothers and pals came unstuck, crooked some of them may have been. But their biggest mistake was assuming everyone was the same. Now a newer breed was coming along. Like Charlie Heinz and many others, they would fuck each other for a quid. it was a case of me, me, me.

You could physically sense their attitude to you and others. If you were successful over a certain level, they would bow their heads in reverence and respect, but all the time waiting to pick your brains or a few tit bits you were prepared to drop. If you were on level, pegging – fuck, all they would react and treat you according to what use you were to them. If you fell on your arse, they would smirk and laugh their arses off because you had confirmed how clever they were and how stupid you are. I found this mentality totally different when I moved into Sutton. People were willing to offer advice or guidance along the way. Here in Devon, I found the attitude the same. Of course, we can't all be the same - not everyone was helpful, after all, we are all in business - but if you can spare a crumb or a morsel, why not pass it on? I suspected one of the fishermen had squealed on me about taking my guests out on my yacht, but he thought I was trying to nick his business. Utterly wrong. I was trying to give him business, but I thought it only fair, after the council had come unstuck, to visit him face to face and explain exactly what I was doing.

It becomes very easy, very quickly, to sus out the users and abusers; but it also becomes quite easy to recognise the decent people: the genuine businessman willing to help, and why not? It's goodwill and no skin off his nose. After all those barren years, it was quite refreshing to me.

It was a small community, so everyone quickly gets to know everyone else. As such, the guy who ran the speed boat - and also did a bit of antique dealing in his spare time - pulled me outside his workshop one day and in his calm measured voice said, "Oh by the way, someone was around here asking about you last week." Puzzled, he got my nose up. Who would be asking about me? I am of no interest to anyone…a guest? No, a guest would know where I am if he knew my name. After further prodding, he said, "Well, there were two of them in a Rolls Royce." Two of them in a Rolls Royce? I'm still looking puzzled. So that's it; someone had dropped down from Brum to have a little nose. This happened quite regularly; some would come and confront me. "Hello, Tom, how are you going?"

Others would just drive down, have a mooch, then bugger off. The agent pulled me one day as he was passing down the Harbour. "Oh, hello, Tom. A friend of yours, a mister-so-and-so, was asking about you last week."

"Mister-so-and-so? Why would he be asking about me?"

"Well, I was showing him around a business just up from you and he mentioned knowing you, so I showed him your hotel." Oh right, someone else having a nose. Collin Lawler would pop down regularly, but he would pop in and say hello face to face. Collin loved the idea of running a hotel and expressed an interest in buying ours. Personally, I couldn't see it. Quite apart from anything else, Collin was a strong druggie. He thought it was perfectly normal to roll a joint and smoke it in front of you. I don't think that would go down to well with the guests. Besides, his missus - well, Annie was fine most times, but when that gob opened up, she could frighten the rest of the customers of. Still, if they were interested and had the money or could borrow the money, what business was it of mine? Another hotel just up from ours was coming up on the market - twice the size of ours and almost the same money. Allowing for Bets recovery, I knew it was a good deal. Sadly, and as expected, Collin and Annie - after many months - came to realise that the hotel life was not for them. It had occurred to Bernard and his wife also. I only found out after a couple of years that their hotel/pub had been on the market all the time, desperately trying to sell it. Small wonder: they hadn't got a clue.

Who should come barging into reception one day in the height of summer but Roger the Dodger Hardiman. "Hello, Tom, how are ya?" I swear Dodger had the biggest gob in Birmingham. Fortunately, he arrived during the afternoon. He had heard the news about me having a hotel and could not wait to get down to me, hitch-hiking all the way. That meant he had no money, and I was going to have to put him up for choice. Not that I minded; he was my mate. After a cup of coffee, I took him over to the yacht. "That's where you're going to have to sleep, Dodger. There's no room back in the inn." Dodger was more than happy. "I don't give a fuck where I sleep, Tom. I'm just glad to see you. Fuck me, Tommy Lewin in a hotel, and a yacht to boot." He couldn't get his wind. Back over in the hotel, Bet put a dinner up for him, "Dodger, now do remember this is a hotel, not a backstreet boozer in Nechells. Try and behave yourself." "'Course I will, Tom." 'Course he will till he's got the booze down his neck.

One of the customers in that week was a family also from Nechells. The guy had rung up the year before. "Hello, this is Les Dawson here, like I'm supposed to know him. I've got the Eagle pub in Nechells Birmingham," in that typical Nechells big gob self-important way. I thought it best I didn't tell him I knew the Eagle, as such I knew him. But Les was a nice guy. Typical Nechells and his missus and kids were nice also, but being a typical Nechells kid, he would just open his gob and whatever he had in there would just spew out. In the bar that first night, Dodger is getting on fine with Les and his family,

Me and Bet on a well-earned cruise

the screws sitting in the background giving disgusting looks towards the bar. I was trying to keep neutral throughout it all. The talk soon got around to Nechells and some of the pubs. Now I don't know if Les had really clocked my name, but he brought up one of the pubs my brother Billy had run. "Oh," he said. "Everybody has heard all about him; he's a right dodgy character. When people talk about having a lock-in, he really does have a lock-in. He locks them in till they've spent all their money!" Dodger, by now having had a few drinks, was about to shout his big gob off. That's T!!!! Seeing it coming, I leaned over to pick a glass up, pinching him hard on the arm. He got the message quick sharpish and shut his gob. It was bad enough running a hotel at the best of times, having people - strangers, at that - getting too pally; made me uneasy. As it happens, Les did get to know me, coming every year, and we became friends. I suspect he did know who I was but never said a word. Whether big gob Dodger told him, I don't know, but thankfully Dodger ducked after a few days, having got a lift home from Les and his family. I heaved a sigh of relief.

Elsie, our waitress and chambermaid, was talking to Bet one day in the hotel kitchen over a cup of coffee. Her son, Mark, had mentioned that the police and social security were watching a hotel at the back of town for DHSS fraud, money laundering, etc. by the owner. Her son, Mark, was fully aware of it because he was living in the hotel. John was an acquaintance I had met at one of the hotelier's dos. He was the owner of the hotel at the back of town and a beautiful ketch in the harbour. It was a beautiful boat and one that I had fell in love with. Having a big cockpit wheelhouse, I gave it a miss because it was too much money for me to spend...or want to spend. At any rate, I wasn't sure if John was the hotelier in question or whether even his name was John. After Elsie had left, I mentioned to Bet that I thought the guy was the one who owned the hotel in question. I was stuck in a dilemma: if it *is* the guy, how do I warn him without gaining his wrath and getting a rollicking for my troubles? Some people can be really funny. It didn't help that half the town was on the dole; we had even had social around our hotel for employing Elsie whilst she had been on the dole. The fact that she had had a nervous breakdown following a disastrous business venture was irrelevant. As landlords ourselves, all of our tenants were on the dole. Most of the landlords in the town made their living from people on the dole in the town. One guy had two hotels doing bed breakfast and evening meal to young dole merchants.

I was mulling over how to warn the guy as I walked down to the harbour. Looking across, I could see he was pottering about on his boat. The tide was out, so I walked over to him. "Alright mate, I like your boat."

"Oh, thanks very much."

"You've got the hotel up the top, haven't you?"

Now how do I fucking warn him? What if it ain't his hotel? What about if its someone next door to him? I could be opening up a right bag of worms. Taking a breath, I said, "My waitress said there's something going of up there with someone." He never said a word, never looked up. I've put my foot in it, I thought. "Well, see you," and off I walked. Getting back to the hotel, I told Bet, "It couldn't have been him." I felt a right prat. He never said a word. The next morning it all came on top; the cops and social security steaming in mob handed. I saw the guy on his boat a couple of days later. Going over and after saying hello, I said, "I'm sorry, mate, I did try to warn you, but I thought it wasn't you and you weren't interested." Through gritted teeth he said, "Well, I wish I'd known earlier."

They hit him for everything. He had actually got two adjoining and interacting hotels. In the one, he opened up to seasonal visitors. Next door he filled up with young unemployed dossers on the dole. Even better, he was registering kids as being on the dole who weren't even living in the place. For this little scam, they split the dole money 50/50, then he was lending them money and charging them top interest to get it back. Better still, he was supplying next door with all the electric from his one hotel meter that he had got fixed. He was - well, had - been raking it in. It seems one of the lads was pissed at being ripped of all the time so decided to squeal. It seemed he had pushed his boat out a bit too far and got a tad too greedy. No wonder he had such a luxury yacht. What surprised me, knowing from experience what people can be like. I expected much of the town to be up in arms, but far from being looked on with contempt by many of the townsfolk. He was treated like a bit of a hero, with other businessmen commenting with a chuckle, "Poor old John. He had a very nice little number going there." When it comes to business, I found that its every man for himself and there is not much out of bounds apart from blatant stealing. Everything else was open season. A couple of 'Publicans were caught out with magnets or diverters on their electric meters. Some of the restaurants and hotels had dubious ways to increase their takings. Many of my neighbouring hotels would throw their black rubbish bags over the sea wall to save themselves from council charges. One day I suggested to Bet that she did a chicken curry for the guests at the same time she was cooking a chicken dinner. When one of the guests in the bar said, "no way," thinking we were using leftovers, I complained to the hotel next door. I was deeply offended; neither me nor Bet would do something like that. The hotelier burst out laughing. "No, no, no. If you're doing chicken for dinner, never do a chicken curry for at least three days after." They will think you're cooking the scraps, The way he said it made me wonder if he actually did that. I suspected a lot of Indian and Chinese restaurants did.

Knowing the background I had come from made me wonder and smile at the comparisons. My old dad was a kitten when it came to making a few dodgy moves to make a few quid, yet he was targeted by the old bill and looked on with some caution and respect by his neighbours who were going out working for peanuts on the building sites or in the factories. Here, the majority of the town who were unemployed just shrugged their shoulders with the adopted attitude of, "well, what do you expect; money comes to money." The businessmen or people who ran the hotels or shops were split into three groups, I found. If they were struggling, they just wished they had thought of the idea first. If another was at it themselves, they would just hunch and look over their shoulders and double check everything they were doing, just in case. The rest, who were doing ok, would just thank their lucky stars that they were doing ok. To be fair, I couldn't blame either one; being in business is an awful risk. It seems totally unfair to me that you can put up all your money into a business, and the first thing you do is get hit by horrendous rates that you have no way of escaping. Miss one payment and you have the bailiffs around nicking everything within site, then you have no alternative but to juggle the books because you can get wacked by the tax man without allowing for any shortfall the following year. Then when you're worn out and want to sell up, the tax man hits you again for capital gains tax. So, I can make 70 grand profit selling my house after one year, with zero - zilch - tax, yet if I make 40 grand profit from selling my hotel, I can be hit with 40 percent capital gains, and all that is without the banks who are even bigger crooks. No wonder so many businesspeople are bent; they have to be. It's a bloody minefield.

It often makes me smile when I look back and think of my older brothers and their friends, all professional villains. They were really pussycats to many of the businesspeople I have come across, from magistrates buying bent gear to Alan the Chandler getting a position as a councillor on the local council, and all the perks that go with it. It had got bugger all to do with the council; his interest was purely self-serving and to enhance his business. When I look back, I cannot blame them for how they sought to earn a living or make money. Their only mistake in my mind was to think it was never going to end, then on the tickles they did have they just pissed it up the wall. They never learned from it after getting the first bit of borstal approved school, or short prison sentence, but as many a wise old copper has admitted, there but for the grace of God go I. And that's how I look at it; whilst I had grown up admiring these people, I was also lucky enough to see the changes in the different generations. From cocky young guys of twenty-five or thirty, boasting about doing six months or eighteen months – "On me head son, no trouble at all" - smartly-dressed in tailor-made suits or black blazers and grey slacks, to a weary fifty-year-old, shoulders hunched from doing a bit too much porridge, their bottles gone from doing another job knowing the next time will result in a few years more in the nick. Now they were tired, wore shabby clothes, and sat in the boozers nursing a pint, grateful for anyone buying them a pint - or even better, a double whisky. Overall, they were not bad people. On the contrary, the people I remember - Jimmy Moore, the Marnie's, the Kirby's Jaggers, etc. - had strong moral boundaries. If you were in trouble, they stood on, were loyal. It's interesting that most of those I knew had wives who stood by them for each time they spent in prison, including my wife. It says a bit about what kind of person they were, for that to happen when you contrast that with the cops who have one of the highest divorce rates in the country. My generation, many who I grew up with, were a totally different kettle of fish. They would stab you in the back for a shilling and grass without a second thought.

We had run the hotel for nearly five years and focused as she was, I couldn't help but feel that running the hotel was taking its toll on Bet. For her to have a breakdown or a relapse, especially at the beginning or midway in running the hotel, would set us right back and cost us a lot of money. I don't know what I was more concerned about: Bet's health or the money. Either way, I wouldn't be able to cope with the stress. To run a hotel, you have to be focused and 100 percent stress-free, be happy, and show a cheerful disposition to your guests. Looking at all the options, considering every scenario, we decided to sell up. We had the local agent around at the beginning of the season. Having looked around, Bill came walking into the kitchen where me and Bet were sat having a coffee. As he sat down, Bill mentioned how busy he was. In fact, he'd got another ten hotels to value that very morning. Me and Bet's face fell to the floor; ten flipping hotels. Christ almighty, we'll never sell. "Oh no," he said. "They're not selling; they just pay me to give them a valuation for borrowing purposes. As the hotel increases in value, they will borrow ten grand, put a new bathroom suit in, then go for a month's holiday in the canaries." Well blow me down with a feather. Me and Bet looked at each other in astonishment. Ten hotels? How many more were borrowing money? How many more were having valuations? The mind boggles; they are just putting further debt on themselves. My whole instincts and logic told us that the first priority is to clear your mortgage. Only on improvements, when you've made enough profits, to borrow money like that seemed utterly stupid. No wonder so many hotels were being snatched back.

For the Easter, the hotel was full. We had got the Clapton's in, plus a few other regulars, then a young couple who had booked in with their child, as under two and, as such, free. Bet clocked on straight away that the child was at least five, so when the mother insisted on her child sitting on a chair instead of the child seat and having her own meal. Bet took the opportunity to point out that a two year or younger child would sit in a child seat and eat off the parents' plate. The couple took the hint and had no choice but to agree to pay half price. It was then given its own meal. Sylvia came up to us after a couple of days and told us the young couple were asking her all about the hotel and if she liked it. Sylvia couldn't sing our praises enough, pointing out that she and her family come at least twice a year and we were always full. That swung it for us; the young couple had sensibly decided to book into the hotel, with the intention to buy. Within a week of leaving the agent's, they came back with a full offer. Of course, we made sure our books were well in order and polished up to just below the VAT threshold.

We didn't expect to sell the hotel so quickly; some hotels were on the market for months, the price being driven down sometimes before the banks jump in and snatch them. In our favour, we had chosen well with the location, position and size of the hotel. With hindsight we were lucky; many more were far less fortunate. Because of the speed with which the hotel sold, we hadn't even bothered looking around. Our long-term plan of building up to a bigger hotel went out of the window and we started looking around for something more suitable. One property was a house with letting rooms. We put an offer in, but the mess abouts pulled out at the last minute. Then our friend John, a builder, mentioned a hotel he had been interested in. He had made an offer which was accepted, but the banks would not lend him the money. The owner was another brummy who had had to keep dropping the price to a ridiculous level. People were going in, trying to buy it, only to pull out when the banks would not lend them the money. The poison went in, the gossip flying like wildfire. It had got subsidence. John reckoned it hadn't, and he'd had a look at it. I decided to have a look. The hotel was a beaut, with a massive Victorian porch on the front made of solid oak on a small dwarf wall that had settled a bit on the front end. So much for the subsidence. Where the real problem lay was in the rear wall. Two floors, including the basement, were below ground at the back, and water was just soaking in. Worse, the whole rear brickwork to the hotel was porous. The hotel had been first turned into holiday apartments, then permanent apartments income coming in from the dole. For some reason, the owner had just let it fall apart bit by bit. Three ceilings had got big gaping holes due to flooding; the back walls in every room were damp. But all this was to our advantage.

John had agreed to render the whole of the back wall for a good price for us making sure he used a good water proofer. We set to making a home for ourselves in the basement, while plastering and treating all the back walls and ceilings. Apart from that, very little money was needed to put the property into a good order, in all giving us twelve self-contained apartments. As each one was completed, we would let it out. The last and best two ground floor apartments we let to Else and her husband, and Louise, our daughter. All the rents paid on the dot every fortnight by social security. Very nice, indeed, too. At least a dozen people in the town were making a fortune from their hotels, flats or houses let to DHSS. Luverly, it was money for old rope, giving us plenty of time to relax take a holiday, and work out our next venture. That's where I lost sight and got greedy.

After a few months, I was growing restless of doing bugger all, all day. I looked at a couple of houses intending to refurbish then renting out, but then a fish and chip shop came up for sale. It never went on the market, just being sold by word of mouth. It was down in the harbour in a nice position and run by two sisters whose brother owned a local restaurant. Bet was feeling a lot better and felt up to having a crack at it with Louise. I went down and made the guy a cash offer, the same rules applying, Bet and Louise going in for a day's hands-on experience. Louise moved into the living accommodation above the shop. We were surprised that the people who brought our hotel never asked for any trials or work experience prior to the final purchase. The wife, we could see, was a know-all snob whose parents apparently had owned a hotel. As such, she - or they - knew it all. This in itself staggered me because within days of moving in, they were on the phone panicking. The silly twat had filled the Bain Marie with water to heat the pots up. I looked at them both with astonishment. This was a four-pot Bain Marie to keep the soups, gravies, peas, etc. warm. I pointed out the heater grids in the bottom, his face looking blank. I had already had previous guests call into us complaining about the treatment they were getting. One family of six who came every year overheard the owner telling another guest that he did not want the [Lewin]crowd in the hotel. What an utter dickhead. How petty-minded and stupid. They had viewed our hotel and questioned our guests, making their offer based on the number of guests we had in and who came back; now he was killing of those very guests.

This is a small two-star hotel, people with money don't come to hotels like ours; they go to smarter hotels or abroad. This idiot was starting to socialise and play golf with the more established higher star rating hoteliers. They had got themselves registered for VAT when there was absolutely no need. We knew that they had borrowed a great deal of money to buy our hotel, and now they were making our guests unwelcome because they were too working-class. Knock me over with a feather; who on earth did they think they were? I was tempted to go and pull them but Bet told me to say nothing; wait till they fall on their arse. Good advice. Another hotel heading for a fall.

We found the chip shop quite steady in its turnover. We had to buy our fish frozen and our chips peeled and cut by someone else. We soon sorted that by buying our own chipper and doing them at home. The mistake I made was in not allowing for the fact the chip shop had no back preparation room. It limited everything we did. The second cock-up I made was not allowing for the small-town mentality of some of the idiots. Not only had I got up the noses of a small group of people who I banned from coming into the hotel, they - in turn - would wind up any newcomer who felt free to have a pop at me after a bellyful of booze.

I quickly came to realise why the Indians Greeks or Chinese are more adept at running places like this or the restaurants. Yes, they make nice money, but they have to take a lot of abuse. We would get idiots coming in swearing shouting and generally making a nuisance of themselves. Now I know why the women were running it. After a couple of weeks, it was decided that it was better for me to stay away from the shop; let the girls run it, with me just doing lunchtimes and early evenings, then picking them up later. Even that wasn't too clever, as while I was sitting there in the corner minding my own business, some prat would come in giving it the mouth in front of my wife and daughter. I found it hard to swallow, especially knowing what the cops were like. I rang Bill the agent up and asked him to sell it or rent it for us, offering him five-grand to sell it. It didn't help that it had a bit of subsidence,

The flats that we had first brought were just around the corner from the chip shop. All the flats had their own electric meters which I would empty every week. This always showed a small profit on the actual bill we were charged. As such, I never paid much attention to how much individually was going into the meters. In one of the flats was Mark, the son of the people we had brought them off. All the kids generally were quite young and on the dole; some in little cash-in-hand jobs. I had very little to do with them. The rent was paid directly to us from the DHSS. Mark was - like the others - a nice kid, but one day I had called into his flat to empty his meter. I was unexpected, and as I went to open the meter, I noticed there was bugger all in it. Nothing at all. I was puzzled. I checked the lock on the front of the meter - nothing wrong with that. It was my lock, my key that fitted it. Looking around, I noticed he had got a washing machine, fridge, and cooker, yet the crafty little bleeder was only using fifty pence a week. Something ain't right. Then I clocked it. After a bit of playing about, I realised what he was doing. The meter came away from the wall and had no back on it, so by easing the meter off the wall, he would simply empty the meter, leaving fifty pence in for me to collect. I couldn't half blame him for trying and had a little chuckle. He must have either forget or been totally skint when I called in. I pulled him about the meter telling him not to try it again. He obviously must have been robbing his old man for a fair whack of time as well. If he'd left the fifty pence in, I would never have thought or noticed it.

Surprisingly, after a few days, he gave me notice to quit. I never told him to leave or gave him notice, so he must have either assumed I didn't want him or felt too embarrassed to stay. At any rate, he left, but a week or so later, I was cooking fish behind the counter and he sauntered past the shop, looking in and smirking. I took no notice till he came back again, then again, sauntering and smirking. I guessed that he was either goading me or inviting me round to the flats, but why? There is a front and back entrance to the flats, so anyone really could walk into them and cause any kind of damage. I told Bet to take over and decided to head off around to the flats. Letting myself in, I looked around. Heading up the stairs, I heard no noise till I got to the top floor. Letting myself in, I shouted up, but got no answer. Walking up the stairs and into the flat, I noticed the tenant in there - another young lad, and Mark, stereo blasting, smirking their heads off. So this was what it was all about. "Ok Mark, you know you shouldn't be in here, now fuck off." With that, Mark headed for the stairs and out as I followed behind him. I'm halfway down the stairs when, totally and utterly unexpectedly, his mate jumped on my back. Mark, in front of me, turned and started to attack me from the front. I grabbed him firmly with my left hand, and gave him a few hard smacks with my right, his mate still clinging like a limpet on my back. Eventually, Mark by now sinking to his knees and realising he'd made a rick, cried out, "Ok, enough!" With that, his mate let go and ran back up the stairs. Mark shuffled quickly the opposite way to the outer doors. I walked around to the chip shop telling Bet, "Quick, get on the phone dial 999 and tell the cops I've been attacked." I don't like grassing, never have, and I would never have pressed charges, but I had come to realise what little rats people are turning into and how stupid and vindictive the cops are. Within minutes, the cops were all over the place; one rushing in through the front door then coming to a complete stop, face stunned. "But-but you've just rung 999?" "Yes," I said as calm as you like. He didn't know what to do, eventually walking back out of the door, bemused. A few minutes later, another cop walked in - equally puzzled. "You've just dialled

999?" "Yes," and explained briefly what had happened. The cop was still puzzled. "But we've got him up the road screaming his head off that you assaulted him. He's got bruises to his neck and face." I tried patiently to explain to him: "Look, I went round my own flats that I own thinking he might be damaging my property. As I was leaving the stairs to the tenant's flat, he jumped me from behind like a monkey. Mark was attacking me from the front. I was holding him firmly round the throat, hence the marks on his neck. The bruises to his face were caused by my trying to defend myself from him and his mate attacking me. What else was I to do?" This threw him, and with that he walked off, stymied. It's a good job I dialled 999. How anyone could consider my actions as anything else but self-defence, I don't know. This is something that we are all seeing in this country on a daily basis. The police, in their wisdom, are encouraging everyone to dial 999 at the slightest excuse. By doing so, they've made a rod for their own back. This would never have happened when I was a kid, but now these kids can go out, cause shit and trouble all over the place, then when they come unstuck, they go screaming to the cops. These little bastards attacked me in my own property, I defend myself then have to resort to calling the cops myself simply to protect myself. For me, I'm a marked man. If you have no criminal record you can smack people all day long, if you have a record, like me, every incident is marked down, even if there is no conviction. The first one to make the complaint is the one believed, only in this instance we both seem to have rung at the same time, and I am completely unmarked. Its completely thrown the cops. A week later I received a letter informing me that I was being charged with assault. Clearly, the cops have got together, studied the evidence, put it to the prosecution who all have my record in front of them, and - ay Mazda - it's me. I'm the guilty one. 'Course, I've got to be guilty, ain't I? I've got a criminal record; I'm automatically guilty. That's why the cops have been watching me, hovering around me since day one.

Within the following week, Mark had gone up the police station and demanded to withdraw his allegations. At first, they did their best to persuade him to continue with his charge, even asking if I had threatened him in some way. Simply put, Mark had realised the dodgy position he was in; he had deliberately set out to bait me, set me up then attack me. There was no way they were going to get out of that in a witness box. His mate was going to have a real dilemma in explaining why he jumped on my back. Another week later I got a letter from the police stating the charge of assault was being withdrawn. I considered I was lucky. The Birmingham cops would have got around it making even bigger charges. Mark would have felt untouchable in a different part of a big city, anonymous. Here, Mark could not have disappeared. Everyone would have known what he had done. At any rate, it gave me more impetus to get out of the chip shop. I wasn't going to have my wife and daughter insulted every other day. Eventually, trouble would raise its ugly head. The cops never apologised, and I didn't expect it. No one visited to apologise; I never expected that either.

What angers and frustrates me is the sheer incompetence, stupidity, and utter lack of common sense - not only throughout society in general but in the police. Courts and judges - the newspapers often refer to it when it publishes some example to illustrate the point, yet this is only the odd scenario. One innocent person charged with the most ridiculous and petty crime only for it to be thrown out as soon as it hits the first court hearing. Fine, but what about the stress that person has suffered for the past twelve-eighteen months? Oh sorry, now fuck off. But lives and livelihoods are at risk here; people have killed themselves through being wrongly charged. When I was in Risley prison before my fit up at Blackpool crown court, a place I had never been to before, I heard young guys crying and shouting throughout the night. It had got one of the highest suicide rates in the country. The problem is you have judges and magistrates so removed from reality, it's beyond belief. Anyone with half a brain could have seen what had gone on in this situation, because the young kids were marked. I'm not. The fact I've already got a criminal record compounds it. Tick, tick, tick - he's got to be guilty.

Ben Stokes is an English cricketer, and now OBE to boot, but a few years ago he was leaving a nightclub when he was involved in a fight. Now, it's a bit irrelevant what the fight was about, but as it happens, he says he was defending two gay men who were being picked on outside a nightclub. At any rate, Stokes has gone diving in, both fists flailing, knocking the two guys out. His mate goes diving in as well, kicking the shit out of the blokes while they were on the floor. Now stokes is known for having a short fuse - plus he's a ginger nut - but the fact of the matter was that stokes, and his mate were knocking the crap out of the two blokes. It was all caught very clearly on camera. Now I'm not whining, but it was no way self-defence. I tell you, the law is a fucking joke. It's happening all the time. Thankfully, Stokes would have the money to pay for a good defence, even more thankfully he was a popular cricketer. Like footballers, I recon they have get out of jail cards free. The bonus is, being all over the media no one is going to mess with him again, are they??

I have never gone out and looked for trouble; I have never gone out looking for a fight. When I was young and boxing, I boxed at welterweight; ten and a half stone and slim, good looking with it, the great advantage I had was a great punch, couple that with a high level of fitness, the ability to take a punch. There are not many people who will beat you. I was never a bully. Boxing generally teaches you all about bullying. It's a great leveller, but the problem I was forever finding - and couldn't work out why - was the regular bullying, or attempted bullying, carried out by other people. Those three coppers who I belted in Nechells all those years ago were out and out bullies. I was barely fifteen, they in their mid-twenties, yet they tried to bully me and my mates. They should have been sacked, yet they had the audacity to mark me out. Yes, I was never charged, being far too young, but I was put on the watch list. I had many a person tries to seek me out as a teenager because I didn't look too much. Stanley Sherrington was a great deal bigger than me when he bounced out of the Monty Carlo to give me a belting coming right unstuck in the process. I never picked on him. I'm not complaining; it's part of life. Many young lads are involved in fights as they grew up; it's all part of the growing up process. What pisses me off is the cops' over-eagerness to make a nicking out of the slightest thing that I'm involved in because of my name.

People think our justice system is the fairest in the world. Cobblers, it is if you've no criminal record, that's why you'll see people being found not guilty of a crime. All common sense tells you he was guilty of. Sports celebrities are a prime example. Every copper likes football, so it's odds on they will be inclined to give a footballer a light ride. Who was shocked, or at least surprised, when Eric Cantona, the footballer, leaped over the barrier and sent a flying kick and assaulting a fan who had abused him? Frankly, I was astonished. The guy was shouting and balling, slagging Cantona off, but that's what fans do. Fair play to him; he didn't get charged. Maybe the fan never wanted to press charges. Maybe it wouldn't look good for him if Cantona was found guilty on his evidence. I suppose there are kudos in being able to boast that. "Eric threw a kick at me." But the fact of the matter is, it was a violent assault, yet he was shown every leniency. John Prescott, the ex-labour MP and deputy chairman, blatantly assaulted a bloke who had thrown an egg at him. Personally, I thought the bloke deserved it, but according to the law, throwing an egg at a politician is par for the course. Tony Blair, as prime minister and an ex-barrister, stumbled for words in the house of commons, utterly embarrassed. "Well, John, is...erm...John, so that's ok then." But Prescot deliberately assaulted the guy on live television. Clearly you can see him step back in shock, hesitate, think about it, then deliberately throw a punch. It was premeditated. Again, I'm not whinging; I don't blame

Prescot for the assault. But it's just clear evidence how the law can and is manipulated by the police to suit themselves. Anyone with a brain who looks at the news or reads the papers. Not all the papers will certainly have raised eyebrows at many other cases, just simply shrugging their shoulders: out of sight out of mind. It's only when it's closer to home that people start screaming.

If that kid had carried through with his complaint, I would have been found guilty, no doubt about it. The judge or magistrate would have had my record in front of him, as would the prosecution. My solicitor, no doubt going to cost me a right few grand, would also have been sent my criminal record by the thoughtful police force. I mean, think about it. Does everyone know I've got a criminal record? Except the jury?—and that's considered fair? And above board?? Ha-ha, it's a fucking joke. I was already picking up vibes from solicitors that I was dealing with. I have had it for many years, dealing with different people: a nod here, a nudge there. Another matter is this principle of self-defence: how can the police or the courts decide to destroy someone's life by interpreting the law weeks or months later in a court of law in the cold light of day? Just over ten years earlier, I was involved in a brawl. That's all it was, a brawl, whilst drunk, with three other drunken blokes. My only shame and stupidity was that I was drunk, as were they. Because we kept our mouths shut, the others went to the hospital and squealed. We were judged the guilty party. This time I made sure I called the cops, and because of my record, they still decide to charge me. Why? They either don't know how to interpret the law or decide I'm guilty because I am instinctively violent, and the kid is marked. Great.

The law states you are required to use reasonable force to defend yourself, but this is where it all becomes a bit grey and liable to any interpretation the law wants to make of it, at its most basic. If someone hits you, you are allowed to throw one punch in self-defence. One bleeding punch? Oh yea, Ben

Stokes did that, as did Cantona. Not. So, if I'm attacked and threatened in a dark alley, I've got to wait till some six-foot Rastafarian attacks me, then give him a punch back hoping that will stop him. Great. This little toe rag, Mark, first set me up, then he and his mate attacked me in a dark stairwell in my own block of flats, one on my back the other in front. How does anyone interpret that? So I would have had to take my chances in front of a judge or magistrate who has all my record in front of him, maybe a word in the prosecution's ear, with the prosecution having a word in the judge or magistrate's ear... "Well, your honor, we do have a bit of a bad un here. And look at the photos; it speaks for itself, the witness was badly bruised and doesn't he look terrible." Of course, guilty.

Thankfully we sold the chip shop quite quickly making a small profit. Me and Bet were just glad to get out. Another lesson learned: think twice about buying a chip shop. We felt a bit claustrophobic in the basement of the bigger flats, so decided to sell up. Bet had seen a very nice, detached guesthouse. This was silly of me. The rent from the basement flat would have paid the mortgage on the guesthouse, but I was having a good run of selling, and allowed myself to be blinded. The flats were doing very nicely and were very easy to fill with generally trouble-free tenants. Calling the agents in, we were very pleased to discover the value of the property had more than doubled in twelve months. It's very hard to resist the temptation of having that money in one's pocket.

We had been on a camping trip over Bodmin moor a few months earlier for a few days. Whilst there, we camped up on a very nice nature reserve. The couple who owned it kept a whole variety of animals on the land including wild boar, wildebeest, buffalo, different varieties of wild deer and ostriches - a mini zoo. To the front was a campsite with a small bar and the kids fell in love with it. We got on very well with the owner and his wife, and before we left expressed an interest in maybe buying it if they ever felt like selling it. Leaving our phone number, we said our goodbyes not giving it any thought. Now, just as we were putting the flats on, the owner rang us up and referred to our previous conversation in which I'd expressed an interest in buying his business. When I agreed, he offered us the campsite, but not the rest of the land or the nature reserve. He mentioned the price, which I thought was more than a tad high. He wanted hundreds of thousands for it, which I thought was about right for the whole caboodle. He wasn't desperate to sell it, leaving us the option to call back if we were interested. Me and Bet spent hours discussing it. We felt the lifestyle could have been idyllic. We had often considered buying a smallholding which was near Bodmin, out of the rat race but - put simply - we both felt he was asking far too much money. When you're talking ten or twenty grand over the odds, you can either lose it or work it, maybe even knock the price down, but on his prices, there was no way he was going to come down to our valuations.

When we sold the hotel, we looked at a twelve-acre smallholding in mid Wales. It was beautiful, an idyllic setting two farmhouses knocked together. Rachael was thirteen and Kristy was eight. We knew it would be great for them. The family had owned it for ten years and had tried to earn a living breeding alpaca for the wool. What put me off were his daughters. Well, not them exactly, but what they told us. They were two beautiful, sophisticated, very smart young ladies. When they first moved to the area, they had to learn Welsh. That was one tick off. The next was that it was made clear to them that whilst people were friendly with them, they made it clear they were outsiders and would never be considered anything other than outsiders. That was another tick. For me and Bet, we couldn't give a shit, but we had to consider our kids. Worse, they told us the job situation was dire. The one had a job for Rentokil delivering plants and tending them around the county, but that was only part-time. The other one was out of work also. They made it clear that when it came to work, the Welsh looked after their own. We both kept a poker face but that was the last tick. Two beautiful girls like that, in their early twenty's, and they were brain dead. As we walked away, I said to Bet, "Imagine our kids in ten years' time." No thanks. We bought the guesthouse.

The guesthouse was fine and gave us a stable home for the kids, as well as a little income, but after twelve months or so, I was starting to feel a tad uncomfortable. The only local school had concerned me. My eldest daughter Louise had been described as university material back in Sutton, but here she was having difficulty settling in. One day in the hotel, Nicky came storming in saying, "Dad, have you heard what the school has been teaching Louise?" We were about to find out. Louise was eight years of age, and one day, the male sex education teacher had been teaching the whole mixed class about oral sex and cunnilingus. Well, this shocked the bleeding life out of me. Worse, the pervert was doing the actions in front of the class. I pulled one of the locals, who was equally shocked, and agreed to visit the headmaster with me. The headmaster had called into my hotel to explain the situation pointing out that the teacher in question was a good teacher and was only doing his job to the best of his ability. "Oh," I said. "So you think standing in front of a class full of eight-year-olds, legs astride, explaining to them how the man stands and the female gets on her knees to give him oral sex, then how he has to lie down whilst the woman lay across him to give him oral sex, is normal?" The head teacher's attitude was very patronising; worse, he seemed to get the other local guy on his side, who just hunched his shoulders down and accepted his explanation. No other child's parents from what I gather was or seemed to be concerned about it.

Eventually, it was suggested that Louise be sent to another school out of town. It was made worse for her by the fact the teachers were seemingly taking it out on her for of all things being a snitch. One of the biggest problems I quickly realised was the number of pupils coming into and out of the school. Parents were moving into the area to buy a business, or just moving out of other - maybe rough - areas to give their kids a better lifestyle. I felt I had no choice but to move her, but at the same time, I decided to put the youngest two in private school. I was taken to court some months later for keeping Louise of school. Trying to argue the case in court, I got up to explain the circumstances, but before I could get a chance to speak, the prosecution jumped up and blocked me by bringing up the new school that she was absent from. I was angry and frustrated. The only thought that could come into my mind was shock value. "Would you like your eight-year-old daughter to be taught how to suck a man's cock??"

I was disgusted and appalled. I thought I had left a corrupt judicial system behind in Birmingham, but it was just as fucking corrupt here in rural Devon. If they had nothing to hide, why should the solicitor have to jump up to shut me up? What was there to hide? No, the fact of the matter is they knew that the teacher was out of order, almost to the point of perversion in my view, and I'd heard one or two stories including one of the teacher taking the kids on a camping trip, encouraging them to drink then run around in the nude. Today it's called grooming, yet these people are defending him. By defending this school and its teacher, the solicitor is corrupt, which makes the judicial system corrupt. This is endemic throughout society today. The average person never sees this. Look, we get up in the morning, go to work, come home at six, dinner telly and bed. Many couples married for forty-odd years don't know how to get on with each other once they retire. It's work, home, telly. Most people have very little interaction or experience of courts, the council, or government. When it comes to dealing with social services, if you have a problem or someone has made a cock-up or been negligent in some way, they all gang up and close ranks. The one who was negligent disappears or is reallocated, just as the bent cops are. The only way any of them get sacked or charged with any offence is if another one squeals on them for whatever reason. It gives me some pleasure to note that the squealing amongst the cops is quite widespread today, with one reporting on a senior officer for drunk driving or something. At the least, this is some consolation having been unheard of years ago. I've had a couple of cops tell me how stressful the job is now. Shame. But according to the one cop, it's all about settling scores or side shifting someone for a promotion. Dirty, but it's just another example of how things are deteriorating in our country. Because of my choices of business or work or my lifestyle, I seem to see more; or maybe I just observe more. Certainly, the older I get, the more I realise how corrupt the judicial system is in our country. Well, in actual fact, corruption is rife throughout the world, but go to Saudi Arabia or Morocco…we expect it. Here in England, we like to think we are whiter than white. We aren't.

One by one we were losing our kids. Bit by bit I was finding it difficult to maintain order. I was not the only one; a few of my friends were having difficulties controlling their kids who were rebelling due to the outside influences. The problem is - and one I had greatly underestimated - is the easy-going lifestyle that young kids can fall into. I had seen this in Skegness, Bognor Regis and other places, where young kids hit the town for the season, drinking every night and shagging all the local girls, but stupidly I assumed a small fishing port would be vastly different. What a stupid mistake that was. In fact, the reverse was true. The very ones who would not have survived in a major town like Torquay or Blackpool found a small port or place where they could be someone. There was also no real sense of family here either. Such was the mixture. In the city, our kids were growing up with a sense of stability. The family, as a core unit, was central to the stability in Birmingham. Whether you lived in a council house or private, it came home to us on regular occasions, if and when we were invited out or to someone's home for drinks, etc. Fred, the local builder, invited us to his home to celebrate the new year. Fred and his brothers had been brought here as kids when his father moved to the area from Wolverhampton. That was fine and I never gave it any thought till the night of the new year. There was a fair-sized crowd in his house, yet no one seemed to know him. Hardly anyone spoke to each other, and it topped it for me when I stood listening to two old born and bred Devon blokes sitting on the sofa, glugging all the free food and drinks, whilst moaning in that strong Devonshire accent, "Oh, you know there's not many of us left now." Looking around the room, his mate agreed with him. "Oh, no, no." Fuck me. I nudged Bet and said, "Listen to these two. They're sitting here drinking all the free booze, yet slagging us all of for being outsiders." I couldn't wait to get out, mentioning it to another friend who had come with his wife Janet. Malcolm agreed. "We can't just piss of now. We'll have to wait at least till after midnight." It was now ten thirty. I felt really sorry for Fred and his missus. All the effort they had put into the evening, yet they were amongst total strangers who seemed to be only there for the freebies. It helped make my mind up - this and other incidents confirmed to me - that we needed to get back to the stability of Birmingham.

Once we made our minds up, it was just a matter of planning; we had got property to sell which was going to be no easy matter. In the meantime, I decided to have a bit of a look around Birmingham and Sutton Coldfield. Whilst I was attending my uncle's funeral, I'd got a phone call telling me Geoff had died, and I was quite gutted. Geoff was a great bloke: decent and polite. He made his living initially as a professional gambler, then he brought or won the Fleur de Lye's club in Birmingham city centre. The club was a very nice and refined cabaret club on the second floor with Ray Mills on the door. It felt a great honour when he gave me a gold card. I don't know how Geoff brought the club; it was none of my business, and we weren't brought up to ask questions. My brother told me he had won it in a card game. A few people had had a crack at the club, including Jonny Prescott. Another mentioned was that he was running it for someone else. At any rate, I thought it was his club, and when he sold it, we would start having a drink together. On a Friday night, Geoff would give me a call or tell me in the club to place a bet on a specific horse running the next day, Saturday. The next day, I would put a fiver on the horse which always came in, giving me a twenty-five-pound win. I never asked Geoff how he got the winners. I know he was well into the gambling with Brendan Joyce who owned the Garry. Brendan owned a few bookies, so I suspected they had got access to a few stables, as such they would be given tips for the winners. I didn't give a shit; twenty-five quid was equivalent to over a week's wages. It took the pressure off me having to find a few quid. My motto is "never rock the boat."

Then I heard Geoff had got nicked. By now, I was in prison for the fight, and he told me when he came up with Bet for a visit. Our well-known pal, John the Gangster, had asked him to sell a load of tom [jewellery], making the mistake of telling him that he would be taking it to London the next morning. Now John was going out with a cockney bird that he had blagged of a cockney gangster who later went out with a bird I knew named Carolyn. This cockney, named Jim, was a bit pissed off with John for nicking his bird, but what can you do. I never found out about this for a good few years after but, Geoff proceeded to tell me that a bird with a cockney accent rang him that night, telling him in what seemed a nervous frightened voice not to go to London the next day. This puzzled Geoff and he couldn't figure out what was going on, who the bird was. Was it a fake accent with someone at the mix? Maybe Geoff had had a drink, or maybe his brains weren't working properly. I said, "For fuck's sake, Geoff, that should have been your warning light if ever you heard one." But Geoff wasn't a villain; he didn't deal with villains. Yes, he always drank with them knew the Krays well - as did a lot of people - but he would never do anything bent normally, so I was a bit surprised. The only thing I can assume is that Geoff needed a few quid, and worse, he'd trusted this very well-known John the Gangster, or who tried to act the gangster. I'd always had my suspicions about John, as I'd had with a lot of these well-known gangster villains who never seemed to get nicked. He'd never got nicked since robbing a post office years earlier in Aston. A guy told me he saw him running up Victoria Road sweating like the clappers with a look of utter fear on his face. He'd never been nicked since. Strange, yet they can bring Pip the Planter in to fit my old man and my brothers up. But some of these gangsters, or so-called gangsters, never get nicked at all. That's because they're all shrewd see. Not like you thicko's.

There was one incident when I heard a group of villains boasting in Erdington sauna, with no thought that I could have been a copper or a grass, about how one of them had got nicked in the local lock-up. One of the dicks approached him with a photo of John. Do you know this bloke? With that the idiot with the big mouth, screamed, no, no, no, thus distancing himself from a known and wanted villain. All this was intoned to the others who sat in awe, which confirmed to them that John was obviously on the big wanted list. I was really tempted to pop up and say well it could be a deliberate ploy to make you say that couldn't it, to throw you of the scent, you prats, but while I was debating, they had obviously clocked on that I was a stranger in the sauna with them. I could feel them nodding before they ducked out. What fucking idiots. No wonder so many get nicked so easy. More just reason that I didn't want to be involved with them. If they're not direct grasses – informers - they get themselves nicked with their utter stupidity.

The next morning, Geoff set off for London taking the tom with him. He got stopped less than three miles down the road by the old bill who were waiting for him at spaghetti junction. For that, the poor fucker got a two stretch. He was the wrong age - over sixty - and by the time he came out, he was knackered. He had lost the instinct and the ability to gamble. He was too old to try anything else. His only hope was for someone to give him a lift up. I loaned him my car for a short period because I'd packed up the taxying, but I had to have it back after a bit as I needed every penny I was making. Now he was dead. His lovely wife Joan had died a couple of years before. Six months would have been a plenty full sentence for him, but the cops and the courts would have none of that. For the rest of his life, Geoff and his wife stopped on the treacle thereby costing the taxpayer thousands. Very clever. Yes, there will be those who say well, he broke the law, he deserved his sentence. Well, to those that say that I can tell you there would be a load around Sutton who would buy it. Remember that old saying, "people who live in glass houses." The cops keep their jobs, even getting a promotion, as do the judges, but nothing is achieved by their persecution, more people are committing crimes today than ever. They are simply spreading out more, they are even being more ruthless, where the old criminals had a bit of integrity. Yes, integrity. Today's villains have none at all, especially certain groups. Today's groups - the Albanians, Russians, Bulgarians - have a totally different mindset. And what about the grass, John? I don't know if he's still alive today; his three brothers are dead. The last time I saw him I was having a drink with Colin Lawler in a pub down in Curzon street. When he walked in, he looked like a right paraffin lamp. He sidled over and asked if I was up for the games, obviously the villainy. I looked at him in disgust. I'd never been up for the games, but I took some pleasure in the fact he was obviously on the floor. The cockney gangster Jim, whose bird left him for John, was later thrown in himself and got a six stretch by someone after doing some business with one of the shrewd miller brothers. Great ay, ha-ha.

I can never understand how grasses can operate. I just cannot get my head around how they think. I'm not talking about honest citizens, the guy who sees some crook robbing a shop factory or whatever. I say fair enough to them for ringing the police, as would most of the old school villains. If a group of guys sees someone robbing a bank and feels inclined to be a hero, then fair play to them. That is the risk that all villains should be able to take. But the villain who has participated in crime only to come out and turn grass – informer - is, without doubt, the lowest of the low. To take on a scrapyard and be prepared to throw crooks in to save your own neck for doing something they would have done a few years previously is absolutely disgraceful. To come out of prison, to carry on thieving, and be prepared to throw someone else in to save your own neck or allow you to carry on thieving is, to me, the worst of the worst. The fact they get away with it, that no one seems to care, is an indictment in itself of the person themselves It's interesting that as they get older their shoulders seem to stoop ever more, like Charlie who walks with a hump, [many call him the hump]the strain of living with themselves, I suspect. Maybe that's why I have so few friends from the "good old days." Historically, events have a way of levelling out by natural dissipation. Finally, after all these years, scrapyards have now really had to tighten up, thankfully. Now, if you go into a scrapyard, you have to show proof of identity.

Then you are forced to accept a cheque, not cash. What the percentage of bent metal goes into a yard now is anyone's guess, but I've had at least three scrap dealers tell me that trade is rock bottom, with a gloomy face. Whether the bunging has stopped, or cases of whisky, I don't know. Frankly I don't care. It's something I don't like to see or dwell on.

Likewise, with the villainy because of all the blatant fitting up. Verballing suspects are now questioned under caution as normal, but this time the whole process is tape recorded, sometimes videoed. These can still be got round though; it just makes it harder for the cops. My son was questioned under caution and tape recorded about the little incident in Sutton. My son told his side of events, the talk was concluded. Afterwards, he was chatting to one of the cops in an informal manner about school and friends they had in common, and my son made a comment that could potentially have been incriminating if it was taken out of context with the rest of the conversation. It was, and it was added to his statement, but outside of the tape recording. There are other ways the police and courts can fit you up, don't you worry, but at least the most blatant ones are becoming fewer and far between. And when you do get fitted up, the chances of getting a fair retrial is virtually zilch. The Birmingham six served twenty years in prison before finally being released on technical reasons. In truth, the cops fabricated the evidence. It took twenty years to find that out.

The Bridgwater four served about the same time before also being released on technical grounds...again...and by the west midlands' serious crime squad, later disbanded...again. No one held to account, no one charged with fabricating evidence or false statements, and what part do the masons play in all of this? Why does no one question that almost every senior judge and police officer in England is a member of the masons? Why would such a large body of people want to join and be a member of such a secret group? In Birmingham, at least it is known that they have their own lodge. Why would they want their own lodge? Because they want to keep their charitable work and fundraising secret? It's laughable, and really, very disturbing. Just a thought, but what is to stop people imagining - or thinking - that by all being in the same group, you might all think the same and you might all aspire to and want the same goals? In America, a film was made called the star chamber with Clint Eastwood. It consisted of a group of judges, chief police officers and junior police officers who had decided that too many criminals were getting away with their crimes. The simple solution? Execute the bastards. 'Course, that was only a film, but I've always been suspicious of the way American films show the prosecution and defence going behind closed doors to discuss a technicality with the judge. Now think about it. How the bloody hell could that be right and proper? "Afternoon, you'r honour. Now David here says we should give way on this point of law. Well, I say no, and I'm sure you will agree with me. Hmmm?? Wink-wink."

It goes on in this country; its widespread. What is to stop anyone's imagination stretching to see a senior inspector and a senior judge discussing a murder, and the possibility of the evidence being thin on the ground?

Who polices the police? Why, it's the police. Who judges the judges? Why, it's the judges, of course, you dumbkoff. It doesn't take a great stretch of the imagination to picture the circuit judge having a gin and tonic in chambers when a senior cop walks in. "Oh, hello Dennis, what are you having? How's things going with the local toe rags?"

"Oh, not too bad, your worship. We've put another three of those Kirby's away, as you know," nudge-nudge. "Quite a few are making things easier for us by giving us plenty of bodies, but those Lewins are still giving us hell; they're utterly feral, antagonistic, very anti-police and very insolent. Worse, they just won't squeal."

"Well, Donald, you need to put a bit more effort in old boy. Now don't you worry too much about the means and the how's. What's Pip up to nowadays? Just bring him in," nudge-nudge. "Let the prosecution see the rabbit, then I can do the rest. I can address the jury accordingly. THEY WILL DO AS I DIRECT, as you know. Don't you worry, another five or seven stretch should see them off." Well, it did, and it did.

Ahh, too much for the old brain cells to take in, ay? Some thirty years ago, a major villain named Kenneth Noy was nicked for stabbing a plain clothes copper trespassing undercover on his land. The cops were so bitter and intent on putting him down, they threw just the one charge at him of murder, so confident were they of sending him down for life. Well, he had a good barrister, and the charge was dismissed. He was found not guilty. The cops were spitting blood. It was pointed out to them at the time that they should have ensured a conviction by throwing in two or three alternative charges. The normal thing. They got him, instead, on another charge of handling stolen gold and he got a six stretch. Not much consolation for the cops, so they were well-chuffed a few years later when Noy's name cropped up again, with the death of a young driver in another car. Following an argument, Noy stabbed the young kid. The cops pulled all the stops out to find Noy and get him convicted, even going to the trouble of taking the young guy's girlfriend to Spain to spy on and pick out Noy. She did. Noy was nicked and brought back to England where again he faced charges of murder.

But this is the really interesting bit: when Noy went before the judge on the murder charge, before the trial, he gave the masonic distress signal. Fingers on tie knot. Shortly after, the judge brought it up in public and to the press and said, "If he thought I was going to help him out on such a serious charge as he was facing, then he was mistaken." THERE WAS NO WAY I COULD HELP HIM ON THAT ONE?? But then that begs the question: what would the judge have been prepared to help him out on?? Did Noy give the distress signal before his trial for killing the cop a few years earlier?—where he was found not guilty? At any rate, the police got what they wanted this time. Noy was found guilty and served twenty years. The police put a bit more poison in by putting it out that Noy was also a grass, thus trying to cause him further grief. They may have been right, but many villains would err on the side of caution knowing how it was put out.

The lives of the Birmingham six were destroyed by their sentences. Maybe they did have something to do with the bombings. At any rate, the families of the victims are now mourning them with no one being convicted of the crimes. No doubt the cops will justify it as they had paid for the crimes anyway. The same with the Bridgewater four. What is the possibility that one or two of them might have been involved in the actual robbery and murder? At any rate, they were found not guilty at a final appeal hearing. They got compensation. I understand the younger one having mental health issues. Now, no one to date, no other suspects, have been brought to justice. Possibly the family of the young boy might feel the real killers were caught and served some sentence. Not much satisfaction, methinks. A few years ago, some of those blacks had formed into gangs over and around Handsworth, the one crowd being known as the burgher boys. Now these boys weren't fucking about. I had come close to one or two of them and I swear they must have come from and been related to the caribs, so named after the Caribbean's who frightened the shit out of any European sailor who dared try landing on their islands in the 16th century. Maybe it was the ganja they smoked, but they just didn't give a fuck about anyone. I know a few coppers were shit scared because a female detective told me she resigned because of them. A bullet missed her cheek by a whisker and that was it, she was out. The blacks decided to set up a trap for the cops by setting a fire in the Barton arms pub to draw them in. When the cops arrived, it went *bang* of with the blacks firing and shooting guns at them. Now fair enough, no one can put up with that in a civilised society, but there are a couple of simple answers. Fitting up ain't one of them, and more than a couple are rumoured to have been fitted up.

The police like to present themselves as being one of the boys, just like Joe public, but they are not; they are a breed apart. I am not really talking about the cop in uniform on the beat - they are the public face of the police force, in the main, I think, decent, hardworking with the aim of serving the public, I have met a few bent uniformed cops, but in the main most of them try to do a good job. It is they who get the brunt of the backlash for any bad feeling rustled up by those hiding behind them. It's the institution of the police that's corrupt. Think about it: what kind of a mentality do you have to have to fit someone up, or bend the evidence, without the fullest of proof? On the basis that if you're not guilty of that one you're guilty of something? Who can walk away seeing someone convicted and sent to prison for life? Let us never forget the body of the police force the institution was founded by the rich, in the form of Sir Robert Peel, himself a wealthy landowner, baronet and former prime minister, to protect themselves against the plebs - the lower orders - in order to do that who did they pick to do the dirty work? Why, the plebs themselves. Those at the bottom of the pile. The prison services work exactly the same. Use the lower order to keep the riff raff locked up. Lock them up, yes. There are better alternatives to that but lock them up. If need be, don't fit people up for a six stretch, it just stores up trouble for further down the line.

Whilst in Birmingham, I decided to look up a few of my old mates, but they were few and far on the ground. First up was Roger the Dodger, who had popped into the hotel to see me. Dodger was well pleased for me having a hotel; no sign of jealousy or resentment at all, but why should there be? Picking the dodger up, he wanted to take me down the Prince in Nechells. My old pal Rudy Swarm was running the boozer and I was excited to meet him. As we walked in, Dodger - as loud and blustering as usual, "Here ya are, who have I got here then?" I was underwhelmed by the welcome - Rudy barely mustered hello - but I put that down to the fact he was tired running his pub. But standing there in front of the bar was my old mate, Wally Barber. Like Rudy, me and Barber went back years, yet here he was with his bird, and he was giving me a total blank. I couldn't bleeding believe it. Hello Wal, how's ya going? Still a blank. I nearly lost my footing. I was in shock trying to figure out what I had done wrong, where had I upset him? I couldn't figure it out, and after a half a lager, I was glad to get out. Walking out with Dodger, I said, "What the fuck was all that about? Have you been saying anything to them?" "No, Tom, I only told them you'd got a hotel in Devon and a nice yacht." Oh, that was it then, maybe they think I've got above myself. But why be like that? I'm still Tommy Lewin. Ok, I've bettered myself, but I never considered myself better than them. To me, if you made good friends at school you were friends for life. Robert Turley is exactly the same good old Turl I used to get my arse smacked with at school. Tony Ally paid me a nice compliment once when he said, "I know you've got a few quid Tom, but you've never changed." And why should I?? But a lot do - have changed a lot think or thought they were more clever or smarter than others. One way to be smarter is to grass on them to get yourself in the clear. Great, ay? What a way to live. What a way to live in the world, ha-ha.

Hitting a few pubs, I found it very much the same. We walk in, Dodger walks up, says hello, they either nod or grunt then carry on. We'd been in Devon about ten years, fair enough I hadn't seen many of them since moving to Sutton years earlier mainly because I couldn't afford to initially then I was too busy, but any of them would have been welcome in the hotel. Yet I get this blank. Is it just me, or is it just Birmingham? In London, you often hear of some celebrity or another who enjoys going back to their roots to drink down the old east end. Maybe that's it. If you're a celebrity you're a hero to everyone, but if you've just got a few quid more it pisses people of. Giving up on my mates, I started trotting around looking at what we could get into once safely back home. There was a little grocery shop up for sale in a little village outside Sutton, so getting back to Devon I told Bet all about it. After a couple of weeks, we drove back up to the village, stopped outside the shop, and I said to Bet, "What do you recon? Could you fancy running that?" "Piece of piss," said she. She never fails to impress me, Bet, yet all the time I just take her for granted. The guy who runs the shop hadn't got a clue, so after a look around we decided to do a deal and buy it. There was a two-bedroom flat above the shops and our plan was to earn a living from the shop using our money to buy houses and refurbish them.

But first we had to sell up to raise the money in the first place. As well as the guesthouse, we had other flats and property, plus some land outside of town. We bought the shop with Bet moving up to the village, the youngest moving up with her, Rachael finishing of her O levels, me trying to sell stuff and get sorted in Devon. Eventually, bit by bit, we started moving up. Bet and Louise were running the shop. I had discovered Brian was still running the Lloyds bank in Aldridge, so went in to say hello and open an account, intending to slowly transfer everything up there. Brian was most welcoming but sadly told me he was going to take early retirement. Well, that was a blow to me straight away. Brian was a great bloke, so I knew there would be no problem borrowing money if and when we needed to, but times had changed. Through the banks' own fault of over-lending on everything from overpriced houses to bad businesses, when things went tits up, the banks lost a fortune. Brian told me he had had authority to lend up to 100k on his own initiative, but now it had been cut to 5000. He felt his balls had been cut off, or worse, his head office had jumped in and forced a few companies into bankruptcy, many of them his personal friends he'd built up over the years. Now they weren't his friends. Brian was not a happy bunny. In many instances the banks had got too close to the customers and allowed their judgement to become clouded. I had seen it in Devon: hoteliers would get a re-valuation every year to borrow money to enable them to have a holiday and only do a bit of work, fine, the hotels did increase in price, but eventually the hoteliers were borrowing more than they could pay back, they were using the top up loans simply to pay the banks back. When everything went tits up, the banks snatched the businesses back the values just toppled. Again, just no common sense. Stupid enough to be in business and keep borrowing, but it's equally stupid of the bank managers to just lend money willy-nilly like they were doing. Now that also cut me off. Now I had no choice but to get property sold so I could finance my house buying projects.

Eventually Rachael completed her exams and I got her up to the shop. I had started buying stuff around Birmingham when Dave rang me up. I had asked Dave to manage my flats, collecting the rent etc., for a few quid a week. He was having problems with one of the tenants who was refusing to pay his rent. This was a middle-aged couple who had approached me a few months earlier for a flat. I'd got a ground floor one that I showed them around, they were desperate, having just moved up from the south coast. Their faces were pleading, and I felt sorry for them. Most of my tenants were young chancers who thought they were proper jack the lads. The odd one tried it on trying to get away from paying the rent. It was par for the course; most paid their rent. With the age of this couple, I thought I'm not going to have any problems when I gave them the flat; they were over the moon, effusive in their gratitude, almost cringe worthy. By putting Dave in to collect the rent, it had signalled to the tenants that I wasn't around, and this gave them the green light to make excuses and stop paying the rent. Dave didn't think his wages were enough to justify putting too much effort in. This was something I couldn't - and wasn't prepared to - put up with. I had got enough pressure on me with everything going on to expect or put up with low life tenants trying to scam me after begging for the flat in the first place.

There are different ways you can get a tenant out. One landlord I knew was notorious in his methods. Nicholas Hoogstraten would just let himself in and treat his tenants like shit. There had been many documentaries on him harassing threatening and terrorising his tenants. If he wanted you out you got out, he had made millions in the process. I could never be like that. The man was utterly ruthless. Another family I was friendly with down in Devon had a completely different method. As long as you paid your rent and kept the places in reasonable order, they didn't see you, didn't care about you and left you alone. All they were concerned about and wanted was their rent, so if a tenant had missed their rent the second or third week, Fred or Joe would pop down and give them a weeks' notice. On the following Saturday, the three brothers would pop down to the property, let themselves in, plonk themselves on the sofa, and say alright son? We've come to give you a hand. The brothers were big lads and the tenants, having got over the shock and weighing the situation, up rapid packed up quick sharpish.

Another friend, a lovely guy, had rented a flat out above his house, to a youngish single woman. After a few weeks, she asked if she could bring a mate in to share. My friend agreed but quickly it dawned on him that they were lesbians, and the one woman was pregnant. Worse, they were making demands. That was putting a great deal of stress on him. He was a lovely guy with a small jewellery shop in the town and my advice was to go in, give them a week's notice, then turf their stuff out. Once she had her child, he would be fucked. He decided to go to his solicitor who advised him strongly against, taking any action and to let them handle it. It ended up with him being taken to court, costs awarded against him of circa five-grand, and to top it off he suffered a heart attack. I felt so sorry for the poor bugger. These nasty bastards had had him right in the net, with his parasitic solicitor who had advised him shrugging her shoulders and pocketing a few grand.

I had decided to adopt the attitude of Fred and his brothers, so on the first Friday I drove down to Devon, popped in to see my pal, and at 10:30 went down and let myself into their flat - my flat. Sitting on the sofa, I waited for them to come home from the pub after another night of spending my rent. Seeing their little faces as they came through the door was a picture to behold. "Oh, oh, oh, heeello Tom." I could see I'd got them on the hop. "You haven't been paying your rent, have you?"

"Well, we can pay it now Tom, we've just had problems, but were ok now."

Well, I couldn't fuck about from now on. "No, sorry, it's too late now, you'll just have to get out. Get your stuff." With that, utterly defeated, they got their stuff together and left, after I'd made sure I'd got the keys of them.

For anyone who might feel sorry for them, well look, if they had been upfront, rung me up or explained to my mate Dave, explained the circumstances, there would have been no problem. I would have sat back and waited, but no, these people were in their fifties, mugs, who took the piss. If I had walked away, they would have carried on not paying the rent. In the event they went to my ex-solicitor, who had acted for my mate in getting the two lesbians out of his flat, suffering a heart attack in the process. Knowing I was out of town, knowing I was leaving the town, they advised these two tenants to sue me, and they eagerly agreed. After all, they'd got all the time in the world, and it was on legal aid. After another couple of months, the case was put before the court. The claimants won their case of illegal eviction, etc., which it wasn't. They were awarded some five-grand, in damages. The parasites got a couple of grand in legal aid. Sadly, I only found out about this belatedly, due to the fact the courts sent the summonses to the wrong place. Well not exactly the wrong house, it was just not my property, it was my wife's property. I am pretty sure the solicitor would have known that because they were involved in the purchase, because I wasn't on the deeds, I couldn't be served with any notices, further, it didn't affect my credit rating at all. The cops wouldn't give a shit, the parasitic solicitors don't give a shit. I kid you not, in business its every man for himself, because no one else gives a shit. The solicitors know you've got a few quid, the tenants have the attitude that its them and us, the unscrupulous landlord ripping the poor folk of. Yet another abuse of the legal aid system.

Dave was curious to know what I was up to. My plan was to buy and refurbish houses. Each house would take me approximately a month to gut and refurbish, three months to sell. Every third house would pay for a fourth house free of mortgage to rent. The plan was fool proof, I thought. Dave wanted a piece of the action and I was more than happy to oblige. With three houses taking a month each, it left me with a lot of time on my hands. I could do with more houses to earn out of. At the same time, talking on the phone about the tenant I had just kicked out it occurred to both of us that we could do some further business. Dave had asked me before

I left Devon if I could do him a little favour. Dave was a businessman in the town who had got a small haberdashery shop. It was earning him a living but not much. A few years earlier he had bought a small three-bedroom house in Birmingham, as an investment, sensibly, he thought. He had rented it to a former university student and computer geek with a solid job charging him forty quid a week. Sadly, the geek was on the ball, and no sooner had Dave turned his back, the tenant got onto the council who valued the property at a reduced rent of eight pounds per week. Dave was only a strip of piss, but he was furious. He went around the house screaming his head off, the little fucker did no more than slap an injunction on Dave, that was it. He was bolloxed. I could see the tears welling up in his eyes as he told, me, that was my pension Tom, ok it wasn't a lot of money, but it covered a few bills. That was eight years ago, so the little prick had been in the house having agreed to pay forty quid a week, only to end up paying eight quid for the last eight years. He couldn't even be bothered to seek an increase each year, what for Tom? An extra five bob a week? He had thrown his hands in on the property. I promised him I would sort it out for him.

The only problem was the little prick was never in. I was going to the house at all times of the day and night, the curtains were always drawn and in darkness, I had to ring Dave up, how do you know he's still here. I'm spending ages watching the house and he's never here? He's got to be there, Tom, he's still paying his rent. Slowly it dawned on both of us, how about doing the deal? Dave was well up for it. We would do a part exchange on my flats for his house. This served two purposes for Dave, after giving me a load of dosh and his house, it left it left him in a good position to borrow some money on the flats to invest with me on houses in Birmingham. It was a win-win for both of us. My only problem was finding the tenant and getting the little prick out. That seemed easier said than done. Any harassment of any kind, and its odds on he's going to go screaming to the cops. I wasn't ready for another eight years of headache. Then I came up with a little plan.

I went round to my old pal Tony Williams and asked him if he wanted to earn a few quid. All he had to do was be a witness. He was up for it, and the next day on the Friday, we drove over to the house, Tony, bringing his son and holding my video camera. "Tone, don't do anything wrong; this is a right mongrel were dealing with here. Any violence he will be straight on to the cops. This is all legitimate and legal, just keep the camera going." The front was impenetrable, the curtains still up. To all intents and purposes, the house was deserted. Going round the back, we found the gate open, and low and behold, the back door open and almost off its hinges. Shouting out we decided to pop back the next day on the Saturday morning. This time, we casually walked in the back through the open door. Tony at the back, camera whirring away, George behind him, me shouting out aloud, "helloooo." The house was a shit hole. Coming through the back door the toilet was full of caked on shit, the bathroom disgusting, the back room full of filth, dirty carpets, fag ends food containers, and the courts are protecting these pricks. Just as were taking it all in, the little scroat comes down the stairs. "Oh, hello there. I'm sorry to bother you but the door was all open." I could see he couldn't get his brains around what's happening, while he was still trying to get his head around what was going on. I followed up. "Now I am a builder acting for the landlord, who has asked me to give an evaluation for any work that might need doing, and there looks like it's going to be a lot, but not to worry, the landlord doesn't want you to be homeless, so he's got another house for you to move in over great Barr. Is that ok?" All this for the camera. He's still struggling. "Look, I'll tell you what. We'll come back Monday, and I'll show you the house ok?" As he nodded, I indicated to Tony, *ok son, lets duck*. Going back on the Monday, as expected, the little shit had gone, the front room full of refuse sacks.

The bedrooms were equally disgusting with fag ends all over the place, curry cartons everywhere. Looking around, Dave had definitely got the best part of the deal. It took ages just to clear the shit out of the place, and this filthy animal was being protected by the full might of the law. It took us six weeks to clear the place out, fumigate it redecorate and refurbish. Dave rang up a few weeks later and said, "What's been going on up there?"

"What do you mean?"

"Well, the cops called round yesterday asking all about the house and the tenant. They recon someone had had a right mace up ordering a load of stuff, furniture etc. in the little shit's name."

I was puzzled. "What do you mean, in the guy's name? I don't even know his name. I can only assume he must have had the mace up himself before doing a runner. Anyway, what did you tell the cops?"

"Oh, I just told them it was nothing to do with me, that I'd sold the place and didn't want anything to do with it. With that the cop shrugged his shoulders and walked off." The crafty little bugger.

The next few weeks and months were very hectic. Bet and Louise were running the shop. She had also been viewing houses in Sutton for us to move into. We were going to live above the shop and for a few weeks we did, but we also realised our two youngest kids needed the stability of a nice house and garden, plus a good school. The headmaster of the private school in Devon had admitted that the Sutton schools were on a par with any good private school. He was right, all our kids had done well in Sutton schools. Bet was doing ok in the shop and was even diversifying to increase the turnover. Some local kitchen fitters had popped in to ask her if she could make some sandwiches. She did indeed and this turned out to be quite lucrative. The more experience we got the more we realised that we weren't afraid or too bothered to have a crack at or run most businesses. There were limits; I knew we couldn't run an engineering company as we had had no experience of engineering. Most business is just a matter of common sense, but there are other factors like competition from supermarkets or discovering customers having no money. Sometimes no matter how much work and effort you put into something, you can find yourself flogging a dead horse. In our case the corner shop was a bit of a dead horse. Along the way was a lovely couple who ran a fruit and veg shop. The locals were just not supporting them, so they set about doing a little bit of canvasing, offering to do free deliveries. The fruit was all fresh, but they were still struggling. A few doors the other side was a Pakistani who ran the newspaper shop. He would get up in the morning, open his shop, set out the newspapers, and run the shop till eight in the morning. Then his wife, having got the kids off to school, would come down and take over. He would then go off to work, return at five p.m., and take over till eight p.m., seven days a week, and then his wife would run upstairs to make the usual curry meal. Neither of them bought from our shop. For all that his turnover was six grand a year. Admittedly, their accommodation would be in that so effectively they were making a bit more. We quickly started to realise that useful as it was having the shop. It was limited. The problem was the setup of the village. Half was made up of council houses who we started to realise had no money, while the other half was made up of private houses who also had no money or very little of it. If either of the people on each estate had money, then they didn't spend it in the village except for the local pub. In short, they were tight. Bet would do specials, like putting bread on as a loss leader to entice customers in. The rest of the stuff was quite competitive as well, but she would see people get on the local bus into town four miles away, get all their groceries from Aldi, come back, laden down, then have the gall to walk into the shop just to buy a loaf. Bet would send me down to the local farmer to get a few dozen fresh eggs, then back in the shop we would put them on display on the front counter. I think we were making about ten pence on a half dozen pack; it was just a service. One day a woman came in to buy another tray of eggs and commented on how nice they were, asking where we bought them from if we didn't mind her asking. "We get them fresh in from just down the road, my love," nodding towards the way. To save ten pence she must have travelled down to the local farms searching each one till she found it; she never returned to the shop again. Without a doubt, running a business in any given area gives you an insight into that place and its people for sure. Brian, our bank manager, had pointed us in the direction of a nice, detached house just a short distance from the shop, but we didn't really want to live in the village. Once we had completed on the house, we set about moving into it. The shop was great for us, giving us a roof over our heads, and with the small profit from the shop, it covered our out goings. But having uplifted them from Devon, we needed to get the kids into a stable environment. Equally as important, I needed to be able to concentrate on the real business of dealing in houses, so we put the business on the market. We had a couple of people view it, but the only person who showed any interest was an Asian Muslim with a six-inch beard wearing a white dress. Now how the fuck was someone like that going to run a traditional English grocery shop? At any rate, he felt comfortable to live in the village, having seen the Pakistani next door. "Oh yes," I said. "That's Fahad, a lovely man; everybody in the village loves him. He even makes us a curry every week." That, and my accounts, swung it. 'Course I hadn't submitted them yet, but they looked quite good. The deal was done, and the only thing left was to do the stock take. Round he comes going through everything on the shelves, and anything with pork in he threw back at us. He was a true Muslim, alright. When it came to the fresh meat counter, his little nose turned right up. No to the bacon, no to the sausages. That was half the deli counter wiped out then if we didn't sell it. We bundled it up and put in in the fridge to eat ourselves. A couple of weeks later, I popped round to see our friends in the greengrocers. They were not happy little bunnies. I could see they were struggling to make the shop profitable. My heart went out to them, but we couldn't do anything.

I was told, "Oh, by the way, that bloke you sold the shop to has been moaning that you robbed him."

"Robbed him? How do you mean?"

"Well, he reckons the turnover is nowhere near what you showed him in your accounts."

"Well, he's got a bit of a fucking cheek ain't he? Look, he's a Muslim; he won't sell bacon or sausages and that was most of our trade, as you know, and be fair...dressed like he does, who's going in there to buy of him? They only go into the Pakistani because his wife runs the shop and its newspapers. No one is going to spend 50 pence on a bus to go and buy a newspaper just to save twenty pence."

"Yes of course."

With that, I went round to tell our Muslim friend the news and stop blackening my name. When he saw the picture, he decided to try something else.

With the houses I was running around like a blue-arsed fly, chasing agents asking if they had got any deals. Sometimes I caught lucky, sometimes not. At the auctions I was up against the Asians. I had looked at a few houses and had marked them in the book. With the top line I was prepared to pay, the first one came up, the bidding went crackers. Then the second. The third one I'd estimated a ten grand profit if I got it at the right price. Blow me if some Asian guy at the back who I knew as a very well of dealer landlord didn't go straight in at the top price I was looking to pay. I couldn't get my hat on. The others looked around the room, saw who was bidding, and you could see their little eyes get all excited. Oh, it is Mohamed; if he is bidding it must be worth it. With that the whole room started bidding, and by the time it was sold it was almost at the top price it would fetch fully refurbished. I couldn't figure it out at first, then, slowly, I did. These Asians weren't bothered about the condition. The house had carpets threadbare and bug ridden, the electrics worked but was all black rubber wiring. It had a bathroom and a kitchen, bare as it was, but for someone used living in a tin hut in Pakistan, it was a palace. Whether it be a cousin or not, he could charge £350 a month rent, and the social would pay it. Very often, the tenant would then rent a room of to one of his cousins for £30£40 quid a week, and that would go straight in his bin. The landlord didn't give a shit; all he wanted was his rent which paid his mortgage. I was slow catching on.

At another auction, I was up against Rahm, who bought one of the two houses we were both bidding on. By now, I had caught onto the fact that as technically the houses were mine, I could let myself in, and by the time came for completion, I had almost refurbished it. As we were finishing off, Rahm came to inspect the house next door. How have you managed to do all this work before I have completed, he wanted to know? I left him guessing. The house was a shithole and in a terrible state. Two sisters had lived next door to each other and neither had done anything. As we pulled of the ten layers of wallpaper, the crumbling plaster came off with it. The kitchen was a nightmare. It was a game just getting the floors levelled. I knew Rahm was minted. Although he lived in a terraced house in Edgbaston, his front room his letting office, he would often boast about his two children who go to private school and his Mercedes car - yet he couldn't read nor write. As we were finishing off, a steady trail of people kept calling up to look at next door. One young couple asked if they could rent my house. I asked if they had a grand deposit. They said no, but were both hard-working, and the girlfriend's mom works in a solicitor's office. I said, "That's no good to me, son; you could walk in here Monday, nick my boiler, and walk out Tuesday and I'm down a grand. Won't your parents pay the deposit?" No. The next couple who came up to view were a middle-aged couple with a disabled son in his late twenties. "Oh, what a nice man Mr Rahm is." I thought that's a bit of a change. The young couple called him a horrible bastard who told them to look through the letterbox or fuck off. "Oh no, he's told us we can do as much work decorating and he will reimburse us our money." Oh really? I don't think he noticed my raised eyebrows.

At any rate, they moved in and started to redecorate from room to room. I was popping back to check on tenants. When I'd come across the family from next door, I asked how they were doing.

"Oh, ok Tom. We've done three bedrooms and the back lounge."

"Oh great, has he reimbursed you for the cost of decorating?"

"Well, no, Tom, but to be fair, he's let us of paying the full rent. After all, he let it to us at £80 per week, but the social will only pay 55."

I didn't know whether to laugh or cry. Rahm would have known what the ceiling was for the rent before he let it. They would be forever in his debt without even realising it. What a clever bugger, and he can't even read nor write? I came across this quite a few times over the years. More than once, Rahm was bidding against me. Once I bid on a very nice house in great Barr. Letting ourselves in to start work, my son-in-law went into the garden shed. Calling me, we saw the shed was full to the ceiling and under the usual pile of garden tools mowers, rakes, etc. was a treasure trove of brand-new shop stock, lighters, gold pens and other stuff. The guy who sold the house at auction was a solicitor who had brought the property ten years earlier as an investment. The house had been raided - whether it was the relatives of the tenants or the landlord. We never knew, but obviously the plum had gone, and no one bothered looking into the garden shed. It was a treasure trove. I never felt inclined to tell the vendor. Besides, the stuff was legally mine. Rahm had come over to me at the auctions and offered me an extra two grand on top if I let him have the house. I said make it five and it's a deal. He shook his head; I'm glad he did.

I came across a few good deals on houses, but sometimes I felt I was too busy chasing my own tail and getting nowhere.

My plan of buying and selling three houses to pay for the fourth-free was great in theory, but it wasn't working out in practice. Sometimes it could take me twelve months to sell a house, and by the time it was sold, I'd spent the profit. I needed another angle - another arrow to my bow. I thought I'd got it with Barclays bank. Calling in one day, I was approached as I was walking out by a nice-looking bird in a pin-striped suit. She introduced herself as the bank manager.

"Oh, hello Mr Lewin. Can I have a word, please?"

"Course you can, my love."

"Well, we couldn't help noticing that you have large sums going into your accounts and then it goes quite for a bit."

"Well, yes, because I deal in property; sometimes houses sell quick, sometimes not."

With that, she insisted I see her financial advisers. These were at another branch but could be called in the next day for coffee and biscuits. I was reluctant. I had realised that banks were bent; the decent old-style bank manager like Brian had been kicked out and now they were being replaced by bloodsuckers/sharks/parasites. It was confirmed to me the next day. As I sat in the office, I was faced with two eager and smiling men in their early forties. I was looking at two sharks. The coffee came out along with the biscuits, but the skin on my body was crawling with nerves. The only time I'd ever felt like that was when the bum bandit who owned the flats next door to our hotel asked me to look at his cooker. It was a summer day and I only had my shorts on. I could feel him slavering over my body as he stood behind me. Well, that's how I felt with these sharks.

"Right, Mr Lewin, what can we do for you?"

"Pardon, you asked me here." I told them what my plans were, what I was doing, and the problems I was facing. I said, "If you really want to help to our mutual benefit, you could lend me the money for one house as I refurbish it. In return, I will give you another two houses." They're trying to think this out. "It's simple, really. You're going to have the security of three of my houses and I will only owe the mortgage on one that I will rent out. That rent will pay the mortgage. Once that's rented, we'll rent the next refurbished house out and so on. You will have the security of each house plus the equity I've put in them."

Well, they weren't happy with that, and then they really shook me. "But Mr Lewin, these houses haven't really cost you anything, have they?"

Well, I was floored. "How do you mean?"

"Well, if you're making twenty-five percent on each house you refurbish and we lend you seventy-five percent, the houses have cost you nothing. After all, you are making profit on other people's misfortune."

I couldn't believe he had come out with that. Excuse me, who made them lose the house in the first place?? I said, "But you will always be holding another two houses in front as security." I don't know whether I was being fucking thick or these sharks were, but at any rate, they wanted my house as well. Now were getting there; they wanted everything including my house. Yes, so they could screw me by the balls. No wonder these banks had got themselves into such trouble. I had never met such stupidity and greed no wonder they make millions.

On the manager's door was a cartoon showing a woman on her knees scrubbing the floor. A customer walks in and asks for the manager. The scrubber on the floor turns and says, you're talking to me. That about sums it up. The banks, are corrupt, to me they can rob you left right and centre, go in and rob a bank. You get ten years in clink. The bank can rob customers hand over fist, and they get a fucking knighthood plus a million-pound bonus. Jeeezzz, if only I'd had a good education.

I'd bought a house in Smethwick blind at auction without even looking at it beforehand. It was a risk, but I was getting pissed off with looking at houses and being outbid by the Asians. After paying my deposit, I shot over to the house to check. I hadn't brought a bogie. I was dead-chuffed; it needed a new roof, but it had been newly double glazed throughout. I had to spend very little on the house completing the work very quickly. A young couple had brought the house. The husband was a mechanic, working a five-day week, his wife stopping at home looking after the kids, then she wanted double glazing because her sister-in-law had double glazing. Soon, her husband was working six days a week to pay for it. When interest rates went up, that was it - they were knackered. We found the house full of catalogue purchases.

Next door lived a lovely couple: Jack and his wife Mary. She used to do a bit of cleaning for us after working, which would pay for her to have a few fags. Finishing off, I rang the local agent up to value and market the house. He turned up on the Friday, and on the Saturday, a little tribe of Asians turned up led by a young lad. I invited them to look around. Walking out, the Asian lad said how much do you want? Well, I ain't dealing with no Asian; they are a pain in the arse to deal with. Tell them a tenner, they will want it for six. Tell them six for the same item, and they will want it for four. It's inbuilt in their nature. Come Monday, the agent rang me up. The little gang had brought it at the full asking price. I couldn't believe it. When another one came up for sale five doors down, I bid and brought that one as well.

Luvverly jubberly, this one was much worse, but if there were Asians out there to buy, then I am selling. Every day, the young Asian guy is walking up and down, shirt open in the sunshine. "Morning Tom," "Afternoon Tom," while strolling along smoking a fag. When I asked him one day, "Aren't you the lad who brought the house off me?"

"Yes Tom, I told you we wanted it."

"Yes, but you ain't working, are you?"

"Oh no, Tom, I'm on the dole." He wasn't boasting; he was just stating a fact. "You whites have to understand, Tom, that when we get of that plane, there is an army of benefits officers explaining to us exactly what we are entitled to. For generations, we have grown used to scraping by on anything. In India, I can live on two pounds a week. When we come here, I can still live on two pounds a week, so on forty pounds a week I can live like a king."

"Yes, I can see that, but you haven't told me how you brought the house."

"Simple, Tom. I didn't buy the house. My cousin bought the house. He has a shop round the corner, so already has a mortgage."

Fucking great, ay? So, this guy buys the house, but it's actually in his cousin's name. His cousin gives him a rent book charging him £350 a month in rent. The mortgage is £240, so straight off, he's making £110 profit. Then he's looking after his mother, so getting a carer's allowance. Then his dole. All in all, he's raking in some £110 a week. Very nice, too. And he can live on two quid a week? Nice, if you can get it.

Jack came down one day asking me for some advice. These houses were all the same: you walked into the lounge, through into the living room, on into the kitchen with the bathroom beyond. Jack had had his bathroom redone five years earlier. All very nice, but there was black mould starting to come through the plaster. I explained to him the effects of capillary action, the heat from inside the room drawing in the damp from the outer walls. Whoever had done the job just never did it right in the first place by treating the walls. An easy job and quite inexpensive. With that, he took me out to look at the roof which had already been turnerised, but he was getting problems. Mary had already told me that Jack had ordered her to cut down her fags, her only little pleasure to five a day. Now he was pressuring her to pack up altogether. Jack, go to the council and ask them for a grant? I've tried, Tom, but they've told me there's no more money left for grants. I pointed to the Pakistani who lived in the house next to the new one we were refurbishing. He was on the dole, looking after his disabled wife. Not too disabled to knock out eight kids. He was selling the odd car from outside his house, plus doing a bit of taxying - he was raking it in. He'd also boasted to us how he'd got a 100 percent grant. Damp-proof course: new doors architrave, skirting, re-plastering, new roof, bathroom extension, etc. It was a proper piss-take, and it was widespread. Jack just looked resigned; shoulders slumped in defeat.

Yes, Tom, but the council is run by Asians. Well, that's it then, look after your own. All around Smethwick and other rundown Asian areas, I had noticed the councils awarding 100 percent grants for new roofs and refurbishment work, yet here was poor Jack and his wife. He'd done his time in the army during WW2. He and his wife had worked all their life, and now all they wanted was to be able to spend their twilight years in a bit of comfort, and here they are scraping for a few quid. I felt heartfelt sorry for them but had no answer. Personally, I felt they should have sold up, spent their money, and gone into an old folks' home. This was nothing new to me; I had seen it time and time again over the years. We go through life in a cavalier way, not thinking about tomorrow, only to wake up with a shock when you're a couple of years from retirement and it hits you how little you're going to have to live on. I felt so sorry for the poor bleeders, decent genuine people.

I had brought a couple of houses in Erdington refurbished, and had got the first one half sold when my youngest daughter came down and asked me about how I could get her a house like I had with the others. I would explain to her and she'd run upstairs to discuss it with her boyfriend, Rob. After a few minutes, she'd pop down again with another question. I was finding the whole thing so funny; both had got good jobs - my daughter as an accountant. Look, this is how it works. The lenders want to see you make some commitment, example in the form of a deposit. If you just go up to them and tell them your dad his giving you his twenty-five percent equity in his house, they will tell you to piss off. What you have to do is go out and tell the banks you have a twenty-five percent deposit.

The banks will bend over backwards. Well, in they both went, and true to form, the banks were bending over backwards, fighting to make a better offer. Choosing the best lender, I gave them a cheque for the twenty-five percent deposit which I got straight back on completion. Finishing of a little bit of decorating, they put the house straight back onto the market, buying their second house in Great Barr six months later. To all my kids, I tried to pass on the benefits of having money and knowing that money makes money. Even here in Sutton I see how the unlikeliest person will have an extra string to their bow. The teacher living in a beautiful, detached house on the Four Oaks estate, then he told me he rents two rooms out. Then the bank manager who lived opposite me - he bought the house unmodernised - borrowing cheap money from his bank, spending a few years doing it up, then making that extra few grand profit. All this I tried to point out and get my kids to see this. They were eighteen years of age, within five years, and in theory, they would own their own house outright or alternatively be in a much nicer house in a better area all by the age of twenty-three or twenty-five. A simple process if you focus on it. One friend, Gordon, guided his daughter the same way. At thirty, her and her husband owned a very expensive house in Sutton.

The thing is, when you've had no money - I mean *really* having no money, your arse hanging out of your pants – you're hungry, you either accept it, thinking if you've got a nice job, a regular wage packet, that's good enough, or you can say fuck this and try going for the jackpot. My kids had been brought up in a modest but middle class environment. If they wanted a foreign holiday, they had it; if they wanted a horse, I got them a horse. They didn't know what it was like to go hungry. The problem with that mentality is they don't think or see what is around the corner. A lot of middle-class kids just assume they have the bank of mommy and daddy. But I read an article once of a go-getting middle-class highflyer who thought she had it all: a good, well-paying job, a nice apartment, nice clothes, money in the bank. But she lost her job. She didn't realise how close she was in reality to that park bench till she was actually sleeping on it. The majority of people go blithely through life just sitting on the thought that they will have a nice pension, its only in the last five years it hits them between the eyes how little there pension is going to be, they then start squirreling away like crazy.

With the youngest now having left home, it meant me and Bet could start enjoying more of our own life - do some traveling, enjoy some holidays. I had more or less given up on the buy-three-pay-for-the-fourth-free plan. I was haemorrhaging money all over the place. Rachael was going to university, which was draining. There was always some excuse to take the profit out of the sale. I had got to find another edge. We restarted the building company up again. In the meantime, we had put the house up for sale with the intention of buying something else to refurb. True to form, the shit hit the fan.

We had booked a fortnights holiday in Crete; the weather was idyllic. We were enjoying the second week of a very pleasant holiday, when Bet started complaining that she'd got a headache. We were walking along the beach and I gave her a right rollicking for not wearing a hat. Dipping my shirt in the water, I placed it over her head, but the headache didn't disappear. Getting back on the Saturday, her headache still hadn't cleared up. She had cracked her head on the television stand before we left on holiday, was it that? On Monday, she went into the doctors, her usual doctor wasn't there. The male doctor was a gynaecologist. Having examined her, he pointed out that she had got a migraine. Giving her a prescription for tablets, he told her to come back on the Wednesday if it still persisted. On the Wednesday, the headaches still persisted so she went down to the doctors again. In my ignorance, I just reminded her to tell the doctor about the bang on the head and that she had a family history of brain haemorrhages. Well, she did. He examined her again for all the usual signs for potential strokes, insisting again that she'd had a severe migraine attack. Getting back home, I queried this as she'd never suffered with migraine in her life. The doctor just doubled the dose of migraine tablets. At six o'clock that night, she'd had a stroke. I was on the phone like a shot dialling 999. At Good Hope Hospital, we were stuck in a corridor for over an hour doctors walked nonchalantly around without a care in the world. My wife had a fucking stroke, no one gives a shit and there are signs all over warning people not to abuse the staff. Eventually, a doctor comes over, takes some notes, does a few tests, and walks away, not saying a bleeding word to me. So I'm just getting very frustrated. Then another one, more tests, off they go. Again, fuck little Tommy. Eventually, three doctors come over to me. Well, I'm assuming they are doctors; one's Indian, the other is an Arab woman with the full Niqab and face covering, and the other is a Chinese guy. The Indian starts doing the talking. "Mr Lewin, we have carried out all tests. Your wife has not had a stroke." Well, that's thrown me. "No, she had a stroke; I saw her face collapse." "No Mr Lewin, I can assure you your wife has just had a sever migraine attack." Well, they are doctors; they must know best. I looked at Bet lying on the trolley. You ain't had a stroke you silly prat, it's bloody migraine. Looking up at me, and half out of it, she said her throat was dry and she needs a drink. The doctor points over to the tap and tells me to help myself. Well, I go over, get her a cup of water, and as I watch over her, didn't think for a minute she was bloody drowning herself. She had had a stroke. These silly prat doctors had wrongly diagnosed a migraine attack. After seeing her tablets that the first gynaecologist had prescribed for her.

Telling me to get home and get some sleep, I left her to do the same, expecting her to rest and recuperate. Returning the next morning, I'm directed to a side ward where I find her swinging her arms wildly at her throat which had got a pipe sticking out of it, and a doctor quietly and embarrassingly hovering around her. What the fucking hell is going on here? A nurse comes up proudly telling me she saved my wife's life in the early hours. Walking past her bed, she noticed my wife wasn't breathing. Screaming for the doctor, he said, "She's gone, dead." The nurse noticed my wife's finger moving. They've resuscitated her giving her an emergency tracheotomy in the process. I was finding this very difficult to take in. I didn't know whether to shout and bawl, not knowing what questions to ask. Saved her life? They had almost killed her through their sheer incompetence

Hospitals are like the courts, and the doctors are like the solicitors and judges: you ain't supposed to ask because you don't know. Shut up and do what we say. I just couldn't get my head around it. One minute we were around the pool talking about how we can start enjoying our life without the responsibility of the kids, the next she's lying in a hospital bed having suffered a stroke, which they are denying she has suffered. I decided that whatever I said or did would be fruitless, so I decided to keep calm, act calm, and pretend it was no big deal. Recuperating in the stroke ward afterwards, the doctors were adamant she hadn't had a stroke. "No, no, Mr Lewin. Your wife has not had a stroke." Why are they so adamant? For all their experience, they were looking at the wrong signs. Bet had had a brain haemorrhage; this had caused the stroke. They were looking for high blood pressure, the classic signs of a stroke. I decided to get the local papers on board, but that was a big mistake. The hospital took it as a sign to kick her out of physiotherapy. Bet wanted to sue the hospital. I spoke to my solicitor who had seen the newspaper article. Mr Lewin, by the time they tell their side of the story it will totally contradict yours. I felt they were right. Telling Bet, I felt she felt I was letting her down.

In many ways, I was quite blasé about Bet's stroke. I had never come across anyone I knew who had had a stroke, and I had quickly realised that a lot of people who had had a stroke were prone to suffer another one. One lady in the bed next to Bet in the stroke ward was in following her second stroke. She had given up and refused any treatment or help, just lying in bed, curled up like a child waiting to die. The doctors or nurses didn't give much of a shit knowing that the odds of recovery were not very bright. I persuaded Bet that her circumstances were very much different. It was very unlikely that she would suffer another stroke. Let's get her better and get on with our life. All she had to do was get better, start walking again and we would get out and about. The building had to go out the window, so we just carried on refurbishing houses carrying on with our plans. In the meantime, I had booked a med cruise to help Bet recuperate at sea getting her massages and therapy, then teaching her how to swim again. It was a bit of a slow process. on shore, enjoying a day out around the port and town. Quite a few passengers did the same, and I commented one day how the doctor of the ship was always around, always bumping into each other. On the last few days of the three-week cruise, whilst she was having her final massage treatment, the doctor came over to Bet and commented on how well she looked, how much better. Bet was quite pleased at this till he followed up. I thought your husband had brought you on here to die?? When she told me I said, fucking great. There was no such thought in my mind, but when I saw a photo of how ill she looked on the first day of our cruise, I could understand. I just never realised.

HOW NOT TO BUY A BOOZER

To my everlasting regret, I was still acting cavalier and blasé about Bet's stroke. Ok, she had had a mini stroke - a brain haemorrhage, no big deal, she'll get better. With that in mind, we decided to buy a country pub in Wales. Ideally, and foreseeing the potential problems with customers, it needed to have a few acres with potential for camping. To me, our income was going to be coming from the caravan site. Initially, Bet didn't want to know, till we looked at a nice little boozer in three acres just outside Tregaron. The setting was idyllic. The pub was never going to be busy, but we didn't want that. The idea was just to open up over the weekend and make a bit of pocket money to see us through the week when we could enjoy the land, keeping a few chickens ducks etc., in the event, the owner another developer wouldn't accept our offer. But by now, I'd got the bit between the teeth - there was no stopping me. We were too young to retire, too old to get into anything too heavy. We were travelling around looking at different pubs, which meant virtually every pub in every village. Sometimes my brain doesn't work right. Eventually, having looked at one pub, a young lad put us on to another, which was run by a London couple that no one liked.

We were on our way to look at a pub in Abergavenny when we passed the boozer. Calling in, I saw an old lady behind the bar, one customer stood the other side. When I asked her if the pub was for sale, she gave me her number and asked to ring that evening to speak to her daughter who was at work. We had pulled up in the car park at the back and I said, oh I'm sorry, I wanted something with some land. Taking me out the back, she pointed out five acres running down to the Wye river, plus it had a caravan site to the side. That was it. Ringing the landlady back on the night, a price was agreed, and we ended up buying the pub. It was one of the biggest mistakes of my life. The pub wasn't in Wales, it was in Hereford. I didn't think too much about it at the time. The pub was in a hamlet, not a village, so we could be out of any potential gossip. I had grown up hearing about Hereford and its people; all you get are funny fuckers, but then I've found and heard the same about the Welsh who have hated the English for centuries. But me and Bet adopted a policy that if we don't like something or somewhere, we get it up for sale quick sharpish and get out... even at a loss. With that in mind, we also brought another bungalow in Four Oaks as a fall back. I had asked our youngest if she wanted a crack at running it. Following our

Bet having a well-earned rest behind the bar, having cooked for 50

Behind the bar with guests, many who went on to become our friends

tried and tested policy, they went and booked into a guesthouse for a week prior to completion.

Chatting one night in the dining room, the landlady said I'm sorry to appear nosey, but did I just overhear you say you had brought the swan? Nodding at her she said, well you have done your homework haven't you?. With suitable confidence, Bet said, well my husband has. Well, I can tell you, I live here and they're a very nasty bunch around here, and then she began recalling how her two daughters worked for a lovely couple who bought the pub in the local village and were very friendly. Within six weeks, the woman was walking around with a face like a Rottweiler that had swallowed a mouthful of wasps, and within two months, they locked up, called my daughters in, paid them up and walked out. When they relayed the story back to me, I felt my bottle go. Within three weeks I knew I had made a big mistake. The pub was magnificent, with an adjoining barn restaurant measuring some fifty-foot by twenty-foot. That's where we were going to make our money, the restaurant and the land. I rang a local architect and told him my plans, and before doing any more, said he would sound the local Hereford council planning department out in an informal chat. Coming back a week later, he was pleased to tell me that Hereford council wished to encourage tourists to the area, as such he suggested that we apply for five vans raised on stilts to avoid flooding. Once planning was granted for five. Any further plans would fly through automatically. To draw the plans up he charged me a grand, money well spent.

By then I'd fully realised what a cock up I had made. The pub had been chock-a-block since we took over. The previous owners had put a boules pitch in, and the pub was made of the local boules players, and the winter darts team both teams were made up of the same group, mainly the local labourers of the farms. The boules were played in the summer, who then switched to darts in the winter. The boules brought in the local farmers and surrounding people during the summer months. They ruled the roost. One night the local boules team captain came in, had a meal, then casually dropped it out to me how they used to play in the village pub a couple of miles down. One night, walking in, he noticed the kids coke had gone up by ten pence. When he pulled the landlord, he explained that he'd got no choice, the costs were going up, he had to pass them on. With that, the team captain put his drinks down and walked out. When he walked out, the whole boules team followed him, inclusive of the darts team. That was my threat. I was on notice. The following week, one of the local inbreeds turned to my daughter and said, in that broad Herefordshire accent, you do realise if you can't speak tractors or cows, you're no good to us around here? After being told another night that she could live there for twenty years but would never be accepted, she said dad, sorry, you never brought us up to put up with this shit, I'm off. I can't say I blamed her.

I had never met such small minded petty insular people in my life; even the farmers were pig ignorant and grunted. The father of our two waitresses were nice girls, quite proficient. Their grandfather had had a farm in Much Marckle and knew Fred West. Oh, it was a shame for Fred. I'd had and seen enough. I rang one of the top agents in England and spoke to Nick. Nick was trying to get his head around it, recalling that he had viewed it a couple of years earlier. The vendors had polished their accounts up by putting their wages in as takings. I went over them again. When I told the agent the turnover, he was well impressed, but why are you selling Tom? How long have you been in? When I told him two months, I could feel him fall of his chair. Before laughing his head off, I said, what's so funny? He said I've never had anybody be so honest Tom, normally it's the wife broke a leg or had a heart attack. I said, look, I vowed before we bought the pub that at the first sign, we were off; life's too short to put up with these idiots. He was up three days later. On the day he arrived, it was high summer; the camp site was chocker, even better with all the cars and awnings out it looked even busier. Tom, this is a "bloody gold mine Tom"! I know, I know I told him. Three days later the pub died. Over the following days, I started putting the mix in to Dave, the local taxi driver with the big gob. By now, the whole village knew about the planning application for the camp site. I let Dave know that I would be closing the pub down, selling off the barn with planning permission for a large, detached barn conversion. He was trying his hardest not to choke. It got back to the locals like a bush fire and when the council held a meeting in the nearby village to discuss my planning application for the camp site, they were up in arms trying to destroy it. Thankfully, the planning wouldn't have it, and passed it despite all the objections. The architect was up for his money like a shot. A few days after Nick, left I clocked a Bentley pulling up on the drive. It was one of the directors for a pub chain company. Nick had sold them the pub on what he had seen. They weren't interested in the turnover or the contents, just put your bill in for fixtures and fittings and we'll pay it. Tony Alli had rung up asking us to book a coach in from the Heartlands social club. I said, sorry Tone, we've got completion two days before hand; they could have had all the booze for free. The pub chain didn't want it. There was nothing clever about my moves; I was just bloody lucky that everything had fell into place. If I'd left it another six months or a year, we would have been knackered. On our first day of opening, the public health turned up prepared to close the restaurant down. All the local had pushed it in our face how we would never be able to compete with the boat inn. Bet had already said, bugger this, I'm not wasting my time cooking fresh food. They're that pig ignorant; they don't appreciate it. One day, a mother and daughter turned up and ordered fish and chips, and pie and chips. Sending the order down to the kitchen, I stood behind the bar. The daughter spoke up and mentioned that she was passing by and that she worked at the Boat Inn. My bottle fell out. The Boat Inn that everyone had been throwing in my face. At the first opportunity, I shot down to the kitchen and told Bet she can't do frozen, that young bird works for the Boat Inn. No cobblers to them. Anyway, its already done, I carried the tray up to the bar handing the couple their food. Walking behind the bar, I stood waiting for the bombs to fall. Finishing off, I noticed they had cleared their plates. Was everything ok ladies? Yes, very nice thank you very much, its exactly how we do it at the Boat. Well blow me down with a frigging feather. That was the very last thing I expected. Told you, didn't I Says Bet? They're pig ignorant. Anyone can tell the difference between frozen food, especially fish...and fresh. The fact is the majority of people are blind to it.

It was with a massive relief that we had got rid of the pub and bought a nice four-bedroom house back in Sutton. The pub chain had either seen the same potential as I had or maybe something else. Nick did his best to find out but couldn't. Their normal plan was to buy a potential boozer, charge the ingoing tenants a fee to take on a lease, then screw them to the ground on rent and beer that they have to buy of them. At any rate, I passed it a few years later only to find it closed up and for sale for a great deal less than what we sold it for.

Settling back in Sutton, we had both decided that the ideal solution for us was to buy a motorhome. We found planes and plane journeys were becoming horrendous. You are treated like sardines, searched then searched again, then crammed into seats barely wide enough to sit in. A motorhome eliminated all those problems. Looking around the amount and variety of motorhomes was utterly bewildering, from little Bambi-type things right up to luxury coaches, but we eventually found the ideal motorhome in an Autotrail Cheyenne. Even better, it had got a garage. It was a six berth, so ideal for having the kids along for short breaks. It was also ideal for carrying a mobility scooter. Following her stroke, we had both felt that slowly Bet would get better and be able to walk again. It slowly grew on both of us that was not going to be the case. Initially, we had the idea of getting a two-seater moped for getting about, especially from out-of-town sites.

I had already been doing a bit of transport and removals before we bought the pub in Hereford. It sat in well with my building work. A transit van, the builder's staple, will carry a ton of sand, a few bags of cement or a few kitchen units which is ideal for property renovation and building work. But after a bit and not doing any building work, I found it was just standing for far too long on my drive. Then I had a Mazda moment: why not swap the transit for a Luton removal van. It's twice the size but uses the same amount of diesel. Ok, I'm never going to make a fortune from doing removals, but as something to run in with my other projects it was ideal and ran in nicely. Even better, it allowed me to fit the little jobs in to suit with my own times. I didn't want full-time contract work, just something to keep me occupied two - maybe three - times a week for the odd couple of hours. Now I found, after getting rid of the boozer, in Hereford the removal van came into its own. I couldn't afford - or take the risk of - working a full day for days at a time while Bet was stuck at home. The van was the ideal solution.

It was also one of the most enjoyable and lucrative jobs or projects I had ever undertaken. I didn't go mad at it, just advertising in the local papers in Sutton or Great Barr. This served two purposes: one, that people recognised that I lived in Sutton, as such they felt more comfortable. Sutton people were naturally very cautious and liked to know who they were dealing with; two, Sutton people were used to paying more. Disabled as she was, I took great delight in coming home after a couple of hours with my takings in my trouser pocket. I would sidle over to Bet. push my hip towards her and tap my pocket. She in turn would give me a little smile, dip her hands in my pocket, draw out a wad of money, count it, then tell me to put it in our pot. Most of our money came from property deals or rentals which were in Bets name, but the removals were in my name. I didn't earn a lot in comparison to other incomes or wages, but I had learned years ago that it ain't what you earn, it's how you handle it. It's surprising how stupid with money so many people are. We had seen so many examples over the years of husbands coming in with the weekly wage packet and the wives seeing fit to spend it willy nilly. We had seen them out paying top whack for a coffee and luxury snack, take that little excursion over the week, and its seventy quid gone.

The plasterer came round one day for his money. I'd love to get into this, Tom, he told me. I said look, you're in a far better position than me to do this; you're a skilled plasterer, and a good plaster finish prior to decorating is what sells the house. No, my wife wouldn't put up with it. Therein lay his answer. I had spoken to his wife a few months earlier asking to speak to him. It was early evening and he wasn't home yet. When I commented on the time, she said I don't care what time he works till as long as he brings my money in on a Friday. I couldn't believe my fucking ears. No wonder he always walked around with a face as long as Livery Street. After he'd left, Bet would give the little look and a nod as I said, fucking hell they make me laugh these comics. They all want what we have but they don't want to work for it. Bet had backed me in everything we had done, whether it be a corner shop to hotels to loading a skip and stripping a house - she had backed me. Further, we trusted each other 100 percent. If you can't trust your partner with money, then you've got fuck all. Nick one pound and all trust is gone. Over many years people would assume I was the boss, that I did the dictating, even our eldest kids assumed it. What they never realised was Bet was actually the boss. Without her, I was fuck all. She could have run out at any time with a great deal of money, yet someone like her sister Pauline would accuse me of being mean because I wouldn't buy a £500 scooter just because it was on sale. They struggled on their incomes and pension, scraping for pennies.

Terry the roofer was exactly the same. Terry was a lovely guy but very vain; he just loved himself. Ex-army, he loved the young birds as much as he loved himself. He kept fit by running to keep himself looking young. He'd have facelifts and little tucks every now and again. I was in the SAS, Tom. Oh yea. I'm just off for a week in my villa, Tom. The lads will do your roof. When I mentioned it to the lads, they said, villa? Villa? He tells everyone that; it's a fucking timeshare. Yes, I'd have liked to have got into this Tom, but I gave too much to my ex-wives. I lost count of how many wives or women Terry had gone through. One was a Philippine half his age. Well, I was making that much, Tom. I gave her the house. She was a nice girl, yea of course, and she'd got a nice little bambino. The last I saw of Terry was when he asked me to move him out of the last house he lived in owned by some woman he had met. He had tried to get his foot under the table but her adult son was having none of it. After a few months, she had kicked him out. I had to move him into a little rented place out of town.

Bill the carpet fitter was even worse. Where have I gone wrong, Tom? A look of total desperation on his face. I would call Bill in for the final finish of fitting the carpets. He was cracking on now well into his sixty's and suffering with his knees. He had had a thriving carpet fitting business with a little shop in Sutton. He was loud and blustery. Then he met and fell in love with a young Philippine girl half his age. She loved him. Getting married, he bought her a very nice little house in a very select part of Sutton. Soon she had a young child. One day, Bill walked in to notice yet again his young wife wasn't looking too happy. She told me she was going to the nursery, Tom, and mixing with all the young girls and it was making her feel old before her time. She was losing her youth. I had to be fair, Tom. I mean, saying in that loud voice, she was only twenty-five. Anyway, she wanted a break for a bit, so I got out and got myself a little bedsit in Aldridge. I pay her money every week and the mortgage. I couldn't get my fucking wind; how old Bill was I don't know. He's sixty-odd, got bad knees, living in a bedsit, whilst his little Philippine wife is living in a lovely drum without a care in the world, and I bet she don't know about the benefits system either. I wonder how some of these people have ever made a fucking living.

Generally speaking, I loved my newfound little job of doing the removals. It also enabled me to meet some really interesting people. Working only a couple of days a week, Bet would build the pot up and that alone would pay for our little jaunts. Our plan was for little, short breaks in or around England, then longer two or three months touring abroad. In between times we would maybe have a cruise. One year, Nile cruise, another a Mediterranean cruise. To all intents and purposes, we were enjoying a very nice quality of life, the only drawback being Bet's reliance on the scooter. By now she had three; one would sit in the boot of the car for little local jaunts around the shops, another bigger shop rider that would sit in the

Delivery of our new motorhome and a bunch of flowers for Bet.
Now for some fun, touring Europe and the world.

garage of the motorhome, then a really big one that sat in the garage. The other thing I noticed, but I could never mention to her, is the people who automatically steer clear of you when you're in a wheelchair. I realised I wasn't alone in seeing this. I noticed other people being treated the same. If you're disabled, people assume you ain't got a brain either. I'm sure Bet must have been aware of this but in my ignorance. I would just go blithely along.

Every now and again, we would pop out down to the old end of Nechells and bump into one or two old faces, but as times change, people change. Bumping into Don and Chrissie Fewtrell one night down Aston, we decided to pop up to Tressines nightclub, which used to be Don's old club, Pollyanna's. Don was on a short trip back from Spain where he had an apartment and lived with big tits Nina. When he sold Pollyanna's, he got on the plane to Spain to make a new life. Unfortunately, no one knew him, and he knew no one over there. Slowly his money ran out. Big tits had persuaded him to put the rest of his dough into a little restaurant in Denia. The problem was Nina had no experience of the restaurant business; she was a cleaner. Eventually, Don came back to England, throwing himself on to the council as homeless, who gave him a two-bedroom flat on the thirteenth floor of a tower block in Sparkbrook. He decided to try and raise a few extra quid by selling his story to the Sunday mercury which really pissed Eddie off, as it was seen as a right come down. He would then fly back every three months to claim his pension, sending it back to big tits, who was trying to prop up the business. Don sadly was never the brains of Britain. He would show me photos of his food display in the restaurant but they had no customers. In Denia he was just another bald bloke with a wig. It was Eddie who had the brains. It was Eddie who had lifted his brothers up and gave them all a great opportunity. Sadly, Don only resented that and used to make up for it by helping himself to some of the takings. Typically, of the time and the people, Don was grabbing the extra few quid, while the girls behind the bar were grabbing even more. One night, Eddie had clocked that all the girls were wearing knee high boots. Why are all you lot wearing bloody boots for in this heat? In exasperation, one bird shouted out, because it's like a bloody river in here with all the booze swilling around [giving Eddie the look to blame him]and looking down, Eddie accepted the logical explanation. What none of them clocked onto was the birds were right bang at it. Ripping off the customers and the club, to the tune of hundreds of pounds a night each. It seems big tits Nina had been manoeuvring things. Don had been prat enough to put the apartment into Nina's name, and whilst he was in England, she started knocking it off with some Spanish bloke. It worked out nicely for her that Don had got himself a flat in Sparkbrook. Ringing me up one night he asked me to pick him up to go to a boxing match that Pat Cowdell, the boxer and promoter, had put on. His brother Chris had latched onto Cowdell and was trying to get himself into the boxing game. Just ring the bell to the concierge and he will let you in. Well, ringing the bell, no one answered. Round I go to the other side of the block, again ringing the concierge bell. Still no answer. Eventually, this black guy comes walking out, looks back at me standing there like a complete dickhead, and when I tell him I'm trying to reach the concierge, he says, concierge? Concierge? With that he walks across, gives the door a good boot, which then bounces open, and says, that's the concierge, mate. With that, I walk in and get into the lift making for the top floor. The mixed smell of piss and curry were making me feel faint. I can't believe it: Fewtrell had been taken to court a couple of times for racism, now here he was having to say good morning, good evening, whilst passing back and forth through all the stink of spew piss and curry wrought iron gates protecting his flat. What a fucking come down.

I was renovating a nice big house on the Slade road when Don pops down and knocks on the door with Chris, Chris looking a bit sheepish. It seems Chris needed twenty-grand to restock his garage. Now I know Chris had been selling cars for a few years from his pitch on Stratford Road, so why would he need twenty-grand? It seems one of his brothers had fucked him for it. Why don't you ask Eddie, your brother? No, we wouldn't ask him, he won't give us fuck all. Obviously, the fall-out had been big. Trying to be polite, I asked who had the freehold to the pitch? Maybe there could be a deal here. Oh, it's not freehold, but I've got the lease. The lease?—I must have a really big stamp on my head saying fucking stupid, because the next thing, he's asking for another twenty-grand on top...forty-grand in all. I couldn't believe the audacity. Here were people I thought were friends, and they are standing in front of me trying to stitch me for forty-grand. In that one little incident, it became utterly clear to me why Don was living in a top floor council flat: they were both skint, and their brother Eddie had sacked them. The arrogance was staggering. Politely, I had to refuse their generous offer of a partnership. Almost all the Fewtrell's had been given a massive lift by their brother Eddie, who had had the brains and ability all those years ago to see an opportunity in the night club game. One by one, he had lifted them all up to positions of respect and prestige around the town, and one by one, they had tried to gyp him or damage their reputations with their arrogance and treatment of others.

Big tits Nina rang up demanding to know why I had got keys to Don's flat and that there were used condoms around the place. The only problem was she demanded to know from Bet. I was fucking lost for words. I'd never stopped at Fewtrell's flat; why would he throw my name up? Big tits had gone through Don's diary, saw my name, found the condoms, and for some reason Don threw my name up, which put another doubt put into Bet's brain. It took a few months for the clouds to clear up. Big tits wanted Don out; the apartment was in her name and she'd persuaded him that a clever move would be getting a top floor flat in a shit hole part of Sparkbrook. Now she wanted him out of her life so she could move her new Spanish boyfriend in. Shrewd move, big tits. I don't think Don ever caught on.

One day, Colin Lawler's wife, Annie, rang up. We had just booked a fortnight in Fuerteventura in the Canaries, Annie said. Colin said, can we come with you? I said to Bet, he wouldn't take the piss by doing drugs in front of us? Yea ok. The first shocker came as we got through security. Bloody hell, that was a stroke of luck. What do you mean? Didn't you see? See what? Colin had put his wacky backy tin in his sock. The customs must look out for signs, so pulled him over and did a body rub down. They missed the tin by half an inch. Fucking great; thanks Col. The fortnight was a fucking nightmare, with Annie and Collin both drugged up to the eyeballs every night. I was arguing with my missis because knowing he was dying, I tried to make the fortnight enjoyable for him. Never again, I vowed. Never again. We never know what people are like behind closed doors.

In comparison, life in Sutton was a complete contrast. People said good morning, and if they had hang-ups, they hid it well. People were well balanced, happy to focus and concentrate on just being normal, doing their jobs, enjoying their leisure times and living a normal life. Another glaring factor that never failed to impress me was the attitude to me as a lowly van driver/removal guy. I would get someone ring me up. Good afternoon, how much to take a sofa from Roman Road to Wolverhampton? Having agreed the price, I would turn up, the house a mansion. The guy came out, no airs and graces, helping me throw the stuff on the van, asking if he could come with me. We set off over to Wolverhampton on the way, chatting without any care in the world, yet he owned a chain of cinemas. I used to find this regularly. Most people with money - even more so, the self-employed, had nothing to prove. Obviously, none of them knew my financial situation. Many just assumed I only had my van and that was it. But it didn't matter; to many, they had been or knew what it was like to be on the bottom rung and had had modest starts. Contrast that with people in less well of areas, rented or council, or first-time houses. And you will often get a different attitude. Some people would talk to you with little noses up in the air, expecting you do all the work while looking down at you. Sometimes it was just so funny to see the faces.

Answering the phone one day, I heard a lady asking me to pick up two sofas from Great Barr and take them to Handsworth. I didn't give it much of a thought. If someone had said Handsworth, my antenna would have fired up, but a woman asking to move from Great Barr to Handsworth threw me off. Normally, I just don't deal - or like dealing - in shithole areas. When I first started the removals, I took jobs in a few of these areas, and inevitably, it always led to arguments or pricks trying to rip you off. Years earlier, one of the reasons I had packed up the taxying was because of the increasing threats and hassle I was getting. Almost every taxi driver carries a tool in his car to protect myself. I could never take that risk no matter what the facts old bill will prod me. Now, in the removals, I always had to try and keep one step ahead.

Turning up on the date and time, I was met by a young girl in her mid-twenties. The sofas were outside the flat, and she helped me get them on the van. I never gave it a thought, assuming she would be doing the same at the other end. Getting to Handsworth she directed me to a courtyard surrounded by maisonettes. Where she was met by a black guy. About six feet tall. My hackles were up, but I had no choice but to carry on. Some smart arsed solicitor once advised me in that patronising way, that I should collect my money first before doing the job, before conceding it was unworkable. Both sofas had to go up two flights of stairs, which should have been more money. Putting the sofas in the flat we walked out, and the black guy bustled his way down the stairs heading for the courtyard. Hi, give me my fucking money? He was ignoring me, the girl, seeing I was serious quietly told him to give me my money, but he's holding out, at the other end of the courtyard was a couple of blacks looking over with interest. I didn't like this at all. I'd got a toolbox in my cab including a hammer. I thought about it and quickly dismissed it, that could only escalate the situation, me with a hammer? No, I was in a predominantly black area. Then I realised I had a jar in the van. I got the jar out, took the lid of then said give me my fucking money or else. Letting his little brain dwell on what was or could be in the jar. He handed over my money and I let him know what a cxxxt I thought he was for giving me this unnecessary hassle. With that I drove off, patting my pocket as I sidled up to Bet, I never gave it a thought to tell her.

Two hours later I get a phone call from some copper at Queen's Road, Nick. Mr Lewin? Who's this? Then what for? It's about an incident earlier. What incident? He doesn't want to say. Well why have I got to turn up? He says, well, you can either turn up and we can settle the matter, or we will send someone to arrest you. Fuck me here we go again, he obviously knows who I am, to use my name. When I get to Queens Road Nick, this Asian cop tells me the woman has complained that she was terrified that I had threatened her with an inflammable liquid. I said are you fucking joking? The copper was sympathetic. I either made a written apology to the bird, with the matter being settled as a local issue, or I would be charged with a different offence. However, he did concede how it must have looked to me the black guy was quite well built. I was fucking fuming, he even had the humanity to look guilty himself, I mulled the options over in my mind. The stupidity of these coppers never failed to annoy me. I get fucking threatened, I get some stupid pricks try to turn me over, yet here again, they go screaming to the coppers for retribution. The coppers, not giving a fuck either way. Take the easy route. I'm yet again the patsy. I know how any minor incidents can be blown out of all proportion by the time it gets into court, the prosecution have worked on it. The witnesses, give their weeping versions, I would be fucked,

Over the last forty or fifty years the government and police have been bringing new laws onto the statute books. Over a squillion new laws cover every eventuality of the one misdemeanour, just in case. Eat a mars bar in your car and there are cameras all over you. Coppers with excited eyeballs springing out on stalks for an extra nicking. Informers are being urged to ring up at any opportunity. On your neighbour. On the guy down the road who has had a drink before getting in his car. Initially it must have been great for the cops. Now it's a major fucking nuisance for them, they've got coppers doing that much paperwork they ain't got time to do their job. And you can't nick a grass for grassing, can you? Because you've been encouraging it? Now it's gone in reverse, they have made a rod for their own backs and are running around like headless chickens.

I made a reluctant written apology; I couldn't afford to be locked up leaving Bet alone. I got home deciding to wipe the matter from my mind and telling Bet there was nothing to it, a misunderstanding.

A 200-year-old cottage came up for auction and I thought it had great potential. I don't know if I persuaded Bet to think the same or she just went along with it. At any rate, I threw an offer in before the auction and the auctioneers couldn't bite my hands of quick enough. It was weeks before the recession of 2007. Where were my bleeding brains? But I wasn't too bothered. I called the architect in to draw up the plans for a very nice large four-bedroom detached cottage. The agent pointed out the ceiling would be no more than 250 grand finished. On the finished size of it, I disagreed. Having instructed the architect Nathan, me and Bet got into the motorhome and set of abroad, driving steadily around France, down into Spain then across on the ferry to Morocco. We had been to Morocco a few times over the years, and this time I wanted to tour and see the underbelly of the whole of Morocco, from Chefchaouen in the north under the riff mountains, right down to the Sahara in the south, through the Atlas Mountains, then doing a leg west to the Atlantic and Agadir before heading back home. We spent three months travelling - a great experience - visiting places like the blue lagoon, or the ghost town, so called because from a thriving mining community employing 10,000 people it had closed, leaving just one Berber family to eke a living out of the ground. To get to it we had to travel over ten miles of dirt track and rickety bridges. My mistake was saying to Bet, the hills have eyes. That was it, without realising it I had put the wind right up her. Reaching the mining village all we could see were little eyes shining out from behind blank open windows. Reaching the village, we were met by the now extended Berber family living in mud huts, no toilets, no electrics, water from a well, it was like we had stepped back over 2000 years. Jesus could have walked out the stable door. I wanted to stop the night for the experience but Bet was having none of it. They could kill us in our sleep and no one would know oh well. After two months in morocco we headed of back home. calling into Benidorm Spain to visit my sister Doris.

A tent village in Morocco, one of many such communities.

YET ANOTHER FIT UP.

Getting back we were sickened to find that Birmingham city council had blocked the planning application. Silly prat Nathan had put the garage on to the side of the house fronting onto the private drive. The neighbours in the small cul de sac rose up and complained. By the time we had resubmitted the plans, we had lost twelve months and the recession had got even worse. In all, it took us three years to get the building finished, not helped by Bet's brother-in-law Clive, who saw it as an opportunity to try and grab a few quid. First, he and Pauline recommended their son-in-law to do the brickwork. Bringing him around, he gave me a price which I accepted. I then gave him the job of building a very nice, detached garage to the land on the side of the cottage. The price was a bit stiff, but being as it was nice facing bricks and he had given me a good price for the rebuild, I accepted it.

When he had finished, I asked him when he was able to start on the main project. Oh, but I haven't given you a price yet. But he had, I'd given him the sizes for him to work it out, having upped the price on the garage it gave him the impetus to try it on even further. Working out his price it was now treble, what he had originally given me. Obviously, he and his father-in-law Clive wanted a bit more of the cake. If it wasn't so serious, I would have to laugh. Because I had never questioned his price for the garage, he must have seen the stamp on my bonce. Why the fucking hell are there so many stupid people about in the main? People who have never taken a risk, never stuck their neck out, never worked for themselves. Clive was struggling to survive on his pension.

Bet's sister Pauline was quite a nice woman, a bit of a snob who was nicknamed miss prim and proper, but Clive was another matter. Having served a couple of years in the army, he had then got himself a job as a door knocker for an insurance company. Eventually rising to manager. Being the spoilt child, he was he convinced himself he was of superior intelligence. While in Spain they had rung us up, asking if they could spend their anniversary with us. Bet, bless her soul, was dead chuffed, but the simple truth was they just wanted a free holiday. Having assured Bet that Clive would not display his disgusting personal habits, we agreed. Bet, dead excited, got the campsite restaurant to put on a nice anniversary meal for them. The owner went to town on balloons and tinsel the lot. It cost us a right few quid. Now, just a few weeks later, they were trying to rip us of. I wouldn't mind, but the guy was thirty and hadn't got a pot to piss in. They were living hand to mouth in a rented house. The guy doing the roof to the garage offered to do all the work, so I gave him the job. I couldn't believe how stupid Clive could be; it wasn't just the one job, it was other future jobs they had lost, I could have helped them with a house, all for stupid greed. We came across it regularly. Bet was gutted. This was happening all the more nowadays, the old saying goes, don't employ family and friends, I'm a slow learner. Unfortunately.

Eventually we put it up for sale at 330k, but still struggled to sell it, then we realised why…at the back of it was a right shithole estate. No wonder. Then, of all things, the bloody boiler packed up. Just as we had a buyer lined up. I rang a couple of plumbers up, as it was a brand-new boiler. But each one couldn't figure it out; then I decided to go to the manufactures, Biasi.

Biasi had their own contractor who looked after all their boilers, and after explaining my predicament, the manager rang his service guy, explained briefly, then put me on to him. After hearing my explanation, the guy very kindly offered to have a look at it then give me a price to fix it, standard practice. On the due date and time, I turned up at the cottage which was twenty miles south on the other side of the city. It was now becoming a chore that I would be glad to get away from. Within a few minutes of arriving at the cottage, I got a phone call from. "Bill, hello." "Is that Tom? Bill here. I'm very sorry, my son made an appointment with you but he's so busy he's asked me to help him out." Turning up, he came into the cottage, admiring how nice it was. He spent thirty minutes admiring the motorhome that was on the side of the cottage and enquiring about my recent journey, telling me that is what he wished to do, as he was now retired having passed the contract with Biasi on to his son. Nothing out of the ordinary - quite normal - then he got to look at the boiler. Going to his van, he explained he had every part necessary in it and could rebuild the whole boiler from scratch. I was impressed, especially considering he was retired and helping his son out.

Coming back in he first replaced the clock. Then as a safety measure he decided to replace the fan, and after a bit more faffing about, he got the boiler working a treat again. Then he hit me with the bill - sixty quid call out charge. A hundred and sixty quid for a new fan, thirty quid for a new clock: in all, £360 quid...for a new boiler!! this couldn't be right. But this was Biasi; surely they wouldn't try to rip me off. I had a hundred quid on me so decided to fob him of by promising to send him a cheque. I could see the panic on his face. Getting home, I tested the fan, and it was working perfectly. I rang Biasi, explained I had just tested the boiler. No sir, a fan is a fan is a fan; if it's working, then there is nothing wrong with it. When I complained, he went quiet and promised to get back to me. He never did, so I assumed that was the end of it. A week later I got a phone call from Bill, so I told him to fuck off and don't ring again. To clarify it, I rang his son, telling him I was on to his scam.

Whether Bill was working for Biasi or not, I never knew; his son certainly was. I suspect this was a regular little scam that they worked and got away with on a regular basis, through Biasi - when the work came through - the son or the father would sus out if it was under contract or like mine, not as the case may be, then pass it on. No customer would have any suspicions aroused because it was assumed it was coming through a reputable company. They would gulp then pay the bill. I was more on the ball because I know from experience that a great many plumbers are cowboys. Many property developers and landlords hate plumbers for that reason. I had spent over 45 grand rebuilding the cottage, but no one likes being ripped off. This was a very lucrative family business for the father, son and grandson. The plumber was in that cottage for no more than thirty-five minutes: he spent less than fifteen minutes diagnosing the fault and replacing a twenty-pound clock. If we said £50£65, that would be top whack. So, he was making 300 quid for fifteen minutes work. Very nice.

Bet worryingly had started having fainting spells while celebrating the new year in Weymouth. She had got up early in the morning, fainted, and crashed out on the floor - bang, white as a sheet, stone cold. I thought she was dead and it frightened the crap out of me. Eventually, she came round but it still frightened me I drove back home like I'd got the wings of hell under my wheels. It took quite a few months and a few more fainting spells before the doctors diagnosed: she had got very low blood pressure. In the May, the practice doctor gave her a course of treatment. I decided that we should drive down into France and spend the summer there relaxing to recuperate. Bloody wrong again. Am I that ignorant that I keep misreading the signs? She had kept complaining about how uncomfortable she was, having pains in her stomach and legs. I'm thinking, fuck me, what are you moaning about? That night I could hear her moaning and groaning in agony. That was it. I couldn't sleep myself all night, so the next morning we packed everything up and drove hell for leather back to Calais, running onto the ferry and back to Birmingham. After one futile meeting, a strongly worded complaint from me, the head doctor called us in. Looking at Bet, he immediately gave me a note and told me to get up to good hope hospital ASAP. I did.

What the first doctor did or gave her, I don't know but she'd had a build-up of fluid in her stomach. This had effectively drowned her organs and caused her to have a mild heart attack. *Well,* I thought, *a mild heart attack.* It later turned out to be a *severe* heart attack.

The plumber rang me up a couple of times trying to get his money, and after telling him to fuck off, he stopped calling. On the early evening of the 22nd of December, Bet had gone to bed for her early evening nap, a regular occurrence now as she was recuperating from her heart attack. To avoid any stress, we had booked a four-day Christmas break in Brean, all food and entertainment laid on, ready to set off the next day. Then the doorbell went. We were living in the bungalow whilst waiting to move into a large four-bedroom house that Bet had just brought in Streetly, ready to renovate. We used the bungalow as a fall back and storage for furniture. Looking at the security camera, I couldn't make out who it was. Maybe my neighbour, Steve. Going to the door, I was confronted by Bill the plumber, who demanded his £360. Now Bill is about six feet, three inches and I'm five feet, nine inches. Whilst I can look after myself, I don't look threatening. Many bigger people make that initial mistake and Bill was making it now. Subtly, he eased himself into the door and in my hallway, keeping one foot in the door. I couldn't believe his fucking audacity. Knowing Bet's condition, I couldn't risk putting one on his chin, so reaching behind me, I grabbed Bet's walking stick. Prodding him in the stomach, I told him quite forcefully to get out my fucking house. As he stepped back, I realised he was badly underestimating me; he thought my bottle was going. Well, it was, but not for him. Pushing him out onto the path, I decided to walk out with him and settle the matter. "Look, there was fuck all wrong with that fan, you ain't getting your money, so fuck off." "Well ok, give me my fan back." "If you want your fan, go back to the house and get it;

you put it in, you fucking get it out." At that, I felt something -or someone - behind me. He had got someone else with him, but he must have been hiding in my side entry. I slowly made my way inside stepping backwards. Bet, hearing the ruckus, came out of the bedroom and to told me to call the police. Bill had put his foot again into the door jam, and I was trying to keep calm, frightened of upsetting Bet. Looking at Bet, Bill said, "Who's going to look after you, Mrs Lewin?" How much did this guy know to say that? At any rate, I picked up Bet's walking stick again and jabbed it up into his neck, put my quite-serious face on, and said, "Get out my fucking house." At that, he stepped back, shouted, "Get back son, he's got a knife!" and the second guy came from around the entry and started walking across my lawn, looking at my car. He then looked at me, shouting "nice car Tom," and the threat was implicit. Bet again urged me to call the cops but I didn't see the need. As they set off walking up the road, I watched them before closing the door. Bet advised me to look out again, saying they were going to come back and put a brick through the car. With that, I re-opened the door and watched them all the way up the road round the corner, then across into the opposite road, then straight to the top, did a left, before eventually reappearing in two vans and driving off. It was a distance of some quarter of a mile from my front door: a quarter of a mile and three roads away. Clearly, they had come to put the frighteners on me - maybe even lay on me. They had come unstuck.

Call it arrogance, maybe over confidence. All my married life I had underestimated Bet. She was just so quiet and unassuming; I always thought my judgement was best. It was only afterward, when I had come unstuck, I'd thought *oh fuck*. This was one of them. There was no way they were going to come back and wreck my car - or even try that trick again.

Over the years, in the building game, I get threatened on a fairly regular basis. Plumbers are the biggest cowboys of all;

you just can't see what they have done. But I've had others - electricians, bricky's - first they give you a price, then their little brains start working overtime. "Ay this is a nice house Tom; how much did you pay for this?" You learn not to tell them; in effect, it makes them even worse. "How many houses have you got Tom?" I'm skint. By telling people you're skint, it has the opposite effect. Then they try upping the price. Try as I might I've got it on a regular basis. If you talk to any of the developers, landlords, or property dealers, they will all tell you the same. You can only build up a small and reliable workforce as you can and be on the ball for the pricks. Many tradesmen accept their prices and are happy enough with that, but there are a growing few who having got the job, started, then allow their little brains to start working overtime. By the end of the day, they become convinced they are entitled to more money off you. After all, you are making big profits.

The next day, on the late afternoon, we set of for Brean. The Christmas was uneventful and something we decided not to do again. We got back late afternoon on the 27th of December, and after a relaxing evening we went to bed. At three o' clock we were woken by loud banging on the door, torch lights shining through the back-bedroom window. They had obviously climbed through my neighbours back garden. Bet woke saying it's the plumbers. I got out of bed hesitant; I couldn't image the plumbers coming in that heavy, it was too obvious. Opening the door with some hesitancy, I was met with a fucking army of coppers, about eight of them in all in three cars. That's when I really lost my temper, my wifes in bed recuperating from a stroke, a heart attack? "What the fucking hell are you doing at this time of the morning?" "Stop your swearing." "Don't tell me to stop my swearing in my own fucking house." They've barged in, no preamble. Bet was slowly making her way into the room and on to her recliner chair. These fucking idiots must have decided, having a quiet night in Sutton, to have a bit of excitement and bring in a couple of female cops with them to show how brave and gung-ho they are. In my hallway up high, fixed firmly to the walls, I had got some WW2, bayonets and other army knives; they had been there for years. The plumbers, obviously realising the shit they had put themselves in - especially with Bet telling me to call the cops - had decided to get in first, calling into Sutton police station and complaining I had threatened them with a bayonet. This was something I had never imagined in my wildest dreams. Trying to explain to the cops the facts, I went to point out the walking stick leaning against the hall cupboard. That was enough for the cops who did no more than arrest me. Arms behind my back and led me out, telling Bet don't expect him back. The problem is, Sutton is generally a very quiet middle class area. These idiots generally speaking must go through from midnight to 8 a.m. bored out of their tits. When the plumber had called in, they've clicked up my name, and without doing any research, sucked it in. Tommy Lewin, the violent fucking lunatic. Let's go boys; we've got a good night here, bring a couple of the girls along to show them how it's done what clever little noddies we are, At the nick, they have put me in a waiting room while they get all their evidence together. Because of my age, they sent a nurse in to ask me what tablets I'm on, expressing a look of utter disgust at my treatment. Of course, only I was registered at the house, Bet at another one of our houses - her own house. The cops - thick as they are - must have thought they had got a great exciting night in front of them, impressing the couple of female cops.

After an hour, these two bozos bring me into a small interview office and switch the tape recorders on. Thankfully, as I thought at the time, everything was being recorded. The duty solicitor had come in to see me, telling me that the obvious conclusion that the cops had come to was that I had obviously tried to avoid paying the plumbers in the first place as I couldn't afford it. Knowing the facts, I found this puzzling. Why the fuck would he assume that? Once the interview started, the two bozos started outlining the case. This plumber had called into the police having passed them after leaving my house. This was some 7 p.m.? Why didn't they come that night? Why didn't they come the next day? I didn't leave till 4 p.m. When I burst out laughing at their allegations, the one said, "Why are you laughing? This is a very serious allegation of assault with a deadly weapon."

"Yes, of fucking course it is. So is being threatened on my doorstep, in my own hallway, in my own house. The plumber had said he saw me lean behind for the knife and held it to his throat, and stabbed him, drawing blood? But the knives were at the very top of the wall by the ceiling, almost eight feet high." Slowly - very slowly - I could see the doubt start filtering through their brains. More so the female than the male; he didn't want to be wrong, did he? "Go and interview my wife while I am here with you to back my story up." They said they would; they never did. "Go and get the fan that I've still got to check it's still working." They said they would; they never did. "And while you're there, go and check the distance to where they parked up hiding before coming to my house." They said they would; they never did.

After the interview, they let me go promising to give me a lift back home. I don't see why I should pay for a taxi. They took their time, but eventually the one brain-dead chewing on his gum like a cow chewing cud dropped me home where I found Bet sitting up waiting for me. I thought that was the end of the matter.

SADLY, I NEVER ALLOWED FOR THE CORRUPT AND STUPID MENTALITY OF THE COPS.

Perverting the course of justice is a very serious offence, quite rightly. Telling the cops your son was with you on the night he killed someone is perverting the course of justice. Telling lies on oath to protect someone is perverting the course of justice. But what about the police? The judges? the prosecution? How many times do they pervert the course of justice? How many times, after a final, successful appeal has it been discovered that the prosecution and the police hid evidence that could have cleared the accused? Great after you've done a twenty stretch.

If the prosecution handpicked the single judge Jarret instead of the usual, two magistrates and a judge to give a balanced judgement and chose to deliberately try the case in a smaller, courtroom at the rear of the courthouse, away from the public and the press. Could that be seen as perverting the course of justice? If the police, the judge and the prosecution knew all along I had a criminal record [spent]whilst keeping my defence in total ignorance and thinking I had no criminal record?-- is that not perverting the course of justice? If the prosecution and, or the judge were fully aware of the letter from our doctor specifically refusing to allow my wife to appear in court but hid or ignored it, would that be considered perverting the course of justice? I went into that courtroom assuming I was going into a level playing field. So did my solicitor, inept as he was. Sadly, we were both wrong.

One way or another, I had grown up knowing most police were corrupt. Every time I had been fitted up in the past I had tried and struggled to justify the police actions. The stolen car when I was nineteen? Maybe it was stolen, just not by me. But it was the single thought that stopped me getting bitter, but as events unfolded in these circumstances the collective, institutional corruption absolutely staggered me. What if I had been convinced the police were the plumbers? What if I had grabbed one of those knives to defend myself, quite justifiably? It was three in the morning and my wife was recuperating from a severe heart attack. I put this to the cop, chewing his gum like a cow chews on the cud, eyes dead like the fucking shark jaws. He said, "We would have just tasered you." Luvverly, and if they'd have had guns maybe shot me? Fucking great; all through two corrupt plumbers and a bunch of stupid cops.

In the light of the next day Bet, ill as she was, was really angry, not only was it very frightening, but she was also recovering from a stroke and a severe heart attack, we had both thought it was the plumbers. What if I had picked a knife up, or any other weapon, to defend myself? Cops have shot people before. She was determined to make a written complaint, and I could understand that. She dictated the letter to Chris Simms, the chief constable of Birmingham, and I typed it. A week later, a uniformed cop came to the door.

"What the fuck have I done now?"

"Nothing, Mr Lewin. I am Dave Sidwell, inspector at Sutton Coldfield police. I have given my lads a bollicking and I've come to apologise."

Oh well, that's a turn up for the book. He even conceded some of his own family think the police are corrupt. A week later, I got a summons to appear in court the charge of assault with a weapon had been dropped. Where Bill had said I cut his throat and drew blood, it now appeared I hadn't, there were no marks, no blood, the charge was to be replaced with a charge of threatening words and behaviour. This was a real coverall charge that could mean anything; it was laughable. So if I told the plumbers to fuck off and farted, that could be construed as threatening words and behaviour? I didn't want to use our own solicitor mainly because they had acted for us for years and had a fair idea of our financial position. Worse, they would be thrown my criminal record up which would sour things for us. If you have a criminal record, you're fucked. I decided to pick out another local solicitor in the town - another big mistake. Hindsight is a wonderful thing.

I was interviewed by a senior partner who immediately filled me with confidence. I could see he was on the ball, assured and able to assimilate the facts. Shockingly, to me, he even pointed out that I had no criminal record. What?—what's going on here then? Why would he say that? Of course I've got a criminal record. Had I better tell him? no, don't do that, I might at least get a fair hearing. Some fucking hope, the solicitor was baffled I can't understand why you've been charged with this. Now we're getting there.

A week later, this clerk from the solicitors called around to interview my wife and take some notes. He was faffing about, nervously interviewing Bet, looking at the area, trying to get a feel for things. To me, he was obviously inexperienced and nervous. Like the cops, he just didn't seem too bothered about the significance of two plumbers turning up and parking three roads and a quarter of a mile away. I was starting to feel a little bit uneasy; all the idiot could see was a very rundown: bungalow, furniture stacked up, wallpaper coming of the walls, and windows in dire need of replacing. It was so familiar to us we never gave it a thought. Penny, one of the office girls, was so concerned she took the trouble of taking the tape-recording home and writing it all down word for word. Penny, bless her, could see something stunk about this. A couple of weeks later I was summoned to appear in court. The solicitors had written to our doctor who wrote a letter specifically refusing my wife permission to appear in court for me. My wife's statement would be accepted in court as a valid statement. Another load of absolute crap. Turning up at Victoria law courts, I couldn't believe what I was looking at: low-life's walking around, wild-eyed and stinking of drugs. The main court rooms are set around the massive hall, reception, waiting area, all open to the general public and press. Normally, you are presented before two magistrates and a judge who directs on any point of law. I had appeared before that exact scenario the week before where I had voiced my concern. The prosecution was not happy about this. Meeting this clerk from the solicitor's office, I discover he's not a clerk at all - he's my solicitor, a fucking junior solicitor. This is making me feel a bit uneasy. Disturbingly, he then directs us to the very rear of the courthouse building

It might dawn slowly how I'm going to get a fair trial! First, I'm arrested, then get a verbal apology then charged, then told I've got no criminal record, right? But then everyone knows, except my solicitor, that I've got a record - the prosecution, the judge, the police. Dave comes to the court to observe and sends a report back to the chief constable and whalla, justice is served.

There is something not quite right about this, but I can't put my finger on it. First there is no one about at all, no public, no press. At the back of my mind, I'm trying to recall the circumstances of when I was directed to the back of the building almost thirty years earlier (that was with my son, Andrew). My record was not read out and my solicitor then described me as a respectable businessman. I guessed that had been manipulated, was this going to be the same. I was approached by the inspector, Dave Sidwell. That's odd, why?

This was a minor petty charge. Dave made a point of telling me to keep calm, don't lose your temper tom. Course, these cops do all the homework, the studies, the psychological profiling, the exact statement to ensure I did lose my temper. Sitting in the court, I was confronted by a single judge, not one judge and two magistrates. But this is a fucking magistrates court? First they bring the witnesses in one by one. First Bill, the plumber who did the job. Now Bill, at over six foot, is doing his level best to appear much smaller by bending over in the witness box, elbows on his knees, his nerves betraying him, shitting himself. Watching him, I couldn't make out. I wasn't 100 percent sure if he had given the masonic distress signal, grabbing his tie knot between his fingers. At any rate, the judge, Jarret, was very sympathetic to his plight. For fuck's sake, this was a bloke who had the balls to call around my house in the dark, park a quarter of a mile away to confront me, and now here he was acting the frightened witness, terrified of big bad Tommy Lewin. And the judge is standing for it! Now take your time, I was wondering if he was going to kiss his arse, I looked at my solicitor, who seemed to have been oblivious to what's going on. Had the police done the usual thing and told the plumbers that I –was known?—to them? The plumber told his story. He had parked up outside my house simply to ask for his money that he was owed. First lie. The solicitor had my fan in front of him, asking him about the fact this was a fully working fan. This was brushed over; it was irrelevant. Then his story changed. Had the police told him? Where I had leaned behind me, as explained in his statement, now I had turned to my right and jumped up on the wall to reach the bayonet. He recognised it fully, as it had the sight on it. The solicitor let this pass and I'm frantically trying to get his attention to ask the witness why he didn't shout out the first time when I forced him out the door. Why didn't he shout out, "he's got a knife" then, instead of waiting? It didn't add up. I'm getting very frustrated and angry, just as Sidwell had anticipated. I knew I would hang myself. Instead I got the roll of paper out on which I had drawn a graph of the exact distance and area where the vans had parked. Hearing the rustling, the judge bawled me out in front of the witness. "Will you keep the noise down?" Fuck me, he was hostile...or is this my imagination? After all, I had no criminal record...right?

You only need a few ingredients to make a cake. It works exactly the same with the judicial system in England. First, a couple of biased cops to nudge it along in the right direction, then a biased and corrupt prosecution to give it another nudge. The third ingredient is the judge who, contrary to what everyone is saying, is made aware that I do, indeed, have a criminal record. Finally, an incompetent defence solicitor who's completely in the dark, knowing you don't have a criminal record, then you're bolloxed. By the time I walked out the witness stand I knew I was fucked.

The next witness, the son, equally frightened, came walking into the witness box giving his side of the story. Like his father he was equally bent over, elbows on knees, frightened of big bad Tommy Lewin. Equally, his story had changed, now from hiding in the entry, he was in front of the door and saw me lean around, reach up high and grabbed the knife. Like his father, he never wavered. First, it was obvious the cops had put my story to them. They had had a rethink, and realised I'd reached up for the bayonet, even doing a physical demonstration of my reaching up. "Can I have a drink of water, please, your honour?" "Yes of course, young man." These guys were clever indeed. I'm starting to wonder if they had police relatives who had put them right, this pair knew how to act, knew how to address the judge, for me, I just confirmed the stereotype. I was steaming angry, no cross questioning. Having explained their loss of serving their customers the judge, very sympathetically, waved them off. Oh, so that's it then, no chance to cross examine them after I've confronted my crappy solicitor. I was furious. These idiots were that blinded by my obvious guilt they couldn't see the glaring mistakes and contradictions the witnesses were making

Next, came the police officer in charge of the case; only him, not any of the others...not the tallest out of the group who had to be called on to reach the bayonets because the others couldn't reach up high enough. Another highly significant point the idiot solicitor never raised. "Did Mrs Lewin look disabled to you officer?" "Well, not to me, your honour, but I couldn't tell, as Mrs Lewin never moved from her chair a smirk on his face." Well of coursed she never moved, you prick, because she's disabled and the chair Was a disabled recliner chair of no consequence to the judge? That ticked the box that he wanted. He also couldn't assess anything else as the house was in such a mess with lots of clutter another smirk. Of course there was lots of clutter, you dickhead pratt! We were waiting for completion on another house and were stacked up with furniture. But the poison was in, and the judge, biased as he was, ticked another box. I was being well and truly stitched up, but why??

Then it was my turn to get into the witness box. Confidently, I was asked to tell my version of events. I had no worries at all; the facts were indisputable. After I had recalled the events, the prosecution got up to question me.

First out of his mouth: "Have you been before a court before, Mr Lewin?"

"Well of cour-" I got no more out of my mouth before the judge jumped out of his chair, waving his hands, saying, "No, no, no, Mr Lewin, there is no need to answer that." I can't get my head around this, but my radar is in full fucking swing, every word now is confirming to me that I'm being fitted up. The prosecutor never cross questioned me on any of my statement or any of my version of events. Instead, he went for my wife Bet.

"Why isn't your wife in court today as a witness for you Mr Lewin?"

"Because she can't, of course." The doctor's letter has been completely disregarded; my solicitor again is letting this pass. Then he went into his well-rehearsed spiel. "Your wife hasn't turned up because you both know she is telling lies; she made the initial statement because she is frightened of you and had to do as she was told. Whilst she made a statement, she has refused to appear in court to back you up because she knows she couldn't carry this through." Now I'm supposed to keep my fucking temper in check whilst he's throwing all these allegations about. If it wasn't so insulting and offensive, it would be funny. I looked across at Sidwell who had been to my house and apologised. He was concentrating on his notes, not paying me any attention at all. He was doing his report for the chief constable following my wife's complaints.

I was dismissed from the box and went to sit down, leaving the court the judge returned after ten minutes—it might have been three minutes, just time to get out and back into the door and did his summing up. Not looking me in the eye, he nodded to the prosecutor and noted that he agreed with him fully. "There was indeed nothing wrong with Mrs Lewin, except she was reliant on him. She wrote her statement out of fear of Mr Lewin." With that, he gave my solicitor *the look*. What was the meaning of that look? It was a look of admonishment — was something being said to him? You should have done your homework? He is a known criminal? At any rate, I was given no sentence. Why not? Leaving the court I was directed to the probation service, but not before seeing my solicitor running around the waiting area like a headless chicken - first forwards then sideways. I could see his body language; he just couldn't get his head around it...you are going to appeal this aren't you?—his eyes were on the swivel, yes, yes. With that I went to see the probation officer, who spoke to me but never asked any questions. Again, in my life I had never seen such blatant collective stupidity, corruption. From the biased judge - so biased it was ridiculous - to the blank and stupid solicitor, to a biased probation officer, it was disgraceful, and I'm supposed to keep my gob shut, show deference and respect to these blatantly corrupt idiots?

A week later I was summoned to appear at the court where I was directed to a proper court hearing with a judge and two magistrates, what I should have had in the first place. Clearly Jarret had been handpicked to find me guilty, then justice being seen to be carried out fairly I was thrown to the proper courtroom, no doubt with the press in attendance. This time I was represented by the head solicitor who passed me a file and asked if I agreed with it. Well, I'd given up by now. Having a quick glimpse, I placed it down on the bench. Did you agree with those comments? Yes. Are you sure? Perplexed, I picked the file back up. There in black and white is my admission, that I had picked the bayonet up and threatened the plumbers!!!—only I never said no such fucking thing! I looked at the solicitor who said he thought it was odd that I should be admitting to that whilst pleading not guilty. What the fucking hell is going on here?? How far across the board does this conspiracy and corruption go? How many government officials, court officials, and police blatantly stretch the truth - tell outright lies - in order to get a conviction?

Being slow it took a bit to hit me between the eyeballs. Having not been in any trouble for nearly thirty years, my crimes were considered spent. Obviously, someone is not happy about this. Collectively someone has decided, even if I may be telling the truth, I needed to be reined in, put back on the radar for future observation. By being found guilty, my massive criminal record was now on show for all to see. Worse - and to compound it all - I was skint?? Whilst we were doing nothing illegal at all, everything - every property - was in my wife's name or our children's names. These dumb clots couldn't see that, neither did any of them ask. The fifty-grand motorhome on my drive was irrelevant. The fucking idiots had added two and two together and come up a mile out of sync. A neighbour in Boldmere pulled me. We had owned two detached houses in the road, and although both houses were in my wife's name, I was linked to them via British telecom. The cops had been around asking the neighbours all about me. Instead of just asking me outright – a trait that popped up regularly -they did their own research and kept coming up with the wrong answers.

A week later I got a letter from the solicitors, now no doubt fully aware of my record, in which they explained that their advice was to not appeal. Well, it will just be your word against there's. Oh, so the ignored lies and facts told by the plumbers were irrelevant then??? The witnesses can be nervous, perfectly normal tell lies just a mistake. And never be cross-examined.

Attending a probation office meeting in Perry Barr, I was advised that I would have to attend an anger management course. The black woman probation officer couldn't look me in the face. "I am not attending any anger management course," I said very angrily. She knew; I could see it in her eyes she was black, she would know how bent the law is. She also knew the reputation the idiot solicitor had. She wrote down a number and advised me to see a solicitor she knew who had offices in alum rock. This solicitor applied for a new hearing, then a couple of weeks later withdrew from my defence. Now it was just a case of picking any fucking idiot out of a hat. Going through the book, I came across a criminal lawyer in Corporation Street opposite the law courts. Having explained to them the situation and circumstances, they agreed to defend me and spoke to the first solicitors to get a fuller picture. Oh, of course, it's like one bricklayer speaking to the first bricklayer to ask why he didn't get paid.

Taking me around to the citadel, behind the main buildings that reminded me of a masonic hall, I was introduced to this

Tom, who was not only a barrister but a prosecuting barrister as well. What fucking chance have I got with him? Going through the paperwork I can see he is puzzled, and before going in, the solicitor urged me saying, "Whatever happens, don't tell him you have a criminal record."? Ahhh, so now he knew? I can see the barrister couldn't work it out. Do you have a record?—following the clerk's advice, I kept my gob shut. Before I had even got a chance to reply, he said it doesn't matter, I can always check that out anyway. He did, and at the new hearing - half an hour before my case went into court - I was told that whilst he was very apologetic, Tom's case had overrun in another court, and as such he couldn't appear for me. That was it; I was thrown to the wolves. Now I was so fucking angry I just knew I couldn't even defend myself. The corruption was disgraceful. Why don't these solicitors just say sorry, your name is that bad were not going to defend you? British justice: it's a joke the evidence was staring them in the face, but they were that blinded to it all they could see was my guilt, my criminal record. I've got no money, no house, I'm on a state pension; not only am I guilty, but I'm also so thick I can't even see I'm guilty, ha-ha-ha.

In court, on the opposite side of the old court buildings, I was placed before another judge and two magistrates, as per is proper, but no one else at all - no witnesses, no press no public. This time the plumbers knew the score. They walked in, stood proud and confident fully upright - no need to appear frightened this time, they knew - and had the confidence to know that the judges were on their side. I knew I was fucked, yet again - double fucked.

My defence barrister didn't cross question them, and how could he - he didn't know me, didn't know the background. The witnesses just whizzed out their story, the judge thanking them profusely for taking the time and trouble and sent them on their way. This is why I suspect cameras are not allowed into the courts, nor videoing the proceedings. My MP was Andrew Mitchell, the chief whip for the conservative party. He had offices in Sutton and was having problems with the police himself. Surely, if there was one man who could help me, it was Andrew Mitchell. How do you interpret corruption? Maybe I'm thick. Andrew had been leaving downing street after a very late session and wanted to get to his club for a drink. On his bike, he asked the police officer on the gate to let him through and the police officer directed him to the single gate to the side. Mitchell, for some reason, wanted to go through the double gates. An argument ensued, and I gather words were passed. The only witnesses to the words being the two people involved. It was next reported to the sun newspaper that Mitchell had called the cop a Pleb, which he denied; another witness turned up who also heard Mitchell call the cop a Pleb, then other cops got involved. Mitchell then decided to sue the Sun Newspaper. The first cop, with the backing of the police federation, backed him - all paid for with taxpayers' money. It turns out the second witness was an off-duty cop who made the story up. One way or another, other cops were -or got themselves - involved. The off-duty cop was found guilty of perjury and sentenced to prison. Some were sacked, some were suspended. To the general public - me included - Mitchell was being fitted up. We all sat back in utter bemusement. Surely a sitting MP, a chief whip, couldn't be seen to be so blatantly fitted up; it seemed utterly unbelievable. If he was telling the truth, surely - he of all people - would understand my position, my circumstances, my predicament. The question should be, if they could do this to a conservative minister, a chief whip, how many times can they get away with it with the rest of us...us plebs? The cops have fitted me up many a time. I know many people who have been fitted up; these are supposed to be public servants - our servants - yet when it suits, they feel they can come out and bend the rules to suit themselves.

I wrote numerous times to Andrew Mitchell. I was given an appointment to meet him in his office twice. Polite as he was, I felt at each stage he was just fobbing me off. His PA, a young guy, was telling me how unfair it was, how Andrew would never use that as an expression. In court, it turned into an even bigger fiasco. If further proof was needed of how corrupt, our judicial system is then look at the court records that were given to the public. The jury are picked to assess the facts and bring in a verdict. The fucking big joke is they are advised and guided by the judge. In this case, at the end of the trial a number of cops being done for lying altering statements, and god knows what else. It's all down to Mitchell and the cop till the judge directs the jury. Referring to the police officer, he advices the jury, "Can you possibly think this police officer could possibly tell lies when its patently clear that he wouldn't have the brains to be able to make up a story - yet Mitchell admits to using a derogatory word two years earlier?" What the derogatory word is: I don't know, but if it was you bastards it's still a lot different to the word pleb. And let's not forget, police are listening to criminal's day in day out, year after year. If anyone knows what signs to look out for in a liar, it's a cop. Any cop worth his salt should be able to lie through their teeth—I know, I've seen them. But according to the judge, out of all the cops who have lied, this one is not. Another judge, his colleague, in advising the jury to find Jeffrey Archer the novelist and MP not guilty, justified his reasoning on the basis of how could this delicate flower [HIS WIFE?]be considered a liar? It turned out both were lying through their teeth. Smart judge.

Andrew Mitchell was found guilty of using such a word. He had to resign from his job as chief whip and re-mortgage his home to the tune of a million pounds to pay of his solicitors and other costs. If that can happen to him, what chance have I got?

I should have realised. Far from being able to help me, Mitchell was fighting for his own political life. I bet he will be pissed off for life. Because of the consistent bias, corruption, and stupidity of the police – who together with the solicitors equally corrupt in their own way - can afford a solicitor? I have to take extra precautions on a regular basis. I had problems with another plumber not long after this incident. He did the job then demanded more money. Being young, his next move was to try coming the heavy. What do I have to do? Dial 999 and two hours later two plods turn up giving me a crime number. I said, "You're a bit fucking late now, ain't you?" Every time I get close to any threats or implied intimidation, I dial, 999. Not that I want to - I despise the idea. I despise informers, but I have to protect myself from past experience. I know what is going to happen, the little rat is going to squeal to the cops. Whenever an incident or scenario crops up where I have to dial 999. I then send a letter to the judges concerned including the senior judge at Birmingham crown court judge Davis QC. To be fair, Judge Davis sent me a letter back, via his secretary, advising me to seek a judicial review, together with the forms to fill out. Well, I filled them out, now where do they go? The prosecution office at Birmingham law courts where they are sent back, inadequately filled. This went on four times, going around the same prosecutor's desk before being back. No case, no appeal, and Inspector Dave Sidwell at Sutton Coldfield nick, none of them ever have the courtesy to answer, public servants? Bullshit. About five times to date, all copies kept on my computer by being blinded to my innocence. These idiots have allowed a family of crooked plumbers to get away with ripping customers of on a regular basis. If they can rip me of, or try to, to the tune of £360, for half an hour's work, how many others are they doing it to??? How many times in the year are they getting away with that? Once a week? That's twenty grand a year? Ha-ha, you clever policemen and judges; I tell you, those plumbers are living of the Hogg alright. Nicer houses I've never seen for plumbers.

It's the knock-on effect that also pisses me off. Me and my wife have worked hard all our lives, far harder than any of these police or judges. Sadly - following this cock up - my wife passed away, thankfully in peace. This time I did sue the NHS who admitted negligence. We had been married 45 years and had built up numerous and reasonably successful businesses, all this despite repeated victimisation, from vindictive, biased, and corrupt police officers and judges. For many years we had planned specifically to spend our later years in very nice comfort. Travelling the world, touring Europe, whilst having nothing to leave anyone anything, except our children. We have lived in semi derelict cottages, only to find people sneering at us for being so poor, before sitting back in shock when they see what profit we made. Thankfully, my mom and dad were never jealous resentful or bitter people, it is a trait I am proud to have inherited.

The cops were not the only fools blinded by the state of our house. We bought it in the early 2000's at the same time we brought the pub. We sat on it, not touching it for years. When it suited us, we would move in for a few months, maybe a year if it suited us. Naturally we never discussed our business with anyone; we always kept it that the right hand never knew what the left was doing. There was nothing devious or corrupt in our mentality, it was just a natural process. Whilst Bet and me trusted each other implicitly, we didn't – sadly - trust other people too much. It's amazing how many people feel they are entitled to a little piece of the pie. It's also a matter of resentment or jealousy. If you had asked me when I was twenty, I would never have believed it. For years, a friend and neighbour had spent many a time chiding me over the state of the house. *When are you going to do something about the state of those windows? You're showing up the street?* After a bit, I started to wonder if he thought I was skint.

Our plan was to move in refurbish it, then spend more time touring Europe. We were already spending short breaks around England seeing much of the country, our winters abroad. Our next plan was to move into the house, extend and refurbish it, and make a nice three to four-bedroom house. In the meantime, Bet left me. I re-thought my plans, rented her house out, moved in, then put in plans for it. But this time I designed it as a semi separate self-contained building with an annex. My friend and neighbour would come over gasping, "Bugger me, Tom, you really are a builder," obviously ignoring the certificates on my walls. After ten years we don't speak now. Ha-ha. It's a funny world.

I now spend much of my time as me and Bet had planned, only this time on my own. A couple of years after she passed away, I rang the WMCA up and offered my services on the food distribution to homeless people. I was thanked but no one got back to me. Later I rang another charity. Between my travelling, I felt quite happy about doing some charity work. After yet another knock back, it was pointed out to me that they would naturally have checked up on my criminal record. That's it then, fucked again. For that, and many other reasons, I have adopted my mother's mantra: "Fuck 'em all."

A couple of years ago, I was driving into Matlock Bath from Derbyshire in my motorhome. Parking up, I went for a walk with a lady friend. Getting back, I was surrounded by about twelve coppers and four to five squad cars. I couldn't believe what was going on. Unlocking the doors, this senior cop turns and said, "Excuse me sir, is this your vehicle?" Well, I should hope so, seeing as I've got the keys. The woman had got into the van, as she heard him say, "Well our cameras have picked up that this vehicle is stolen. Would you mind stepping into the car?" A whole pile of coppers? What the fucking hell are they expecting? Getting into the back of the car I've got two country bumpkins in front, wanting to know all about my motorhome. 'Course a simple check inside might make then sit up and wonder. I'm having to be polite because they have already given me the threat of settling the matter at the police station. Oh, it was a Saturday. I could be in nick all weekend. In the meantime, my girlfriend was approached by a female cop who asked her if she knew me. This obviously made the woman very nervous, especially when she was informed that she might have to make her own way home. In short, it frightened the crap out of her.

All this was for nothing, over nothing. Two years earlier I had been visiting friends who had a farm in France. My rear number plate was missing. Not wishing to take the risk of driving home without it, my friend took me to the local garage who made me a new number plate up. Unfortunately, they made a U as V almost, plus they didn't space the letters as in England - plus, it had an EU badge, little dumb-dumbs here decided to blank the EU off and never gave a thought to the letters. I had been driving about in the van for over a year; why did you cover the EU up? Because it had got EU on it, not GB. All your letters are not right. Well, what's wrong with them? He couldn't answer me. Almost shouting, "Everything's wrong, yes, but what?" 'Course, I'm that thick they think I've altered the rear number plates but not the front. Eventually they realise no offence is committed so after at least an hour, I'm released. The one cop is pissed off. At my request, the other one agreed, reluctantly to explain to the woman that I had committed no offence. I could see it was killing him, having explained. I could see he wanted to tell her about me, warn her off. I said, "Is there something else you'd like to say?" No, off he goes. A week later I got a £100 fine for an incorrect number plate. I still don't know what was incorrect. BUT I GOT DOUBLE BACK.

The woman knew I had been in prison - I'd told her. She explained, well, after you had gone, I looked around the van. It's my extended home; it has photos of my wife all over the place, clothes cutlery the lot. Pretty obvious it wasn't nicked if the idiots had looked. Ok, maybe it was a natural mistake - it's understandable - but why twelve cops - cars all over the place, hemming me in? How fast can a big van go?

As an experienced landlord, it's not in my interests to treat tenants like shit. Some do; a lot of Asians do, I don't. I will buy, refurbish and then let a property in good order. Most landlords work the same way. But we do run a business. For the wheels to run smoothly, it's in my interests for the tenants to be happy. Happy tenants pay their rent with no problems, but some tenants can be total idiots. There are two things to remember: you are the rich landlord, and they are the hard, done-by tenants struggling to pay there rent. Not all, but a few. The new build property was built as an annex, so therefore I would be renting out rooms. I had had a married couple in for two years before leaving, I instructed a local agent to find me a tenant. A guy in his mid-20's turned up, his Asian girlfriend an hour later, both telling me they loved it. My instincts were telling me not to have them in. I text the agent but then changed my mind. His girlfriend assured me that her boyfriend was so fussy he would want to clean and redecorate – if that was ok. They had been given two months' notice from their previous flat, and I was getting the warning bells but ignoring them in my eagerness to get abroad.

They started straight away; they must have seen the stamp on my head. First the lock on the side door was stiff. That was resolved a week into my tour, and whilst in Croatia, I got a text screaming that they had caught fleas, then the agent rang telling me they had called into his office screaming their heads off and demanding a major discount on their rent. I offered them £40, and if they are not happy, get out. These pair are at the scam, that's why they were given notice to quit it. All went quite till I got back two months later. On my first night I got a text asking me to keep my voice down as they couldn't sleep. That's me in my own home, I text suggesting again they were not happy so should get out. The next day the toilet started leaking, and whilst I couldn't prove it, I guessed they had loosened the pan deliberately. He didn't want me to fix it, but wanted me to get a professional in. I am a professional and I fixed it. He just wanted me to spend money. It went on and on: they deliberately blocked my car in on my own drive, then videoed every situation, so when I asked him, are you a total cxxxt? he went screaming to the agent, showing him his tape. The idiot was a compete piece of work. Then he called the police in on another incident. Now I know how that's going to look don't I?—corrupt and stupid as they are the cops, know me, don't they? So whatever I say or do their mind is made up before I even open my mouth. I've got a criminal record, ain't I?

People today know how to act; they know how to play the police. All it needed was the know-all cops to tell the tenant I'm known to them. They've then got the green light to wind me up even further. I have seen this time and time again, and if I had, how many others have? People go out and cause trouble, drunk or sober, and when it comes on top and they come unstuck, they use the coppers to exact their revenge. For the coppers, if they are faced with two guys each with no criminal record, they have a difficult quandary: who do they believe? If the ones got a black eye, simple enough, do the other fucker with assault. Two black eyes? Assault and battery. The cops have no guilt; they are brainwashed to nick people - it's all about promotion. The fact your life could be destroyed is irrelevant, ain't it? As the voice says, the law is the law. If the ones got a criminal record, well, its simple ain't it? To Joe public they are just seen to be doing their job. To the ones who do the squealing, it's a win-win. One, they get their revenge; two, they stop the other going back at them. Some tenants know how to put on the hard, done-by. Poor little me, I'm just a hardworking chappie trying to get by in life whilst being ripped off by a ruthless landlord. Out of all the tenants I had dealt with, these pair of scum bags were really adept at it. For my part, I was concerned about my position; for their part, the silly prats thought I was frightened of them. Calling the cops out. He would act all innocent, and she would act the typically timid Asian wife.

I had different options open to me: I could have cut their water and heating off or I could have blocked the whole drive off. Either way, I would look the big baddy - especially if the cops were brought in, none of whom would have experience as a landlord. Plus, these tenants were very good at manipulation, putting an act on,- videoing every situation. Eventually, I got them out without too much hassle. They took the front door key - which is theft - they took the remote controls to the fire - which is theft - then they broke the backdoor lock. They also caused damage to the hallway which needed redecorating.

What the prat never allowed for, as it was not a separate house, is that I was allowed to keep their deposit. This really pissed them off; it's something they never had the brains to foresee. Obviously, they had built up a little catalogue of complaints, videoed and all. They left on the Wednesday night midnight doing a flit. I text asking for my keys and controls before considering their request for deposit. On the Friday, I dialled 999 asking the police to visit and assess the situation. After a few pauses I was then asked my full name. Click, then my full address? Click. Then my date of birth – click. Half an hour later I got a text: your report has been crimed as criminal damage, crime number 20BE217759X—then, this case has been closed. Why am I not surprised?? Here we have a collective body of cops. With no experience of property rentals, most never having been in business. Making an assumption about me based on the criminal record I have achieved through those same corrupt bodies having fitted me up in the first place.

On the Saturday I got a text of the lowlife asking for his deposit. I text him back telling him he would be owing *me* money, decorating the hallway alone coming to more than his deposit. The phone went dead, and the next afternoon at three, he pulled into the drive with eight or nine others. in two cars. I was half asleep on the sofa, balaclava'd up. They've jumped me while the ex-tenant robbed my house, nicking a cherished gold bracelet from my wife plus other valuable watches, etc. I recognised the tenant as I half grabbed his balaclava. Fuck it, I rang the cops, who turned up. This is all wrong, this is. They need catching. Not only had I got it on video, a neighbour had got even more on his CCTV camera, including clear readings of their number plates. Surely a simple matter of tracking the cars. For some reason, Sutton nick didn't want to handle it, so it passed to Stechford.

A few days later I got a phone call from a female officer from Stechford police station. Maybe my local nick didn't want to know. I couldn't make out what she was on about: they had nicked the two owners of the cars who were not driving them at the time, and they hadn't arrested the tenants. They did have someone in custody who, for some vague reason, seemed to suggest some previous tenant had robbed and assaulted me. No one visited me, no one interviewed me. If truth be told, and true to form, they didn't want to know did they. I don't think they even spoke to the right tenant. Whatever the scam is. A month later after several chases by me, two cops turned up with my CCTV hard drive to tell me they couldn't find any evidence or proof of who was involved. Neither one could look me in the eye. Fucking great, ain't it? They didn't want to know. Maybe they thought Tommy Lewin was getting his just rewards. What concerned me more than anything was the fact this team set up wasn't a one off, it was well planned and very well organised, and it was over in a few minutes. How many more robberies like this had they carried out? There was a spate of similar robberies within the area, yet I suspect the cops - bright and embittered as they were to how they perceived me - were blinded to all else. Fucking great, ay?? Worse, I was bloody hesitant to defend myself because of the experience with the plumbers a few years earlier and others. And I'm supposed to stand for that and do bugger all?

Just a few short years ago, whilst doing a house clearance a customer gave me a solid bronze bar with a rubber, bicycle-type hand grip. She told me her father had been given it by a policeman for protection after he had been burgled. For myself I thought that was a kind gesture. I keep it handy myself for the same reason, however I am fully aware that if I were to use it, in my own house, whether against the bent plumbers, or the little toe rag tenant: it will be me that is accused and found guilty of assault. Most taxi drivers I know carry some form of protection in their car, quite rightly too, it can be quite frightening, I could not take that risk, hence my getting out of the business. This is how corrupt the law is in this country - that old boy would have been held up as a courageous OAP, defending himself and his property, quite rightly. Me, I'd be nicked, thrown into court and painted as a violent nut case in front of a judge who thinks he knows me.

Assuming I am telling the truth in all my recollections - and why would I lie, what have I got to prove? - I have had my life and I'm still enjoying it. After a great deal of considerable thought over the years, I felt it only right that I put the record straight. This fitting up is going on all over the country. My dad was not a bad man, he had worked hard all his life, but his life was almost destroyed by corrupt police. The bastards have had a good pop at me. Any good barrister who is not corrupt can look at all the mentioned convictions and pick holes out of them. My dad nicked. Pip the Planter, me and my dad nicked for the Blackpool jewellery? Pip the planter. My brothers, Reg and Johnny? Pip the planter. There are dozens of others. I've never had a good solicitor. This applies to 99 percent of those convicted today and sent to prison. Clearly most would, and are guilty, but even if only two percent are innocent, that is a hell of a lot of people. If this has been happening to me, how many more have been victimised???

A lady doctor named Amanda Brown has written a book on her experiences of working in one of the largest women only prisons in Europe, HMP, Bronzefield, The Prison Doctor. In the book, she recalls some of the female inmates she has treated, some clearly really nut jobs, yet she states that she feels the majority of the prisoners shouldn't be in prison citing how it costs circa £65,000, per year to keep a person in prison. Most of them for a few weeks at a time and drug-related, whilst I have no time for any drug user. If that 65,000 was spent on really helping those women, it would be better spent. The same applies to the men's prisons; yet if no one is going to listen to her, what chance do I have? I have often wondered what the real agenda is of those in power in this country.

The police, having been called into a crime, are then supposed to find the suspect then find the evidence. What they actually do in far too many cases is make the evidence to fit the crime. The prosecution deliberately hides the evidence that might help the defence. This also has happened many, many times over many years and in many cases. We slate the American police for fitting people up, killing black people, but we are doing exactly the same here, in this country. IT IS WRITTEN SOMEWHERE THAT IT IS BETTER TO LET 100 GUILTY PEOPLE GO FREE, RATHER THAN ONE INNOCENT PERSON BE FOUND GUILTY. I THINK THE JUDICIARY DON'T GIVE A SHIT ABOUT THAT.

To Joe Blogs or any innocent citizen who reads my books: I can well envisage the reaction to my recollections. My story. Ahh, your first thought is it's a load of cobblers; the cops don't target or pick on people like that. No, of course not, I'm making it all up. But think on; the police have been picking on the blacks for years, during the miners strikes they were queuing up to serve on the lines, simplyif you're on the wrong side of the line you become a target. Your second thought - and looking back at the events, I can understand the thinking - is that maybe I'm a major or persistent criminal who the police are justified in keeping under observation. If I had been unemployed or constantly on the dole, wasting my life, I could understand it. Possibly, when I got done for a stolen car, I was running a business, a warehouse. I was nineteen; anyone with half a brain would or could see I was trying to do something with my life...and if not? It would have come out eventually. I was never asked about that car stolen or otherwise. I will never know the facts, but I was driving with insurance. I believe the car was not stolen. I certainly never stole it or received it as a stolen car. The cops never even asked me. This was all about a young vindictive copper who wanted to score points, backed by his colleagues. The real question people should be asking, is if I'm saying this...if I'm telling the truth... why should the police, the judges, the judiciary conspire to fit people up? Obviously, they think they are acting in the public's interest, when in reality the exact opposite is true...look at the statistics. Look at the facts. More people are becoming more corrupt; more people, like me, see how corrupt the system is. What do you do??

The jewellery stolen from Blackpool: I'd never been to Blackpool in my life. The first time I ever went to Blackpool was in mid-2000 for my wife's birthday and found it a shithole. To this day, I don't know whether I pleaded guilty to robbing the shop or receiving the jewellery. At any rate, I had been working at Pilkington glass, having had the day off, when Pip the Planter arrested me and my dad. I was never questioned; I was never asked to make a statement. I have no doubt Pip the Planter had put something down to us. I have tried to analyse all the facts and circumstances of that time and period: why did Charlie Heinz bring that jewellery?—if he didn't squeal, how would the grass scrap dealer Caswell know the exact draw? Heinz had seen me put that jewellery in? Why would you leave the house? Go straight to Caswell, and tell him the exact draw, the exact spot, where the jewellery had been placed?—coming to our back door, maybe one-two hours later…how would Pip the Planter know exactly what draw in the cabinet to go to?—after walking through three rooms?—no, it was a blatant fit-up. Villains, like Heinz, or john the gangster. I believe, like the scrap dealers, were [engaged,]by the police to fit someone up, like my family, like my uncle Geoff Elliot, if they weren't paid they were given free rein to carry on with their own little misdemeanour's

Think about it for a moment! The scrap dealer was allowed to carry on buying bent metal week after week after week, knowingly;; so long as he threw the odd body in. Certain villains were given or allowed to carry on with blag after blag, robbery after robbery,- so long as they threw the odd body in, so for throwing Geoff Elliot in, who was not a fence or a villain; john the gangster was allowed to continue on his robbery sprees,-- haha,- now I ain't the brain of Britain but somehow the figures don't add up. How do I know this? Well because Wilko, told me when he nicked me within a couple of weeks of opening my scrap yard.

In Stafford prison I came across a guy named Miller. Miller was, I found, the new breed of professional crook around today. Miller strutted about like he was the cream of the bunch and above everyone else. He equally was screaming that he had been fitted up and had got some independent organisation fighting his case. In actual fact, I believed him. From all my experience and knowledge, it was something that I knew happened on a regular basis. Miller was a clever crook; he was also a snide to me. He was the new breed of thief that strutted around Birmingham - clever in the same way as Charley Heinz, never saying much, they just had a permanent smirk on their faces. They would let you do all the talking simply so they could pick your brains and pick out your faults, all the time giving the impression that you were the focus of their admiration. Miller, like many more, learned his lesson from his time in Stafford, further proof if needed of why any form of fitting up, or the judicial system anyway, is outdated and a waste of time.

When he came out, he turned to the new easy way of making money by becoming a drug dealer. What no one else knew was that he also covered his back, along with his brother. By turning grass and throwing bodies in. A cockney, who had done some business with peter Miller and got nicked shortly afterwards, facing a six stretch. He guessed Miller had thrown him in. It's a funny quirk of human nature that because you're getting away with villainy, other villains want to do business with you because they think you're clever. This gives them more bodies to throw in; one body doesn't know who the other body is, and by the time anyone starts working it out months later, in nick it all becomes Chinese whispers. They have a constant supply of new bodies. It often made me wonder if that's why Peter Miller's wife was an alcoholic. I know from personal experience how easy it is for the coppers to fit someone up; all they need is an inkling, or someone throwing them in. The coppers very rarely kill the golden goose, and no one can actually prove who the grass is.

My experience with Charlie stood me in good stead; it opened my eyes up to what snides there were about and how gullible, disloyal, and stupid the people were who I thought were family friends. It took my brothers a while longer to see the print really. They were that decent and naïve - they couldn't believe that so many people friends, could be such rats.

KNOW YOUR FRIENDS AND KEEP YOUR ENEMIES. IN SIGHT

I do not pretend to be lily white; trying to find my way in the world has caused me to skate on the edge a few times, along with a lot of people. But neither me nor my family were anything like we have been painted. My dad wasn't a villain: after serving in WW2, he came out to work on the barrow, as did my mother. They were both hardworking people, as was Billy, nor me. I had realised as a kid that villainy was stupid and mainly unprofitable. In actual fact, if truth be known, I became far more of a crook when I got into business. Charles Richardson, the London gangster, once said in passing the houses of parliament, that that's where the real crooks were residing. The older I got the more I realised he was right. Once I got into business, I really started to see the crooks... morally bankrupt and crooked. That's when I first started to really learn and wake up. All the time those many years ago I was thinking I was being jack the lad selling gear to various people around Kitts Green, I never gave a thought to the fact there were people out there informing the cops that oh yes, Tommy Lewin was round here last week selling bent gear when I was'nt. I never gave a thought that all the time, going right back to when I quite justifiably smacked those cops as a kid, I was building up a portfolio of hate along with the rest of my family. What comes first, the chicken or the egg? I grew up knowing most coppers were bent. Every copper I came across took a back hander or nicked something.

One of the most favoured viewing programmes of the police was the Sweeney, when on it was the most viewed. Sweeney Todd, flying squad, concentrated on Jack Regan. Jack would delight in knocking the crap out of and fitting up known villains. Any spare bent money lying around would dissipate by the time it got back to the nick. That says it all really, and I found to be exactly as it was.

If I never actually knew of them stealing something, they were party to the fitting up, which in itself is corrupt. Our only crime really is in not being police informers. One of us wouldn't have stood out the whole family. Being the same made us a target; it magnified everything we did. THE COPS LIKE TO THROW UP THAT THEY ARE JUST LIKE THE REST OF US?? Yea right. Just bear in mind there are a lot of nasty people in this country. We are known for tearing people down after lifting them up. This in itself goes back to those old days of serfdom: all for one, one for all - unless you've got a bit more food on the table than me. We are known as a nation of bullies. It's inbuilt in our character; maybe it comes from that Saxon German heritage. At any rate, the average policeman in this country comes from a working-class background. It doesn't stretch the imagination too much to imagine the joy a person would get once he's got that uniform on, backed up fully by a judiciary that was formed over 600 years ago with the wigs, meant solely to intimidate us. If anyone is susceptible to be targeted, then me, my family and friends are prime targets, along with the blacks, of course. At least I've got the advantage of being white. Until my face is recognised, I'm on safe ground. If it was black, I'm fucked before I start. Yet despite everything, all of my family have done reasonably or very well; all own or have owned their own houses, all their children have done very well in life and out of life. I'm very proud of that knowledge. Most of my kids are professionals, two in the top five percent of earners in the country. All own their own houses. For myself, I'm quite happy with what I have achieved in life. Could I have achieved more if I hadn't had coppers breathing down my neck throughout my business life, whether it be the hotel or in the building, with poison being put into customers? I honestly don't know. I didn't much think about it at the time; it was something I was used to accepting so just took it on the chin. But without a doubt, I look back on it with some resentment.

Without a doubt, I look back on a Tommy Lewin, which is greatly at odds painted by corrupt coppers and biased judges. I consider myself lucky, despite everything. I have a very nice lifestyle; I travel the world at my leisure and spend months at a time touring Europe. My only bitter regret is that my beautiful wife, Bet, is not here to share and enjoy that lifestyle. We both aimed for the stars; we set our goals high and she followed me unflinchingly and without hesitation. Learning from our parents, we declared a deliberate policy - a plan of making sure we were able to enjoy our later years after first doing the best we could for our kids. We didn't, and have never starved, but we were always careful. For all that time I just took her for granted. Its only now I look back and realise how much we achieved together, how clever she was, how talented, how determined she was to back me. Now I have all the fruits of what we both worked for, yet without her to share it with. We both climbed a mountain.

Looking back at life also makes me think of those far less fortunate than me: young kids who never had the benefit of a hardworking savvy bloke like my dad, or a hardworking determined mother like mine. I have seen those kids at school, and I've seen them in prison, fucked and lost before they even start. I've seen them in later life: older, wiser, more bitter, no criminal record but worn out and knackered. Maybe they should be forced to carry a sign on their bonce for all those cops and teachers to carry on kicking them. Because trust me, in my lifetime I ain't seen things change much. A classic example is the treatment of the blacks in this country that manifests itself in the treatment of the families who came over on the good ship Windrush in the early 60s. These people were brought over as cheap labour following the loss of our workforce in WW2. That was bad enough. I saw them on the railways, in the factories, segregated, made to feel segregated. I used to watch my elders and the way they looked down at them and treated them. Without a doubt, they were never brought in as equals.

Some did ok, some did quite well, others didn't. In later years I've moved them from one room in a shithole house to another, worn out and defeated, on a crap pension. Then I've met their sons; Handsworth is full of them - alone and isolated from the rest of society. Robert and his mates in Stafford nick who were really nice kids, but fully aware of the situation their parents were in - had lived - and were equally determined to say fuck you, lot. It's still happening today, with the eastern Europeans, the Polish, Bulgarians, Romanians...they are prepared to live eight to a room like the blacks and the Asians did before them, but their sons are going to look around and say fuck you, I'm not going to live like this.

I well remember a detective inspector making the point that he could understand many people turning to villainy after the war due to the hardships suffered by so many people. I personally can't reconcile this in financial terms to the benefits available today. I know people who live very comfortably, be it modestly on the dole and drawing benefits. Before and after WW2. It was a completely different story. I well remember the hardship suffered by such a lot of people: single mothers bringing up kids in the slums of Birmingham, old ladies or men before they were forty. My own mom had me and Kenny late in life, yet I can only remember her as an old lady, so yes, I can fully understand my older brothers, family and cousins and friends, turning to villainy. Their biggest mistake, in truth, is that they all thought - for the most part - it was going to last forever. Shopkeepers and factory owners were asking them to rob them so they could claim on the insurance. I well remember one factory owner thanking his lucky stars for being robbed. Where he had had a few hundred pounds nicked, he put in a claim for a couple of grand. They at least made the most of their good fortune buying more stock etc. The people I knew just pissed it up the wall, pubbing and clubbing it every night living of the hog. The shrewd ones invested in a scrap yard, a night club, or some other business.

Today I see no need or justification for anyone to have to resort to thieving, hard as times are. I think there are lots of opportunities for anyone to do well and get on, but hindsight is a wonderful thing. When you're uneducated, skint from a poor background, the temptation to steal is only too obvious. If it gets hard, then the easier route is into the drugs, get nicked? It gives you more incentive to carry on. Tragically, this is where the law really lets the public down. Celebrities are shown to boast about taking drugs with a blind eye turned in most cases. Who's going to say ay, Mick Jagger does that, it doesn't harm him? Even politicians boast about having taken drugs, thinking it gives them street cred. Nick some jewellery and you get heavy porridge…the fence who buys it gets treated even harsher. No fence? No one would steal. Right? With drugs it works the opposite way. Pop stars boast about taking drugs. The singer Amy Winehouse has been pictured clearly drugged up; the newspapers saw her, the cops did bugger all. Today she is dead.

Drugs are rife throughout the country. Very clever. Sadly, I think these young kids are not given any encouragement at school. How many, like me and my peers, were told our only hope was a job in the factories or building sites? Some future, methinks. Then you have footballers or pop stars strutting about flashing thousands of pounds in cash, plus very expensive watches, against that. You have the immigrants, many desperately fighting to get into England, believing the streets are paved with gold. Well, they might have been years ago, to certain races who had the ability or sense to work at something, but the more that are allowed into the country means there is less to go around. The cheaper the labour costs become for those at the top of the pile. Great really, ain't it?

There are probably more slaves around today than there were three hundred years ago in the cotton fields of south America.

If I've offended anyone by naming them in this book, then I apologise. I was actually paying my respects to you. In life, people's stature can either grow or diminish in our memories. As a kid, Johnny Prescott was my hero: a brave warrior with a big heart, a ready smile that he threw at anyone. Who will ever forget his fights with Billy Walker? He died skint, but he had a great life shagging some of the world's top models. My only sadness was I felt a lot of people used him, but that is the way of life. Charlie Taylor and Billy Monaghan were another couple of great boxers from the Morris Commercial, but there were many more. Wally Cox, a great trainer, a lovely man, we were his kids. Johnny Beards, David Parry, Robert Turley: never changed, never altered throughout their lives. Truly, I feel privileged to have grew up and known you all.

Then there were and are the mongrel's, the scrap dealers, the gangsters, the steel stockholder and his sister who threw their weight about - used people just bunging them a few quid whilst demanding total loyalty, never mind the unpaid bodyguard bit. - the grasses, maybe still strutting about, sticking the chest out, being the big shots, yet at the first opportunity throwing someone else in to save your own neck, worse, like the plumbers here, exact your own revenge. Far too many others even worth mentioning. Have a nice life, me and mine are.

I have made many mistakes; I wear them on my sleeve. Tomorrow I will make many more, and the day after. But in the meantime, I'm seeing the world. To my kids, I say don't worry about making mistakes, as long as you learn from them. Have a good life, and as my mom will say, 'fuck 'em all'.

So you think those scales of justice are evenly balanced eh? So when you go to court you will get a balanced and fair trial? Cobblers! In life, accept that everyone else is corrupt, from the police to the judges, and you might fare a lot better.

My life Is good and enriched, through good genes I am fit and healthy, I also have a nice lifestyle, travelling Europe in our camper or seeing some of the world, from the Nile to the Caribbean. My only regret is my wife bet is not here to share it with me, she more than anyone deserved the rewards we had both worked so hard for, without her I could not have done it. But is she watching over me? I don't know, I hope so. What I do know is following tense words with my youngest daughter days after my wife passed away, a wall clock, the first present I brought her fell of the wall where it had hung for ages. Was my wife chastising me ?

Within weeks of her passing, everything came together for me. Properties, rentals etc. sometimes I find it difficult to reconcile knowing she is not here to enjoy the benefits. No matter what happens, when it's my time I will be buried with her, with my family where hopefully we can dance and smile again without the stress we had in life.

EPILOGUE

The attitude and my treatment by the police and the courts are still ongoing. I don't think I'm the only one. Having been in various moderately successful businesses over the last 50 years, I consider myself fairly savvy. However, I feel the police have a little file under the desk somewhere, marking me out as some thick violent thug who will steal your wallet whilst you're not looking.

There are a lot of cowboys and crooks out there. Especially plumbers. Any landlord or developer will tell you the same. I can get robbed or threatened by some cowboy, yet I'm ignored if I call the cops. I'm given a crime number then forgotten about. Yet the plumber can ring the cops. Tell them I've threatened them, even in my own house, and they are out with all guns blazing. And trust me, they don't need much help to stitch me up.

The police are supposed to be public servants. They are increasingly not. Between them and the government, they are coming out with new laws every five minutes. We are encouraged to inform on our neighbours and every uncle in the area. Now that many are squealing, the police can't handle it. They are running around like headless chickens, crying they are overworked. Yet all these laws never apply to themselves or politicians. They can fiddle their expenses or take backhanders with impunity. When will it end?

COMING SOON! MY NEXT BOOK:

TOURING EUROPE ON A BUDGET

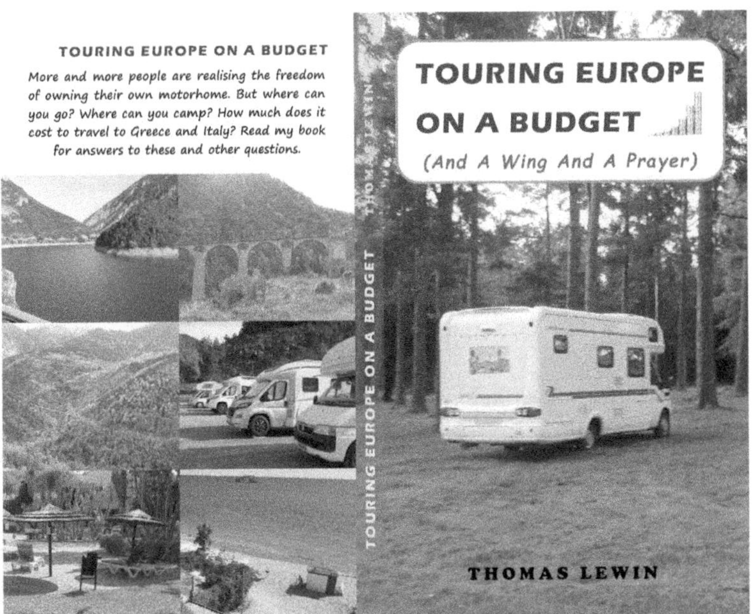

Milton Keynes UK
Ingram Content Group UK Ltd.
UKHW030804170924
448459UK00006B/346